Trade for life

Making trade work for poor people

Mark Curtis

D1347917

Christian Aid
We believe in life before death

Published by
Christian Aid
PO Box 100
London SE1 7RT

© Christian Aid 2001

First published 2001

ISBN: 0 904379 49 3

Christian Aid is campaigning as part of the Trade Justice Movement, which includes ActionAid, CAFOD, Fairtrade Foundation, Friends of the Earth, Intermediate Technology Development Group, Oxfam, People and Planet, Save the Children Fund, Tearfund, Traidcraft and the World Development Movement.

Design and typesetting: King Graphics
Project management: Ginette Casey
Cover photograph: Christian Aid/Leah Gordon
Printed by Jamm Print, London

Contents

Foreword

We cannot tolerate a world where the fortunate enjoy quite unprecedented wealth, while one in three of our neighbours experiences desperate poverty. Globalisation and trade should bring the world's rich and poor closer. The evidence shows that often the opposite is happening. Is there a better way?

Yes – the rules of global trade can be changed radically, so they work in the interests of the world's poorest people. No 'one-size-fits-all' free-market model can magically empower poor people to compete successfully in world markets. But the world's rich countries can agree to trade systems that are specifically designed to help poor countries succeed.

In this book Mark Curtis shows how decision-making in the World Trade Organisation is biased against poor people, how trade agreements often fail to give poor countries the support they need, how in many areas there are no rules where rules are needed, and how the growing power of giant international corporations needs to be controlled.

Our report reflects Christian Aid's prophetic vision as an agency representing 40 UK and Irish churches. This vision is deeply rooted both in the Christian gospel of *'good news to the poor'*, and in our experience of the extraordinary work of partners in the developing world. In the words of Proverbs we must all:

'Speak out for those who cannot speak, for the rights of all the destitute. Speak out, judge righteously, defend the rights of the poor and needy.'

A just world is one where all men and women receive fair shares of the earth's resources and can flourish as equally important beings in the eyes of God. Love for our neighbour can be expressed in the way we trade together as well as in our individual contacts. Today the benefits of trade are concentrated in the hands of the few, and we do have the power to change this.

In the Last Judgement at the end of Matthew's gospel, it is the nations *'who fed the hungry, gave drink to the thirsty, clothed the naked and visited the prisoners'* who are welcomed to the Kingdom. Christian Aid's book is rooted in the Gospel imperative to make this happen.

Dr Daleep Mukarji, Director, Christian Aid

Acknowledgments

This report benefited from research and comments from many people. The lead author was Mark Curtis. Research and writing of case studies and specific sections was done by Talitha Bertelsmann-Scott, Claire Melamed, Mark Farmaner, Sharon McClenaghan, Philippa Saunders, Jasper Corbett, Andrew Pendleton, Mira Shiva, Roger Riddell, Moira Nash and Paul Ladd. The editor was Jon Barton. Sub-editor was Irena Hoare.

Comments were provided by Myriam vander Stichele, Kato Lambrechts, Kate Phillips, Martin Drewry, Mary Bradford, Jon Davison, Danny Graymore and Jenny Brown.

Christian Aid is grateful to the following for their advice: John Samuel, National Centre for Advocacy Studies, India; Nicola Bullard, Focus on the Global South, Thailand; Egidio Brunetto, Landless Movement, Brazil; Christopher Sinckler, Caribbean Policy Development Centre, Barbados; Alida van der Merwe, Centre for Rural Legal Studies, South Africa; Benjamin Castello, Church Action, Angola; Samir Amin, Third World Forum, Senegal; Hubert Lubyama, Christian Council of Tanzania.

Preface

We live in a global world where finance and trade move with increasing ease across the continents. The liberalisation of trade and the globalisation of the international economy have brought unprecedented wealth to some. But those of us who enjoy its benefits live as neighbours with 1.3 billion people who survive in abject poverty. Christians, along with others of good will, find this morally and spiritually unacceptable.

We must identify what needs to be done to create a different world in which justice, compassion and peace benefit all people. The globalising of the world's economic order has been rapid and is here to stay. Yet it has not shifted the harsh reality of poverty in some of the most vulnerable nations of the world.

Many of our partners in Christian Aid, who are seeking to deliver justice to the poorest, remain deeply critical of the way the present system of trade works – or does not work – for the benefit of the poor. The conviction is growing that unless there is a change in the way globalisation proceeds it will fail to reduce the growing inequalities between rich and poor.

Listening to the voices of our sisters and brothers who work close to the poorest, Christian Aid has launched a new trade campaign. We argue that global trade rules, and the processes of bodies such as the World Trade Organisation, need to be changed, if poor people are to be included in the benefits of an expanding world economy. In this way we reflect the prophetic vision of Christian Aid which looks towards 'a new earth where all shall be included in the feast of life'.

This report makes a vital contribution to the debate on globalisation. The challenge it presents is sharp and urgent.

I hope it will stir us all to work for a better future for all.

The Right Reverend John Gladwin
Bishop of Guildford
Chair of the Board, Christian Aid

Executive summary

Making trade work for poor people

All over the world, many poor people suffer as a result of current global trade rules. In some cases their needs are ignored or by-passed; in others the benefits they receive are minimal or short-lived. For a decade, these rules have been negotiated through the World Trade Organisation (WTO). They cover not merely trade issues but also investment, services, agriculture and intellectual property rights. The rules will soon be renegotiated, transforming still further the workings of the global economy. In turn these changes will shape the lives and livelihoods of billions of people around the world.

People everywhere must act now to make sure that the rewriting of global trade rules does not deepen or extend poverty, or further marginalise more of the world's population. Trade can be made to work in the interests of poor people. Christian Aid believes that the international community now has a great opportunity to rewrite the rules to serve the poor rather than to continue to favour rich, powerful countries and global elites. The Jubilee 2000 debt campaign showed beyond doubt that concerted international action can convince decision-makers that they should change their policies in the interests of poor people.

What is wrong with current global trade rules?

- **The decision-making process is biased against the poor.**

The WTO is in reality dominated by the governments of rich countries, so its rules mainly reflect their interests and those of the large corporate interests and transnational corporations (TNCs) based in them.

- **Many WTO agreements harm rather than help the poor.**

The global rules impose uniform policies, which can prevent poor countries from doing what they need to promote sustainable development and root out poverty.

- **Sometimes there are no rules where rules are needed.**

  There is no adequate national or international legislation to regulate large transnational corporations, despite their growing size and influence, and despite the fact that the activities of some can, and do, undermine poor people's livelihoods.

Losses for the poor

Analysis from five United Nations (UN) agencies shows that for many of the poorest people in the world the effects of global trade policies have been either to increase poverty and vulnerability, or to bypass or ignore their needs. Our report illustrates this with examples from around the world. Of course many poor people benefit from international trade, though under current rules they are still highly vulnerable to changes in global markets or the unregulated activities of transnational corporations. Also, benefits that have been achieved have often been short-lived.

Poor countries generally depend more on trade than rich countries. Overall they earn eight times more each year from trade than they receive in aid. But the world's 49 least developed countries together accounted for less than half of one per cent (0.40 per cent) of world trade in 1999. Though the poorest countries have expanded their trade, their share of world trade has fallen by a half over 20 years (it was 0.80 per cent in 1980). The benefits of world trade expansion have simply passed them by. At the same time the terms of trade (the ratio of export prices compared with import prices in any year) are worsening for many developing countries as prices of many of their principal export commodities have fallen to the lowest level for 150 years. This means that these poor countries are having to export much more, just to be able to import the same range of products. Rapid globalisation is not bringing the expected prosperity to the world's poorest people.

The WTO agenda and corporate protectionism

Christian Aid has been shocked to see the world's powerful states and corporations force their priorities through the WTO, often in the face of mass opposition from developing countries and strong counter-arguments from UN agencies. As a result, the interests of poor people have often been neglected.

- Issues only marginally relevant to trade, such as intellectual property, have been added to the WTO agenda. TNCs now have unprecedented private monopoly rights over much of the world's natural public resources. The United Nations' Development Programme (UNDP) describes this process as 'a silent theft of centuries of knowledge from developing to developed countries'.

- Aspects of the global trading system which benefit rich countries (for instance tariffs which protect their producers against cheaper imports from developing countries) have been largely retained. But changes have been forced through which reduce the protection of developing countries through tariff and non-tariff barriers. The United Nations' Conference on Trade and Development (UNCTAD) estimates that by the year 2005, developing countries could earn $700 billion more each year from expanded exports if rich countries opened their markets by removing tariff barriers.

- Critical development issues, such as the need to subject TNCs to legally binding international regulation, are not currently being discussed in any international forum.

The trade agenda of the world's richest nations is primarily driven by a desire to help their companies to expand production by breaking into profitable foreign markets. The freeing of trade is the aim, not the promotion of a trade system which works in the interests of poor people in the poorest countries. The main beneficiaries are the big global corporations, based largely in the rich countries. Powerful governments are promoting an agenda which not only opens up poor and vulnerable economies to the power and force of these massive global players, it also prevents developing countries from choosing economic and trade policies which violate global free trade rules. The result, in effect, is a Robin Hood policy in reverse – one of corporate protectionism for the strong pitted against the decreasing power of the already weak.

The WTO's ambitious vision of 'progressive liberalisation' now includes the opening up of markets for government procurement, investment and services. If this process continues, poor country governments will be left with no meaningful protection against cheap goods and imported services, and with even less power to develop, deepen and diversify their national economies to ensure they maximize economic opportunities for their people, and protect them from the external shocks caused by the process of globalisation. Once again, the main gainers will be powerful private global corporations.

Global rules are certainly needed to regulate trade, and this inevitably restricts national policy-making. But greater flexibility is needed to enhance the ability of poor countries to use trade policy to promote development, not to reduce it. There is a very real danger that WTO agreements will lock developing countries into a one-size-fits-all straitjacket, which gives them minimal freedom to follow policies appropriate to their local conditions. Countries which have most successfully reduced poverty in the past (for instance the industrialised West and more recently in South-East Asia) have often pursued policies which are very different from those currently prescribed by international bodies like the WTO. Governments have judiciously intervened to help build up viable and competitive national firms. Many of these successful trade and development policies are banned under WTO agreements. Christian Aid believes that poor countries must be able to retain the *option* to pursue what they consider the most appropriate policies for development and poverty-reduction.

In its present form, the WTO challenges the right to democratic decision-making. In theory, the WTO operates by consensus and some developing countries are successful in making their voices heard. But in practice, decision-making is dominated by the powerful countries, often meeting behind closed doors. Equally important is the power of organised business lobbies, some of which have successfully shaped EU and US negotiating priorities. By comparison the interests of the poorest people in the world have been marginalised, and the representatives of these people play next to no role in shaping contemporary trade policies.

Christian Aid believes that the WTO's power should be used to create overarching global rules only where they are strictly necessary. In particular, its ability to set global rules which impinge on national sovereignty needs to be limited. In accordance with the principle of subsidiarity, more decisions on trade policy need to be taken at local, national and regional levels, to increase the likelihood that they reflect country diversity, and to ensure that policies suit the national context and the need to eradicate poverty.

The UK government and world trade

The British government has articulated a number of positive policies in the trade negotiations. It has acknowledged the need to make international trade work for the poor and for developing countries to be able to pursue policies in their own development interest. However, it is also a leading champion of the liberalisation model for development: '*everywhere* it is clear that openness is a *necessary* – though not sufficient – condition for national prosperity'. Plus, it supports the inclusion of issues such as government procurement, investment and competition policy in the next WTO round, in the face of continuing opposition from most developing countries.

In addition, the UK strongly believes that liberalisation works in the interests of the poor, and has pressed in effect for the implementation of a free trade, 'one-size-fits-all', model on all countries. But if it is to help steer the WTO towards trade policies which deliver prosperity to the world's poorest people, the government needs to pay closer attention to the factors it has pinpointed as impediments to the practical workings of the model. These include the failure of rich countries to reduce trade barriers, unbalanced markets dominated by powerful actors, ineffective governments and widespread corruption. It needs to curb its enthusiasm for unfettered globalisation and recognise the need to focus on issues of equity and on the importance of policies to promote pro-poor development. The government must also acknowledge and help to meet the very significant costs poor countries have to face in adjusting to changes in the global economy.

The seven deadly rules

Agreements already made in the WTO risk deepening poverty and extending inequalities. But issues that are currently on the negotiating table may make this situation worse.

- Transnational corporations are increasingly securing access to (and often control over) markets in developing countries in areas previously denied to them.

- Developing countries are being prevented from promoting policies in their own development interest.

Christian Aid identifies seven specific trade rules which lie at the heart of this process.

Rule one: **limits protection against cheap food imports**
Developing countries are restricted from intervening in order to raise adequate barriers against cheap food imports, while export subsidies by rich countries are allowed to persist.

The outcome: *a flood of food imports into developing countries which undermines or threatens to undermine the livelihood of many poor people.*

Rule two: **limits government regulation of services**
Countries which agree to sign up must open up their services sectors to foreign suppliers by abolishing restrictions on access to those markets.

The outcome: *the renegotiation of the WTO's services agreement may result in health, education and water services being run and controlled by profit-driven foreign corporations.*

Rule three: **limits regulation of foreign investment**
The WTO's investment agreement bans policies and regulations favouring the use of domestic over foreign products.

The outcome: *poor countries are denied some important ways of supporting the development of viable local industries over foreign producers. A new investment agreement would further strengthen this rule.*

Rule four: ***limits use of agricultural subsidies***
Developing countries are limited in their freedom to increase subsidies to agriculture. Some (the non-least developed countries) are required to reduce them. Particular types of subsidy are banned altogether. Meanwhile the EU and US are still permitted to spend huge sums on agricultural subsidies themselves.

The outcome: *poor people's food security is being undermined by restrictions on subsidies which deny poor countries an important tool in development.*

Rule five: ***limits use of industrial subsidies***
Governments are prevented from using industrial subsidies to promote the manufacture of domestic products over imported alternatives. Some subsidies of special use to poor countries are banned, while some of special use to rich countries are permitted.

The outcome: *poor countries' industrial development is being hampered by taking away a critical policy tool to help develop their own industrial sector.*

Rule six: ***blocks exports from developing countries***
Rich countries can retain high import barriers or other restrictions against key exports from developing countries.

The outcome: *poor countries lose much needed export revenues and the economic growth rates of affected poor economies will suffer potential losses.*

Rule seven: ***gives business rights over knowledge and natural resources***
This WTO rule requires countries to introduce effective patenting laws, including plant varieties and seeds, which can give TNCs rights over those products for 20 years. This in effect legalises biopiracy of natural resources and knowledge.

The outcome: *poor people's food and health security can be threatened if TNCs are successful in securing monopoly control over knowledge and natural resources.*

Transnational corporations and the need for regulation

Over the past two decades of expanded trade and globalisation, TNCs have secured unprecedented power across the world economy. The largest 200 account for more than a quarter of global Gross Domestic Product (GDP). Many transnational corporations provide benefits to poor people, for example through creating jobs, supplying a wide range of cheaper consumer products and, indirectly, through higher levels of government revenue which can be used to tackle poverty. But unregulated TNC activity can lead to environmental degradation, undermine human rights, threaten the livelihoods of the most vulnerable and create great instability when corporations choose to disinvest. The economic management of developing countries must not be distorted simply to cater to the demands of transnational capital.

TNCs have grown as trade, financial flows and investment regulations have been liberalised. This has allowed companies to reorganise themselves to exploit their size and realise new opportunities to obtain security and higher returns. For many of the larger TNCs, the recent wave of mergers and acquisitions has radically increased their overall market power. Desperate to attract investment, governments of developing countries frequently compete with each other to offer foreign investors the best deal. So under pressure from powerful countries and companies, laws have been enacted which are far less favourable to the individual national interest than might have been achieved within the framework of a more collaborative inter-national approach. The mobility of capital gives TNCs the freedom to move around the globe in search of the least restrictive conditions in which to operate. Fundamental rights like the freedom to organise and work in safe conditions are often compromised.

That is why regulation is needed to protect the interests of poor people. But currently there are no binding international regulations to hold TNCs to account for their activities. Most national legislation does not make TNCs responsible for the activities of their subsidiaries: they are usually not obliged to apply 'home' standards across all their operations. Most national laws fail to address adequately the global structures and strategies of TNCs. Instead of binding regulation, there are voluntary codes of conduct like the OECD's Guidelines on Multinationals and the UN's Global Compact. These remain incomplete and inadequate in the prevailing climate of rapidly growing corporate power.

International law on subjects like human rights, the environment and development is the responsibility of the private sector as well as of governments. But strengthening legally binding regulation to uphold ethical standards is not currently on the agenda of the WTO, the UK government or the governments of most other rich countries. Fashioning a new system of international rules to address the growing power of large TNCs is crucial to enhance the positive role that the foreign private sector can play in development.

Alternatives and recommendations

Global trade rules need to be rewritten in order to benefit poor people. New trade rules should champion diversity and protect the rights of governments and people, especially in the poorest countries, to decide how best to develop their own economic activities. These should ensure that trade is a means to promote sustainable development, not an end in itself.

Many principles upon which the WTO agreements are based need to be reversed. Currently the WTO:

- tends to treat all countries the same, with strict limits on 'special and differential treatment' for poor countries
- restricts regulation of the private sector by national governments
- treats domestic and foreign companies the same
- enforces the primacy of global rules.

But the WTO *should*:

- treat rich and poor countries differently as a matter of course
- encourage sensible regulation of the private sector by government
- treat domestic and foreign companies differently
- emphasise the primacy of national and local decision-making while still tackling global problems through global rules.

Christian Aid believes that global trade rules must be rewritten:

1 *To ensure their impact on the poor can be assessed, and changes made where they are needed*
An impact assessment of existing agreements must be conducted urgently, as WTO members promised under Article XX of the Agreement on Agriculture (and Article XIX of the General Agreement on Trade in Services).

2 *To contribute explicitly to the reduction of poverty*
In its mandate, the WTO must replace its commitment to 'progressive liberalisation' with a more explicit promise to promote trade policies which help to reduce poverty and promote sustainable development.

3 *To narrow the focus of the WTO to enable more decision-making on trade policy to take place at local and national levels*
The WTO's ability to set global rules which impinge on national sovereignty needs to be limited. Under the principle of subsidiarity, more decisions on trade policy need to be taken at local, national and regional levels. The principle that developing countries need to be treated differently as a matter of course must become a key tenet of all agreements.

4 *To ensure rules are decided in a fair and democratic way*
All major decisions must be taken with the active participation of all WTO members, ending the practice of rich countries agreeing deals behind closed doors. The capacity of developing countries to formulate and negotiate trade policy needs to be strengthened.

5 *To guarantee that rich countries as well as poor countries abide by the rules*
The dispute settlement mechanism needs to be changed to replace the current bilateral system with more effective multilateral mechanisms. The legal aid system established in Geneva should also be widened.

6 *To regulate transnational corporations effectively*
People in developing countries need the legal right to take TNCs to court on issues relating to the activities of their subsidiaries in the developing world. A legally-binding global code of conduct for TNCs needs to be established enforcing agreed environmental, human rights and development standards. A new Global Regulation Authority should be established to police this code.

The seven deadly WTO rules should be rewritten to give a high priority to the needs of the poorest people.

Rule one:	**protect adequately against cheap food imports** Developing countries need to be free to choose effective import tariffs to ensure they are not flooded with cheap and disruptive food imports, and export subsidies in rich countries should be made illegal.
Rule two:	**require no mandatory opening up of services sectors** Poor countries in particular should not be required to open up their service sectors to foreign companies without careful analysis and without their explicit agreement. No future services agreements should be drawn up until detailed analysis of their effects on poor people has been made, and they have poverty alleviation as their priority.
Rule three:	**ensure appropriate regulation of foreign investment** The WTO agreement on investment (TRIMs) must be rewritten to ensure that foreign investment can be fully regulated by developing countries. The ban on policies which discriminate in favour of domestic companies should be lifted.
Rule four:	**promote national and local food security policies** Developing countries need to be able to support their farmers to maximise food security for poor people. Either the WTO agreement on subsidies should be rewritten or the issue taken out of the WTO altogether.

Rule five: **support domestic industry**
General global rules outlawing some industrial subsidies and other support mechanisms need to be reversed to permit poor countries to intervene in ways they deem appropriate to establish viable, competitive industries.

Rule six: **enable fair access to rich country markets**
All exports from least developed countries should be able to enter rich country markets duty-free. Tariff peaks and tariff escalation on processed agricultural products must be eliminated. There must be an increased burden of proof on rich countries seeking to use sanitary and phytosanitary measures to ban imports from developing countries.

Rule seven: **protect against biopiracy and misuse of patenting**
Intellectual property issues should be negotiated through the UN, not the WTO. To prevent biopiracy, companies taking out new patents must be required to demonstrate the prior informed consent of the original holders of any resources or knowledge applied in the development of patented products. Developing countries must have greater flexibility in overriding current patent protection, especially in public health emergencies.

Christian Aid believes that developing countries should not be forced to put all their faith in international trade but be free to pursue policies suited to their local situation. This may mean prioritising production for the domestic rather than international market. Securing greater access to rich country markets can reinforce dependence on a few primary commodities, and reduce food security.

The WTO must be reformed. But making it more democratic and transparent will not on its own ensure that new trade rules work in the interests of poor people. We need a global body able to set rules democratically and work in the interests of all, both rich and poor. Christian Aid believes that to ensure that poor people derive maximum benefit from trade, decisions must be taken as close to them as possible. In some ways the WTO does not so much need to be reformed as to have its focus narrowed. Its ability to make rules which impinge on national sovereignty needs to be limited. It is currently too powerful and sets global rules too rigidly. But at the same time more power is needed for the international community to hold global businesses, and especially the larger TNCs to account. Christian Aid is calling for a re-balancing of global governance to ensure that decision-making on trade takes place at the right level.

Christian Aid's view is not that we need a world trading system which enables rich and poor to compete on equal terms. Instead we believe that in an unequal world it is our responsibility to create a global trading system which explicitly and deliberately favours those who are currently severely disadvantaged, one which gives priority to resolving the problems of acute poverty *before* it begins to create systems based on fairness and equality of outcome.

The sharp contrast between the limited life-chances and opportunities of 1.3 billion people who are forced to live in extreme poverty, and the expanding opportunities of the rich is morally unacceptable. The current global economy is failing to resolve the problems of poverty of so many of the world's poor. This is manifestly unjust. Because they are relatively powerless, poor people in developing countries have the right to demand from the rich an international environment which works to meet their basic needs and fulfil their core human rights. It is our duty to help ensure that this happens, and happens fast. One major way that this can be achieved is to make trade work for poor people – to root out poverty and improve the life-chances of the world's most vulnerable people.

1 Why trade matters to the poor

Over the past decade, many of the rules governing the global economy have been agreed through the World Trade Organisation (WTO) on trade, investment, services, agriculture and intellectual property. In the next few years, these rules will be renegotiated, transforming the global economy in ways that will shape it for decades to come. The WTO affects the lives and livelihoods of billions of people. One of the biggest questions facing humanity is whether these rules can be made to serve poor people. Or will they continue to serve primarily the rich, most powerful countries, and marginalise the poor?

Señor Gabriel and his family live in the far north of Mozambique, where cotton has been produced for over 50 years. During the 16-year war in Mozambique, farmers could not sell their cotton, and production fell. So Señor Gabriel could no longer earn the money to buy clothes, fertiliser for his crops, cooking pots – or any of the other things he needed which he couldn't grow or make himself. When the war ended in 1992, Lonrho, a UK-based transnational corporation, made a contract with the government of Mozambique to start buying cotton from farmers in the area. Lonrho repaired the roads, provided farmers with seeds and insecticide on credit, and promised to buy their cotton at the end of the year. For the first time in twenty years Señor Gabriel had a guaranteed income.

At the end of the year when the farmers sold their cotton, traders came to the village selling bicycles (made in China), household items like torches (made in Taiwan), radios (made in China), and cooking pots (made in Tanzania). People from other villages brought meat and fish that they had caught locally.

The cotton was bought from farmers in the villages and transported to Pemba on the coast. From there Lonrho exported it to Asia, the USA and Europe, where it was made into fabric and clothes. These were sold by other large companies like the Gap, Next and Marks and Spencer. Some clothes eventually found their way back to Mozambique, where they were sold as part of large shipments of second-hand clothes. Some even ended up in the village, to be bought by Señor Gabriel's sons.

International trade like this connects people across the globe.

- It enabled Señor Gabriel to earn an income to buy things from all over the world for his house and his farm.
- His sons could buy t-shirts with the latest logos on them.
- Lonrho were able to make a profit from buying in one part of the world and selling in another.
- Workers in textile factories in Asia, the USA and Europe were employed in industries which otherwise would not exist.
- None of these people would be able to trade if it weren't for all the others. They are connected in a chain that encircles the globe.

But in the global trading system not everyone is equal. Between 1996 and 1997 the price Señor Gabriel received for his cotton fell by 25 per cent.[1] This was because of the fall in cotton prices on the world market, which Lonrho passed on to producers rather than cut its own profits. In 1997, the company stopped buying cotton from Señor Gabriel's village. The price of cotton was so low that it was no longer profitable for the company to buy from such remote villages. Lonrho still buys cotton from other parts of Africa, cotton still reaches the clothes factories of Asia, the USA and Europe, and UK consumers still get the products they want. But Señor Gabriel does not have anyone to sell his cotton to. Traders no longer come to the village, and farmers' only source of income is the small amount of maize they sell at harvest time – maize which they might have to buy back later in the year for very high prices if their stocks run out.

Señor Gabriel's experience shows both the good and bad sides of inter-national trade. When poor people secure access to markets on favourable terms, trade helps them to increase their incomes, and gain access to goods they need but cannot make themselves. But when they are excluded from markets trade can make people more vulnerable. The most vulnerable are the poorest who do not have the options to pack up and move somewhere else. If conditions change Lonrho can shift its operations to other parts of the world. Señor Gabriel and his family can't make that move. They depend on what compa-nies like Lonrho can offer them where they are. If the company pulls out, they lose their links to international markets and are left with deepening poverty.

Ways in which poor people are affected by trade

Like millions of poor people, Señor Gabriel is connected to people he will never meet through trade. Villagers in remote areas of Mozambique can buy second-hand Gap t-shirts in the local market while shoppers in London buy vegetables flown in daily from every continent. People watch the same television programmes in New York and New Delhi. Brands like Coca-Cola, Marlboro,

International brands for sale in Bolivia.

and Levis are instantly recognised across the world. Boardrooms in New York, Frankfurt or Tokyo decide the futures of workers thousands of miles away.

Most people of the world are involved in trade, agreeing to swap one or more items for others. One side of the bargain usually involves money, which gives the opportunity to set a range of prices from very large to very small. Money is given for items that people would have otherwise not been able to make or grow, and received for goods that they have too much of or no longer need.

Goods or services can be traded across the world and involve transport over vast distances. But most trade takes place locally, in markets organised by communities. People come to market believing they can make themselves and their families better off: having access to a range of different goods is one way of doing this. But it also means that they are dependent on markets to provide them with a price for the goods they wish to sell. Prices are negotiated in markets by producers and consumers – so that demand equals supply. Whether a fair bargain is struck depends on how much power each side has to influence the terms under which this trade takes place. And prices can change quickly.

The extent to which individuals, businesses or countries can cope with the changes that result from trade will depend on their resources and their capacity to use them efficiently. These resources are not just economic – they can be cultural, social and political. They can have positive and negative consequences: markets create incentives for the movement of not only goods and services, but also people, ideas, expertise, and sometimes even disease. This report argues that richer and more powerful bodies involved in trade are currently much better placed to deal with the negative effects that come from rapid change in a globalised trading system.

Opening up international trade can have many unintended consequences for poor people.

- **Working conditions:** Millions of people in developing countries are employed in the factories of transnational companies making goods such as trainers, computer chips or t-shirts for export. They benefit when companies pay high wages and provide good conditions of employment. When wages are low, working contracts temporary, unions forbidden and factory conditions dangerous, then employees are simply exploited as cheap labour.

- **Unemployment through cheap imports:** Local production can be undermined when governments open up markets. This may benefit consumers but destroy jobs. In South Africa, 43,000 people, or a third of the workforce employed by textiles and clothing manufacturers, lost their jobs when the textile market was opened up to foreign competition.[2]

- **Unpredictable movements in prices:** Señor Gabriel's story is repeated across Africa. The prices of many primary products have been falling for many years, forcing producers of primary commodities into a bleak struggle for survival. This can contribute to social disruption and conflict, as in Rwanda and Burundi.

- **Pressure on natural resources:** Production for export (commercial farming, mining or tourism) can result in resources being taken away from domestic producers. In Kenya, for example, the flower farming industry provides employment for around 50,000 people, but other farmers around the shores of Lake Naivasha now struggle to obtain water for their food crops.[3]

- **Increased dependence on imports:** Trade can make agricultural inputs cheaper and increase the range of goods on sale. But it can also make poor people more dependent on imports for essentials like food. They become more vulnerable: external changes over which they have no control can raise the price of essentials beyond their reach while the alternative of self-sufficiency has disappeared.

- **Inadequate protection for health:** When imports are liberalised without effective health and safety regulation, consumers can be vulnerable to unsafe goods. Britain continued to export cattle feed that was potentially infected with BSE to Africa, long after it was banned in Europe. Exports to non-European countries quadrupled after the EU ban.[4]

- **Reduction in government income:** Increases in trade can mean increases in government revenue, but reductions in trade taxes under liberalisation can deprive developing countries of a major source of revenue to tackle poverty. On average one third of developing countries' tax revenues come from trade taxes.[5] Customs duties contributed nearly half of Mozambique's total revenue in 2000[6] and between one-fifth and one half of government revenues in most Caribbean countries.[7]

Particular effects on women

Two thirds of the world's poor are women and they are the poorest of those poor. The number of women financially responsible for entire households is increasing, as divorce, war, or migration in search of work cause husbands to move away from households. Women are particularly vulnerable to neglect by policy-makers keen to promote export-oriented trade.[8]

In agriculture, emphasis on export crops has displaced women workers in some countries from permanent agricultural employment into seasonal employment. Women subsistence farmers have been adversely affected by the sale of land to large companies, leading to reduced food security and a consequent adverse effect on women's health.[9] The disappearance of small farms in favour of large agri-businesses means that women are less able to supplement their income by subsistence farming. Technological advance is welcome, but women in poor countries are often incapable of finding alternative employment after machines have replaced them, due to training shortages. An example is the loss of women's agricultural jobs in Indonesia and Bangladesh resulting from the introduction of mechanised mills and post-harvesting processing.[10]

In industry, one UN report has shown that global industrialisation 'is as much female-led as it is export led'. This is particularly true in export processing zones (EPZs) and other special economic zones where labour-intensive industries have relocated in search of cheap labour. Women provide up to 80 per cent of the workforce in some EPZs, especially in textiles, shoe and toy-making, data-processing and semi-conductor assembling industries. In EPZs, unionisation and collective bargaining is often impossible and poor pay the norm.[11] Though globalisation has brought much needed employment to these women, inadequate international regulation allows many to be exploited.

Globalisation has also resulted in an increase in the trade in women. Increased poverty and unemployment in many developing countries have meant that many poor women have turned to overseas markets for work as domestic helpers. They enter foreign countries as illegal immigrants or asylum seekers without legal rights, and subject to large-scale exploitation. The WTO promotes the free movement of goods and services, but has made little progress on the free movement of people. In Thailand alone between 800,000 and 2 million women have been driven to prostitution in order to supplement income.[12] As the global economy expands, too many women are being left on its margins.

The importance of trade to poor countries

Poor countries are generally more dependent on trade for securing income than rich countries. One-third of Africa's GDP, and half the GDP of the least developed countries, comes from trade, while OECD countries earn on average less than a fifth of their GDP through trade.[13] The poorest countries earn eight times more each year from trade than they receive in aid.[14]

This carries huge risks. The larger share of trade in GDP for developing countries means that these poor countries are far more vulnerable to changes in demand for traded goods. Countries that are most dependent on global trade are for a number of reasons the least able to cope with the risks associated with an open global economy.

This dependence on trade takes place within a trading system that is fundamentally unbalanced.

- The world's 49 least developed countries together accounted for less than half of one per cent (0.40 per cent) of world trade in 1999 [15] – half of the level 20 years previously (0.8 per cent in 1980 [16]).

- In 1998, the whole of sub-Saharan Africa earned less from trade than Switzerland.[17]

- Very few poor countries have trading companies that can influence prices and secure a high added value from their activities. This compares with numerous

Christian Aid/Gideon Mendel

Tobacco makes up 26 per cent of Zimbabwe's and 64 per cent of Malawi's exports.

Coffee prices

According to the International Trade Centre, 'the protracted period of low [coffee] prices is seriously impacting on producers who are unable to cover the costs of harvesting. Almost all growers are losing money now; in some countries berries are being left to rot on the bushes. The higher-cost producers may be forced out'. Meanwhile, there are some who are not losing out – the 'world coffee trade, the roasting sector and instant coffee manufacture are increasingly concentrated in the hands of a very small number of international companies'.[19] And yet the World Bank has promoted the expansion of primary product exports in many poor countries, a policy which has directly led to over-production and the associated fall in prices.

TNCs, mostly based in rich and powerful countries, which are able to control the production, marketing and distribution of many of the world's most important commodities.

- Three quarters of the least developed countries are dependent on two or less commodity exports for over half their foreign exchange earnings. At the same time world prices for many of those commodities are at their lowest levels for 150 years. Coffee prices are today at their lowest level for 30 years (see box on this page) while cocoa prices were at their lowest level ever in 2000.[18]

Table 1: Source of main export earnings, selected countries

Country	Main export	% of total exports
Burundi	coffee	82
Bolivia	metal ores	15
Côte d'Ivoire	cocoa	48
Haiti	women's outwear	25
Jamaica	metal ores	52
Kenya	tea	24
Malawi	tobacco	64
Tanzania	cotton	17
Uganda	coffee	73
Zimbabwe	tobacco	26
UK	motor vehicles	5
Ireland	data processors	14

Source: *UNCTAD Handbook of Statistics 2000*

As Table 2 shows, the terms of trade – the ratio of export prices compared to import prices in any year – is worsening for sub-Saharan Africa in general and for many other developing countries. For example, Mozambique's terms of trade have fallen by an average of almost seven per cent each year from 1980. In 1998, Ghana's exports bought less than half what they did in 1980.

Table 2: Terms of trade, selected countries (index: 1995=100)

Country	1980	1990	1995	1998	Average annual % change
Sub-Saharan Africa	179.4	116.6	100	93.2	-4.7
Burundi	134.4	74.6	100	74.0	-3.35
Ghana	203.9	99.7	100	98.1	-5.8
Kenya	96.1	67.6	100	105.5	0.5
Malawi	126.4	115.5	100	108.9	-0.9
Mozambique	221.8	161.1	100	104.2	-6.5
Senegal	106.1	115.7	100	108.3	0.1
Zambia	136.1	131.1	100	83.8	-2.9
Zimbabwe	87.4	100.0	100	104.7	0.9

Source: World Bank, *African Development Indicators 2000*

Christian Aid's approach to trade

Christian Aid campaigns for policies that increase the likelihood that trade will help poor people. We oppose policies that harm poor people or provide benefits only to the rich. Policy making that affects poor people should take account of the fact that they are already disadvantaged and need to be provided with the tools needed to participate more fairly and effectively in trade. And we are concerned that anything that provides disproportionate benefits to the wealthy will widen inequality, and further distort access to the world's resources.

Christian Aid works with partner organisations in a huge variety of situations around the world. From this we know that global trade rules should reflect the realities of life for the poor – and the best way of achieving this is for poor people to be centrally involved in formulating them. Current global trade rules, and policies promoted under the World Bank/IMF Poverty Reduction Strategy process, fail to involve poor people or their representatives in policy formulation, even though this is their intention. Christian Aid believes that, within a framework of global rules, countries should keep the right to put in place policies that they believe will promote sustainable development and reduce poverty – even if these do not conform to the free-market consensus of the WTO.

Whether poor people benefit or not from trade reflects the ways they are connected to the markets as producers and consumers. Many are not able to secure any short-term benefits from trade because there are simply no roads or other reliable means of transport to get their goods to markets. This is compounded by other problems: ill health, illiteracy, lack of land rights, no banking facilities – or sometimes that the weather is bad and crops fail. So in order for poor people to get more from trade, it's clear that poverty needs to be tackled over a period of time in its most basic forms – through investment in health, education and infrastructure that empowers people to make choices to improve their own livelihoods and reduce risks.

Poor people are particularly vulnerable to the volatility of markets, especially rapid changes in prices. They have little to cushion themselves against such shocks. They benefit when they have the opportunity to process primary products and add value to the crops they grow and the commodities they produce. This adds to their security and lowers the risk of engaging in uncertain markets.

Trade that makes economies grow

Trade can drive wealth creation through more efficient allocation and use of resources, and greater access to knowledge and expertise. But what determines the impact on poverty is the way in which the benefits from growth are shared: there may still be many losers. It can also happen that trade – especially on unequal terms – can lead to a lower growth path than would otherwise have occurred. This happens when countries which have the capacity to industri-alise are unable to do so because they are not given enough time to adjust to international competition. Global trade rules need to be more flexible to make sure this does not happen.

Christian Aid wants more poor economies to grow in ways that benefit the poor and allow them to participate in shaping the world of international trade. When trade produces higher growth, government can raise more money through taxation. This feeds through into spending on essential services such as health and education, or other areas of productive public investment. This is more likely to happen when budgetary systems are strong, and governments are democratically accountable. In the worst cases extra resources generated through trade and growth are used to enrich the lives of a few.

If we recognise that in the right circumstances trade can help to reduce poverty, then we must also accept that trade expansion can increase these bene-fits. But where the rules or practices are unfair and less powerful economies do not have the capacity to adapt to the changes trade brings, opening up global trade can threaten the livelihoods of the most vulnerable people. Expanding trade will help poor people if the process is accompanied by rules and systems to compensate for its potentially negative effects.

The world of the 21st century is one where major changes are taking place as a result of technological changes. The pace of change is far more rapid than in the past. Christian Aid views with deep scepticism analyses which 'show conclusively' what the effects of trade on different groups of poor people are likely to be. History teaches us that it is right to be sceptical about any economic prediction.

Trade to reduce poverty

Because trade liberalisation leads to change in the market, inevitably some poor producers lose out. This happens most obviously when the goods they are involved in producing do not have the potential, either through price or quality, to be competitive in larger markets. This leads to job losses. But often during trade liberalisation, products are not given a chance to become competitive. Indiscriminate tariff reduction means that protection is suddenly withdrawn, and domestic producer prices crash. And poor consumers can also lose out during times of trade liberalisation, particularly when they have traditionally been purchasers of subsidised products.

These problems can arise in situations where markets function perfectly well. But the costs of adjustment to poor people are exacerbated when markets do not work very well. Market failure can occur for many reasons: the lack of basic information, dominance of the market by a few key players, weak economic governance or poor enforcement of the law. This is a particular danger in developing countries, and greatly reduces the likelihood of economic growth and poverty reduction. Ultimately, the solution is to level the playing field and correct the market failure. But in the short and medium term, poorer countries need to retain the right to implement policies which they believe will help to overcome market failures and weaknesses, even though these may not be allowed under WTO global rules or the conditions linked to World Bank/IMF loans. These options are currently being closed down.

Poor communities can also be at particular risk from sudden changes when markets are opened up. They have less power to influence the price of what they buy or sell, and with subsidies outlawed, prices are determined solely by demand and supply. This creates much greater volatility. Demand may fluctuate because of changes in fashion, health scares, technological progress, or recession in other parts of the world. Supply may fluctuate because of a crop failure thousands of miles away, or industrial action, or price changes in things which go to make up final goods. The large open markets of the modern world are highly flexible. This may be an advantage in sharing out resources to the best users, but can lead to dangerous volatility.

Poor communities are not well placed to cope with volatility. They rely on the production of a small number of goods – often primary mineral or agricultural products. Changes in the markets of these few products affects them a lot. Even where the products they are selling are competitive, they can be at risk because they are locked into inflexible production chains. This can leave communities high and dry when demand falls and the goods they produce are no longer needed.

Irresponsible and poorly regulated business practice can compound the costs poor people have to pay as their economies adjust. Sometimes domestic or foreign companies do not pay the full cost of the resources they are using. This is particularly acute for poor people who live in rural areas and are dependent on natural resources. Unregulated business can – in the worst instances – expose people to employment practices that undermine their basic human rights (see chapter 5).

There is no magic guarantee that poor people will gain when trade expands. Everything depends on circumstances. There is always potential for long-term gain through economic growth and overall efficiency. But a whole range of safeguards are needed to help disadvantaged people adjust to more open markets, and to help them address their basic needs. This means that national governments must retain the option of promoting distinctive development policies of their own. And it also means that richer countries who are pressing for more open markets must commit themselves to providing the extra resources needed by poor countries during the process of adjustment.

Safeguards to protect poor people

What safeguards can be put in place to help poor people in the face of change and economic vulnerability? The answer is simple: the same safeguards that are employed in richer countries which have the resources and capacity to put them in place.

Developed countries often protect their own domestic production through tariffs and other means. This is particularly true in the case of textiles and agriculture, products that developing countries can often produce more competitively. These policies are not cost-free, but the decision to adopt them reflects national sovereignty and political priority. Less powerful countries lack the resources to take similar action when a measure of protection – especially in the short term when it relates to food security or industrialisation – might be the best policy for growth and poverty reduction.

Resources are also needed to look after people who have had their livelihood suddenly taken away from them, or if the prices of the products they used to buy under protected markets suddenly shoot up. This can stop people slipping back into poverty. More importantly, resources are needed to invest in education and re-training so that poor people can quickly find alternative livelihoods.

For volatility that arises after trade liberalisation, there may occasionally be a case for market stabilisation policies - these do not always undermine markets. We do recognise that market distortions generally lead to inefficient use of resources, with attendant costs. Some people may win in this situation, but poor people may become worse off. A proper assessment is needed as to whether the short-term benefits from stabilisation outweigh its costs.

Adjusting to change can be a slow and painful process. Development agencies recognise that the time bought through asymmetrical trade agreements is not enough to level the playing field within the space of ten years. The resources they make available are pitiful compared with the scale of the problem. Christian Aid believes that if richer countries want to gain from free trade, they should help to put in place a framework through which all people in the world can gain.

Developed country governments display massive hypocrisy when it comes to trade liberalisation. They fail to practise what they preach. They preach that unbridled trade liberalisation is in the interests of all. They practise something very different: restricting access to their own markets for the products of most importance to the poor, most notoriously agriculture and textiles. When poor countries have the capacity to make good products more cheaply than rich countries, they find the gates of these same rich countries locked against them.

Worse still, developed countries preach that subsidies distort the workings of the market, leading to inefficiency. But when poor countries do open their markets – often as conditions within World Bank and IMF loans – they are sometimes flooded with subsidised exports from rich countries. It's not surprising that developing countries are deeply suspicious of the motives behind the trade liberalisation agenda.

But worst of all, the same rich countries, which call on poor countries to open up their markets, pour billions of dollars into helping their own citizens adjust to economic change – but are reluctant even to talk about providing similar resources to help poor countries with the massive social and economic costs of adjustment. Indeed, during the last decade when rich countries have been urging poor countries to open up their markets, and the need for assistance has been greatest, the amount of official aid governments have provided for development (rather than emergencies) has dropped by almost a half in real terms.

The hypocrisy of the rich world comes from the simplest of motives: self-interest. This is natural – but it fails to recognise the moral imperative of lifting 1.3 billion people out of poverty, and the economic common sense of building trade, with bigger and richer markets developing to the benefit of all. Rich lobbies within developed countries finance political parties and are extremely successful at influencing the positions their governments take in bodies like the WTO. Trade policy driven by these forces is almost certain not to match the best interests of poor people on the other side of the world.

Poor people's central role in policy-making

Christian Aid believes that poor people need to be at the centre of the decisions which affect and influence their lives. If rich governments are serious about development, they will make sure that poor people have an indispensable role in making trade policy. This must not be a tick-box exercise, but a recognition of how different people are affected differently by trade. When people are asked their views about trade and trade policy, they should be presented with informed options and their consequences. But this hardly ever happens in current WTO negotiations. Unless efforts are made to give poor people a greater voice in decisions about trade made on their behalf, it is unlikely that they will benefit as much as they should, and likely that many will become worse off.

As the experiences, resources, skills and opportunities of poor people in each country differ, we would expect the policy emphasis to be different. A 'one-size fits-all' approach is not appropriate. We would like to see stronger national sovereignty and greater flexibility in the way global rules are decided.

But setting good policy through participation is not cost free. And poor countries face many pressing needs, not least in building up education and health systems as the backbone of future economic growth. It is very difficult to justify a diversion of scarce resources away from these needs in the interests of economic liberalisation. Instead, richer countries must shoulder greater financial responsibility for the development needs of poor people. This should be primarily through grants rather than loans, which simply delay the burden.

Christian Aid has a long tradition of strengthening the voice of poor people whose rights are ignored or eroded, or whose livelihoods are under threat. We will be a channel for the views of poor people who are at the moment adversely affected by international trade rules and policies. Christian Aid is not 'anti-globalisation'. But as some rich countries prepare to launch a new trade round in the World Trade Organisation, we need to make sure that globalisation works in the best interests of the poorest and least powerful players in the world trade game.

2 The World Trade Organisation

The WTO: basic facts, basic problems

The World Trade Organisation, based in Geneva, began operating in 1995 following the 'Uruguay Round' of trade negotiations which set today's trade rules. The WTO evolved out of the 1948 General Agreement on Tariffs and Trade (GATT). Since 1948 successive rounds of negotiation expanded the general agreement until the Uruguay Round established the new organisation.

The WTO provides the framework for the conduct of international trade in goods and services and the protection of intellectual property rights. It administers the implementation of a set of agreements, or rules, which include enforcement of rights and disciplines on governments. This ultimately occurs through a dispute settlement mechanism that allows member states to apply sanctions against other members who violate its agreements.

The WTO currently has 142 member states who have signed up to two important principles:

1 Non-discrimination among members. All countries must trade with other countries in the same way, without preferential treatment.

2 Non-discrimination between domestic and foreign goods and services. All domestic and foreign products and companies must be treated the same way.

The agreements include those on market access, on trade in food and other agricultural goods (the Agreement on Agriculture), on services (the General Agreement on Trade in Services, or GATS), on intellectual property rights, including protection of patenting (the Agreement on Trade-related Intellectual Property Rights, or TRIPs), and on foreign investment (the Agreement on Trade-related Investment Measures, or TRIMs).

The aim of the agreements is to liberalise trade between countries. This includes opening up the economies of developing countries to global markets and 'freeing' markets from government intervention. Tariff protection on imports and on domestic subsidies are being reduced, and export-oriented strategies encouraged. In investment and services equal treatment must be given to foreign and domestic firms, reducing governments' scope to intervene to regulate their activities.

In theory, all members have an equal say in the agreements and decision-making in general works by consensus. All members are required to abide by the agreements, although certain exceptions apply to developing countries, which mainly involve longer periods of implementation. This is termed 'Special and Differential Treatment'.

In practice, however, developing countries often miss out.

- **The decision-making process is biased against the poor.**

Decision-making can easily be dominated by rich country governments. Consequently, trade rules mainly reflect their interests and those of the transnational corporations based in rich countries.

- **Many agreements harm rather than help the poor.**

WTO rules impose uniform policies which can prevent poor countries from pursuing policies suited to their national situation. While rich countries massively protect their agriculture and industry with systems like the European Union's Common Agricultural Policy, poor countries are prevented from adequately protecting themselves against imports that undermine local producers. At the same time they are denied access to rich countries' markets for some of their most important exports.

- **Sometimes there are no rules where rules should exist.**

There is no adequate national or international legislation to regulate the activities of TNCs, despite their size and influence and the fact that some of their activities can undermine the poor.

Losses for the poor, gains for the rich

Five UN agency reports have recently demonstrated how current global trade rules are failing to protect the interests of the poor.

- The *United Nations Development Programme* has calculated that from 1995-2004 the least developed countries would be worse off by $600 million a year as a result of the Uruguay Round agreements – sub-Saharan Africa would be worse off by $1.2 billion.[21] The UK's Secretary of State for International Development, Clare Short, admitted that 'sub-Saharan Africa may face a small welfare loss' as a result of the Uruguay Round agreements.[22]

- A study of 14 developing and least developed countries by the United Nations *Food and Agriculture Organisation (FAO)* shows that, after the Uruguay Round, 11 of the 14 are importing much more than they did before, but that their exports have not risen by as much. The result is that most of the 14 are worse off in balance of payments terms after the Uruguay Round than before. The FAO also notes a worrying trend towards the concentration of farms and absence of safety nets to support marginalised small producers whose food security is decreasing. Key agricultural sectors are being undermined through the competition from cheap imports.[23] The conclusion of a group of 11 of the developing countries was that the report shows that so far 'developing countries on the whole are not benefiting economically from agricultural liberalisation. In fact, the balance of payments situation has worsened. From a socio-economic perspective, food security, employment and poverty seem also to have deteriorated.'[24]

> *'Major violations of human rights are carried out under the legal imprimatur of international trade, negatively impacting the well-being of countless millions of people around the world.'*
>
> Background paper for the United Nations Development Programme [20]

- A UN *General Assembly* report states that 'liberalisation of international trade has not reduced food insecurity. Cheap food imports are threatening local food production and can under some circumstances lead to greater food insecurity.' In the majority of least developed countries 'there are no safeguards to protect fragile industries from abusive competition, and this has resulted in the closure

Christian Aid/Gideon Mendel

Losses for the poor, gains for the rich.

From one of the winners...

'The trade gains that the United States has won through the WTO
agreements and other trade policies have been a major contributing factor
to our thriving economy. Studies estimate that the effect of full implementation
of the WTO agreements will be to boost US GDP by $125-250 billion per
year (in 1998 dollars). We have a great stake in expanding opportunities for
US companies and workers in manufacturing, agriculture and services
industries through the WTO.'

Office of the US Trade Representative [28]

... and one of the losers

'Kenya has faithfully complied with its basic commitments on agriculture in
belief of benefits from freer trade. The results of implementation, however,
have been extremely disappointing. The reform process has neither helped
the sector nor improved food security. The annual average growth of our
agricultural value added fell from 3.3 per cent during the 1980s to 1.4 per cent
in the 1990s without compensating growth in the industrial or the services
sectors. Increase in imported foodstuffs displaced rural farmers from the
domestic market. Without an alternative source of income, farmers have found
difficulties in purchasing imported foodstuffs however cheap they may be,
hence exacerbating poverty, food insecurity and malnutrition in Kenya.'

Government of Kenya statement to the WTO's Committee on Agriculture[29]

of many domestic industries, worsening the situation of unemployment.' The
least developed countries 'have been marginalised in world trade' while 'some
of the problems facing them within the multilateral trading system relate to
difficulties in the implementation of WTO agreements'.[25]

- The *United Nations Conference on Trade and Development* judges that 'the
downside risks' of the Uruguay Round global trade agreements 'have proved
far greater than expected'. 'The predicted gains to developing countries from
the Uruguay Round have proved to be exaggerated' with poverty, unemployment and income inequalities all rising in developing countries.[26]

- The UN's *Sub-Commission on the Promotion and Protection of Human Rights*
describes the WTO as 'a veritable nightmare' for developing countries. In its
view, 'the assumptions on which the rules of WTO are based are grossly unfair
and even prejudiced. Those rules reflect an agenda that serves only to promote
dominant corporatist interests that already monopolise the arena of inter-

national trade'. It also believes that 'women as a group stand to gain little from this organisation [the WTO]' since they have been largely excluded from its decision-making structures.[27]

The WTO and rich countries are unable to show convincingly that the agreements have worked for the poor, since they are refusing to carry out the promises clearly stated in the Uruguay Round's Agreement on Agriculture to conduct official impact assessments of the agreements. Referring to the liberalisation programmes of recent years, a senior World Bank official has noted that 'little has been done to determine what the impact of trade reform on the poor would be.'[30] In the absence of this evidence, they continue to push ahead with more of the same policies. Since the majority of the world's population lives in poverty,[31] and the global rules have global reach, the failure to assess such impact can only be regarded as immoral.

The world's poorest countries are being left further behind the richest, with their terms of trade worsening and the prices of the commodities they export at their lowest level for 150 years. The world's 49 least developed countries are falling further behind other developing countries. In 22 of them, GDP per person either declined or was stagnant in the period 1990-98.[34] Globally, inequalities between people are rising. Between 1988-93, for example, the incomes of the poorest 80 per cent of people in the world actually fell, while the richest fifth of the world's population were the only group that saw their incomes increase, and within this group, the richest one per cent saw their incomes rise the fastest. In Africa, the poorest half of the population became poorer between 1988 and 1993, according to the World Bank.[35] This appalling

Trade liberalisation – conflicting views

'Trade liberalisation has accelerated the free movement of goods and services and has brought benefits to the richer countries. But the benefits have yet to be enjoyed by the least developed countries. In some respects their condition has worsened. An example is the way in which globalisation has intensified the movement of people across borders as many seek to escape dire poverty. For them, the choice is often between poverty at home, or discrimination abroad.'

Mary Robinson, UN High Commissioner for Human Rights[32]

'Trade liberalisation and reform are indispensable key elements contributing to the 'integration objectives' of faster growth, increased earnings and reduced poverty. To this end, strengthening the multilateral trading system and ensuring that progress in liberalisation and reform continues unabated is urgent.'

World Trade Organisation[33]

record of increasing inequality is repeated within countries which are already unequal: the poorest fifth of the population have less than one twentieth of national income in, for example, Brazil, Chile, Gambia, Mexico, Senegal, South Africa and Zimbabwe.

Not all these growing inequalities can of course be laid specifically at the WTO's door, and some of the trends predate the implementation of WTO agreements. But trade liberalisation has so far tended to reward the strong and either bypass or punish the weak. Many people are benefiting from current

> 'That the Least Developed Countries remain committed to the WTO, and optimistic that there are better times ahead, is a tribute to their patience.'
>
> Richard Eglin, Director, Trade and Finance Division, WTO [36]

trade rules, but the evidence suggests that many more are losing out. They see no tangible short-term gains or secure prospect of longer-term improvement. Further, the gains that some poor people have made have often been temporary, and have left them vulnerable to changes in global markets or the whims of TNCs. In this report, we show these effects with regard to people in Sudan, Brazil, Mozambique, Tanzania, the Philippines, India, Peru, Haiti and Uganda.

The WTO in principle and practice

The World Trade Organisation was set up with some lofty ideals. In the preamble to the agreement establishing the WTO, these principles are set out:

- 'relations in the field of trade and economic endeavour should be conducted with a view to raising standards of living, ensuring full employment and a large and steadily growing volume of real income and effective demand...

- 'allowing for the optimal use of the world's resources in accordance with the objective of sustainable development...

- 'seeking both to protect and preserve the environment and to enhance the means for doing so in a manner consistent with their respective needs and concerns at different levels of development...

- 'recognising that there is a need for positive efforts designed to ensure that developing countries, and especially the least developed among them, secure a share in the growth in international trade commensurate with the needs of their economic development.' [37]

If only WTO agreements were always shaped by these impressive principles! But as we will demonstrate, the current practice of the WTO often undermines their implementation. It is good that there is a rules-based system for the conduct of international trade which commands the assent of the powerful as well as the powerless. But we will show how some of the rules are stacked against poor countries and why it is much more difficult for developing countries to use the WTO's dispute settlement mechanism than it is for the rich.

WTO rules also provide a framework within which to tackle rich country trade policies that damage the poor, such as rich country import protection and export subsidies. However rich countries honour these commitments slowly and grudgingly, if at all. Change rarely comes free, and developing countries are often pressed to make equally far-reaching policy changes, either in the same areas or others. This is fundamentally unfair, since the starting point for rich and poor countries in international trade is very different.

Developing countries under the WTO *are* accorded special and differential treatment (SDT) in several areas of the rules. The world's 49 least developed countries are paid particular attention. However, SDT is very limited, with many of its provisions only allowing developing countries more time to introduce the same policies. SDT is not as special and differential as it needs to be to allow poor people to take advantage of globalisation.

The WTO agenda – 'corporate protectionism'

Few issues have shocked Christian Aid as much as seeing the world's powerful states and private corporations forcing their priorities through the WTO, often in the face of mass opposition from developing countries and against the reasoned arguments of UN agencies. They have succeeded in placing onto the trade agenda issues of only marginal relevance to trade, such as intellectual property, and ensured that other critical development issues, such as subjecting TNCs to legally binding regulation, have been left off the agenda and are currently not being discussed in any world forum. One TNC leader, President of the ABB Industrial Group, Percy Barnevik, was extraordinarily candid in his description of the advantages of globalisation:

> 'I would define globalisation as the freedom for my group of companies to invest where it wants when it wants, to produce what it wants, to buy and sell where it wants, and support the fewest restrictions possible coming from labour laws and social conventions.' [39]

The WTO agreements represent a fundamental change in human history in that for the first time agreements made among a small number of people have genuinely *global* coverage.[40] No global institution in history has had such influence over the economies of other countries. Rich country governments, and the companies which so clearly influence them, have succeeded in forcing through regulations which may have major negative effects on poor communities.

Open for criticism?

The WTO, World Bank and IMF have a memorandum of understanding that they agree not to undermine each other through the advice they give, agreements they make or conditions they impose. A recent paper by the chief trade economist of the World Bank argued that certain WTO agreements are not economically viable for poor countries since they cost more to implement than is justified by the potential benefits.[38] However, the memorandum of understanding prevents World Bank staff from warning these countries accordingly. In effect, Bank staff will be forced to argue for implementing policies they know will have negative effects.

The ideological underpinning for this strategy is liberalisation, not a concern with economic justice or the need to help poor people. There is little allowance for ends such as human rights or the preservation of the environment.[41] The primary beneficiaries of such liberalisation are commercial enterprises based largely in rich countries, especially the largest, in whose interests the rules have largely been shaped. And promoting this agenda in the WTO has required massive intervention by the governments of rich countries. Liberalisation can thus be seen as a form of corporate protectionism.

As globalisation has advanced over the last two decades, TNCs have become increasingly influential global players. They have lobbied so successfully that a liberalisation consensus is now so entrenched in policy-making circles that calling for alternatives can appear to be just going against common sense. Trade liberalisation has opened up national economies so TNCs now penetrate almost every major economic sector in every country in the world. They can control developing countries' economies, especially those most vulnerable and struggling to develop, by influencing domestic and international trade policy (see chapter 5).

'We see the new group of supra-states, the multinationals, contributing to more than a fifth of world trade just by trading among themselves. Taking advantage of economies of scale, location, sourcing of inputs and in pricing, they have begun to dominate markets. In some cases they have even followed predatory practices, which make strong economic sense from their perspectives. Least Developed Country firms are unable to compete, and our legal and institutional structures are inadequate to ensure fair competition.'

M.D.Abdul Jalil
Bangladeshi Minister of Commerce [42]

TNCs can and do often provide benefits to the economies of developing countries and enhance poor people's economic opportunities. They can build or finance infrastructure, and provide employment and technology. Their investments can support local businesses and stimulate domestic economic activity. But in many developing countries TNC-led globalisation has led to greater environmental degradation, the undermining of human rights and threats to the livelihoods of the most vulnerable.

Despite their size, influence and impact there are no bodies, governmental or intergovernmental, with sufficient power to regulate or even monitor these large corporations. There is no system of accountability to match the scope of their activities. Trying to make a TNC legally accountable to a government for human rights violations or environmental destruction committed overseas is virtually impossible, and even more so for poor people with no resources to spare for litigation.

'One-size-fits-all – the basic WTO approach'...

A senior World Bank official has, in Christian Aid's view, captured some of the key issues:

'A key issue for developing countries is to ensure that global rules that are negotiated in multilateral bodies support the development process. One message that emerges strongly from recent research is that one size fits all – the basic WTO approach – is not appropriate in a number of areas where there are substantial implementation costs and critical institutional development needs. Developing a position on priority areas for global co-operation and reform is important to support autonomous reform actions that are taken by developing country governments. In doing this, we must draw on country-level experience in determining what types of cooperation (rules of the game) will support the development process.' [44]

The UN's Development Programe has warned:

'The rapidly increasing multilateral agreements – the new rules – are highly binding on national governments and constrain domestic policy choices, including those critical for human development. They drive a convergence of policies in a world of enormous diversity in conditions – economic, social, ecological.' [45]

... which has advantages for some

'You just adjust less because the markets are becoming more and more similar all the world over. We read more or less the same magazines, watch the same films and listen to the same music. That's good for us: we don't have to adapt too much. Maybe it's a little bit boring that all countries become the same but it's good for a global business such as ours.'
Stefan Persson, Chairman, H&M [46]

Global rules are certainly needed to regulate trade. They inevitably place restrictions on national policy-making. But the 'limited domestic policy options'[43] that developing countries have under the current trade rules are far too limited, and do not allow them effectively to pursue policies that help to eradicate poverty. Global rules should make it easier for poor countries to use trade policy to promote development – not more difficult. The key lesson shared by all civil society groups working anywhere in the world is that development happens differently in different places. There can be no single prescription for eradicating poverty. So any set of global rules which is insufficiently flexible to reflect such diversity will be inefficient and likely to fail.

Policies of liberalisation do sometimes benefit groups of poor people within countries, and sometimes those policies can have a positive overall impact. But rigid adherence to this one economic model prevents countries from choosing or pursuing alternative policies, and even from suggesting that an alternative might be what the poor in their country want. It is precisely the intention of WTO agreements to lock developing countries into pursuing a single economic model, a straitjacket of 'one-size-fits-all' liberalisation.

Not only is *any* single model doomed to failure, but the current dominant model is far removed from that pursued in the past by many successful developers, for instance in East Asia, and many developed economies like that in the US. One of the greatest scandals is that many of the global rules within the currently dominant model are specifically preventing poor countries from using policies that had a very successful track record in reducing poverty in the past.

The main WTO actors (which include some large developing countries) demand global rules which open up new markets for their own companies. This imposes a single economic model on all developing countries and in the process severely hinders their ability to promote policies of sustainable development and poverty eradication. Liberal trade rules can leave the smaller, under-resourced industries of developing countries at the mercy of fierce competition from large, established companies from the North or the South. The unintended effect is to stifle development, not promote it.

Reasons to be cheerful

Despite the obstacles, there are strong reasons to be optimistic that trade agreements can be made to serve poor people. Developing countries were able to block the strategy of the rich countries to launch a 'Millennium Round' of trade negotiations at the Seattle ministerial meeting of the WTO in 1999. Although policy-making in the WTO is dominated by the rich countries, developing countries acting together can at least block many proposals that would undermine them.

Since Seattle, the WTO has moved to the front pages of the newspapers for the first time, demystifying an institution that had operated without public scrutiny. Although the motives of some demonstrators were questionable and the methods of a minority contemptible, WTO negotiators are now in the spotlight as never before.

Faced by clear evidence of deepening poverty in many areas of the world, institutions like the World Bank, IMF and WTO are being forced to think again about their strategies. The IMF and the World Bank have started to review their policies to achieve better results in the battle against poverty. So far the WTO has done precious little to rethink the impact its rules are having on poor people, but is beginning to feel the pressure to do so.

And finally, Jubilee 2000 has shown how a focused campaign can mobilise people and press policy-makers to make changes. This is part of an even wider movement among civil society groups around the world. There is an emerging consensus on many key issues – and one of them is that the WTO is one principal cause of a manifestly unjust global economic order. The opportunity exists for this ever-growing movement to reshape the global institutions to promote sustainable development and human rights for all.

The next two years are critical in the WTO negotiations as the key policy areas are all subject to review and rewriting. The opportunity to help shape the rules to benefit the poor is one that the world community cannot afford to miss.

3 The seven deadly rules

The agreements already made in the WTO are having two outcomes that are deepening poverty and inequality for many poor people.

- *Protecting companies*

  Transnational corporations mainly from the rich countries are securing greater access to (and often *control* over) markets in developing countries. This is happening in areas previously denied to them – especially in agricultural trade, through foreign investment and by securing patent rights to natural resources and knowledge.

- *Limiting development strategies*

  Increasingly, developing countries are being prevented from promoting policies they believe to be in their own development interest.

  Supporters of the WTO argue that the system has built in adequate protection for the special interests of developing countries. In practice this flexibility is absent for two main reasons.

- *The first is that although there are some formal exemptions and safeguards in WTO rules, developing countries cannot properly take advantage of them.*
  The rules are very complex. It is extremely difficult and costly to invoke the formal investigations that the WTO requires to implement them. Few poor countries have the legal capacity or the funds to do this. The UN's Food and Agricultural Organisation notes that the safeguards 'are not useful for many developing countries. Rather, they would need more accessible and simpler instruments'.[49] Neither would many be prepared to risk the economic or political fall-out of proceeding with an investigation against rich countries. Though quite impressive on paper, the safeguards are in practice virtually unusable.

- *The second is that these formal exemptions and safeguards are often overridden by rich country pressure outside the WTO.*
  For example, the World Bank/IMF's Structural Adjustment Programmes (SAPs) in the 1980s and 1990s virtually eliminated countries' ability to use agricultural

subsidies and protect themselves against cheap imports. These policies continue with SAPs' successor – the Poverty Reduction Strategy process. PRSP is seen by WTO officials as a primary means to promote trade liberalisation outside the WTO's formal remit. Also, new *bilateral* trade agreements, especially with the EU, are reinforcing liberalisation policies in developing countries.

These pressures combine to make the formal exemptions and safeguards in the WTO rules almost meaningless. The WTO can in some ways be seen to be a de facto police force for imposing liberalisation policies on developing countries across a range of world bodies. Indeed, with its dispute settlement mechanism, it is judge and jury, too. The result is to impose on developing countries a single economic model.

The negative outcomes of the WTO rules can be illustrated by looking at seven specific trade rules, all of which need to be rewritten so that poor people benefit from the appropriate choice of development strategy.

What the rules forbid: how the WTO agreements prevent choice in strategies for development

'The Uruguay Round produced agreements which have limited the policy options available to the remaining late developers. Today, many of the policy measures that were applied so successfully in the transformation of the South and Southeast Asian region are no longer possible under these agreements. That is why OAU member states take the view that the provisions on special and differential treatment in these Agreements need to be expanded and strengthened.'

Organisation of African Unity [47]

'Although developing countries need policy flexibility to support and promote their enterprises, investments in production and marketing, and export expansion and diversification, latecomers now face more stringent policy conditions than those which prevailed previously.'

UNCTAD [48]

Rule one: limits protection against cheap food imports

The flood of food imports into many developing countries that has followed trade liberalisation is taking away the livelihoods of many poor people all over the world. WTO rules do not allow developing countries to raise their tariffs on imported food and many have been forced to reduce them. The rules also allow subsidised exports from Northern countries – for example under the EU's

Common Agricultural Policy – to be dumped (exported at below market price) on food markets. The beneficiaries are mainly Northern export companies.

What the rule says

Developing countries are being prevented from protecting themselves adequately against cheap imports, which undermine local food producers and food security.

The presumption in WTO agreements is in favour of allowing imports, except where countries are allowed to retain some tariff barriers, or allowed to invoke special safeguard provisions under the Agreement on Agriculture (see page 40). Developing countries generally are required to reduce tariff barriers on agricultural goods by an average of 24 per cent by 2005 (36 per cent for developed countries). The least developed countries are exempt from these reduction commitments, but all countries – even the least developed – have to 'bind' their tariffs on agricultural products. They are not allowed to *raise* their import tariffs beyond a certain level to protect themselves from cheap imports.

> *'On agriculture, the promise was liberalise and things will get better. The opposite has happened. Now we have food insecurity.'*
>
> African official involved in the WTO negotiations, October 2000 [50]

There are three ways developing countries can *in theory* protect domestic production against cheap imports:

1 Under the first way – the '**general safeguard provisions**' in the WTO rules – countries must clearly demonstrate that such imports are causing serious injury to *all the producers in that industry* (it is not enough to demonstrate that a small number of producers are affected). A lengthy consultation process with all WTO countries affected follows, then a meticulous investigation. At the end a country can, if successful, impose only a temporary safeguard measure (maximum of ten years for developing countries) to allow domestic industry to adjust itself to the competition from imports.

2 The second way – the '**special safeguard provisions**' (SSP) – is for agricultural products only. Here, countries are not required to demonstrate a negative impact on domestic production. The SSP provisions are complex. Essentially, developing countries can invoke SSP either when the price of the import has fallen below a prescribed level (usually calculated as the average cost, insurance and freight import price) or when the quantity of the import has reached a prescribed level. Under SSP countries cannot restrict the actual quantity of the imports but can increase the import duty on them. Notice has first to be given

to the WTO's Committee on Agriculture and every other country concerned has to be consulted.

3 The third way is **anti-dumping measures**. Dumping is defined as exporting at a price less than the comparable price of the product in the producing country. Developing (and other) countries can in theory take action if there is injury to the domestic industry. However, the agreement rests on very difficult determinations of what constitutes the export price and what constitutes the 'normal price'. And the investigation procedure is so costly that it is only available to a few developing countries with sufficient capacity and resources, and only for large-scale impacts.[51]

The Agreement on Agriculture

In most developing countries agriculture is the major employer of labour. It produces most of the food eaten by the poor, and provides a large proportion of export earnings. In most European countries and in the USA, the number of people employed in rural areas is tiny, and agriculture's contribution to the economy is very limited. But farmers are a very influential lobby group. For this reason, agriculture has always been hugely controversial in trade negotiations. For a long time, it was virtually excluded from negotiations. That changed with the Uruguay Round which led to the founding of the WTO. For the first time agriculture was discussed, and delegates agreed to treat it more like other goods in trade talks.

The Agreement on Agriculture (AoA) negotiations were dominated by disagreement between the US and EU over protection and access to markets. The final agreement reflects the agendas of the developed world. It covers three main areas: domestic production subsidies, export subsidies and market access. Developing countries were brought into the negotiations only at the last minute, when the agreement had in essence already been written. The issues relevant to least developed countries – like market stability and food security – were never properly addressed. Many developing countries disagreed with the AoA, but it was presented as a package which had to be accepted on an all-or-nothing basis. They hoped that greater access to rich country markets would be forthcoming in future negotiations. The AoA is currently being reviewed in negotiations at the WTO, which are expected to continue throughout 2002.

For developing countries food security is paramount. This means making sure food is available at all times, and that everyone is able to get enough of the right sort of food to support a healthy life. In theory there is no reason why a country cannot meet its food needs through imports: sometimes this may look sensible in the short-term. But trade policies which undermine the position of poor and marginal farmers can endanger food security. In practice most

developing countries find it difficult or impossible to meet all their food requirements through imports. Access to remote communities is often impossible due
to infrastructural deficiencies, and often these communities do not have the
cash to buy imported food. Reliance on international production also leads to
higher risks, as national governments have no control over what and how much
is produced.

If cheap imports are allowed to flood developing country markets, local
producers can be pushed out of production. Dependence on imports can make
developing countries vulnerable to price fluctuations on international markets,
and when there is very little foreign exchange to buy imports, a sudden increase
in the price of essential goods can cause havoc with the balance of payments.
Governments need to be able to choose the policy which best serves the long-
term interests of their people.

Many countries have become less self-sufficient in food after opening their
markets to food imports. As a group, the least developed countries have
changed from being relatively self-sufficient to being net food importers – what
the Secretary General of UNCTAD, Rubens Ricupero, has described as 'one
of the darkest stories of the last 25 years.' [52] Some case studies from UNCTAD
can be found in Appendix II. Other examples of the effects of liberalisation
policies (often combining WTO agreements as well as structural adjustment
programmes) follow.

- In Sri Lanka, food imports have significantly increased since 1996 leading to
a decline in domestic production and a drastic fall in rural employment.[53] An
UNCTAD report notes that Sri Lanka's fixing of tariff rates and elimination
of non-tariff barriers 'led both to a surge in food imports and to a reduction
in domestic production of certain food crops in recent years'.[54]

- In Guyana, imports of food and drink have shot up since liberalisation, replacing domestic production. Even products where Guyana might be expected to
be able to compete are not immune – fruit juices are being imported from
France and Thailand, undermining local producers.[55]

- In Trinidad and Tobago, an UNCTAD report notes that domestic production of some of the major staple crops has been damaged, with self-sufficiency
in rice being halved compared to the situation before the Uruguay Round level.
Meanwhile, 'multilateral trade liberalisation did not improve the export performance of major exports such as sugar'.[56]

- The Philippines used to be almost self-sufficient in food. However, since 1995,
tariffs and quantitative restrictions have been removed and the Philippines has
become a net food importer. Millions of peasants are losing income because
cheap maize and rice imports make it difficult for them to sell their own crops.[57]

- In 1996 Mexican subsistence farmers faced inflows into their markets of US cereal supported by export credits and government subsidies in the US. This created an enormous glut that forced local prices down by 20 per cent compared to previous years.[58]

- In Gambia, EU subsidised poultry exports are being dumped, undermining local producers.[59]

- In Brazil, the wheat, rice and cotton sectors have seen production shrink because of the competitive pressure of imports. The agricultural sector has been transformed through liberalisation, with large-scale farming promoted at the expense of local co-operatives. This has undermined the livelihoods of many farmers, particularly those involved in maize and soy-bean production.[60]

There is overwhelming evidence that cheap food imports are undermining local producers and food security in numerous developing countries, which is why UNCTAD and many developing countries are pleading for WTO agreements to be rewritten. In UNCTAD's words, developing countries 'require flexibility to apply urgent measures to safeguard small farmers against import surges and unfair trade practices, particularly those affecting the production of key staples of domestic diet.'[62]

'Food imports... have further demoralised the small-scale farmers. Having produced maize, rice, soybeans, rabbits, sheep and goats, Ghana's farmers cannot obtain economic prices for them, even in village markets. Their produce cannot compete with imported maize, rice, soybean, chicken and turkey. Farmers are producing as much food but receiving lower prices. Smallholder incomes have fallen and malnutrition among the rural poor has risen.'

Christian Aid partner in Ghana [61]

Ironically, while the liberalisation of agriculture is intended to increase competitiveness, it can have the opposite effect. Developing country governments used to be able to protect their farmers by imposing import tariffs and non-tariff measures on agricultural products coming from abroad, so that their farmers would at least be able to compete in the domestic market. However, even before the Uruguay Round was agreed, many developing countries had to lower their import duties as a condition of structural adjustment lending from the World Bank and IMF. As an UNCTAD experts meeting noted:

'Rapid market liberalisation and reduction of domestic support under structural adjustment programmes, which many least developed countries and net food importing developing countries have undergone in the last 15 years, may have harmed the competitiveness and the viability of their agricultural activities through, inter alia, an inflow of imports of key staples.'[63]

The Agreement on Agriculture has made many developing countries feel that they have been pressured into agreeing to something that has made their situation worse. Many industrialised countries still subsidise farmers to produce food domestically which could be imported at lower cost. They do this partly because they recognise the insecurity which comes with over-dependence on food imports. Why should rich countries deny developing countries the opportunity to operate the same safeguards?

One possible explanation can be found in the candid words of the former US Agriculture Secretary, John Block, expressed at the beginning of the Uruguay Round negotiations in 1986:

'[the] idea that developing countries should feed themselves is an anachronism from a bygone era. They could better ensure their food security by relying on US agricultural products, which are available, in most cases, at much lower cost.'[64]

Straightforward commercial motives are also involved. A 1993 report from the US Department of Agriculture (USDA) argued that 'because the domestic market absorbs a smaller and smaller share of production, US agriculture must compete more and more effectively with other countries for share of world market – or else accept a reduction of productive capacity'. USDA estimated that the Agreement on Agriculture would create market opportunities of $3 billion for American producers, mainly in south-east Asia. Forcing open poor countries' economies is allowing food exporting US TNCs potentially massive commercial benefits.[65]

So while developing countries are unable to protect themselves sufficiently against cheap imports, most rich countries continue to use domestic and export subsidies to protect their own producers. These subsidies – which can include direct payments to farmers or payment to reduce export marketing costs – are used by rich countries to offload surplus production at prices lower than in their domestic markets. They are therefore a direct cause of dumping. Export subsidies have been especially damaging to small-scale producers in developing countries who have few resources to compete against subsidised exports from the rich world. They also increase the instability and variability of prices on world agricultural markets.[66]

The Government of Bolivia puts this argument in stark terms:

'The adverse effects of the production and export subsidies granted by some developed countries have a direct impact on food security in developing countries and jeopardise their political and social stability by increasing the poverty of their populations, especially in rural areas, thus creating an ever-increasing migratory flow to urban centres and the proliferation of belts of poverty in cities... The opening of markets as a result of the current negotiations will not benefit countries such as Bolivia for the simple reason that Bolivian producers will once again have to compete with their counterparts in rich countries who receive billions of dollars in production and export subsidies. We shall embark on the same vicious cycle. The benefits of greater market access will accrue to countries which distort trade in agricultural products and they will take up the new market opportunities by dumping products.' [67]

The EU is the largest provider of export subsidies. It has agreed to cut them substantially but according to UNCTAD, by July 2000 'five years after the implementation of the Uruguay Round, there has been very little reduction of world market distortions in this area.' [68] Together with huge levels of domestic subsidies to agriculture, UNCTAD notes that export subsidies work 'against the interests of developing countries as it causes the unfair advantage which the farmers in developed countries have over those in developing countries. Therefore, developed countries should eliminate totally their domestic support and export subsidy immediately, the latest by 2005'.[69]

The myth of 'symmetrical liberalisation'

If all countries remove trade barriers at the same time, do poor countries gain the same as rich countries? The answer is 'no'. The main reason lies in the nature of the poverty that poor countries experience and the way markets operate.

Poverty often occurs when markets are either non-existent or distorted. Poor communities lack the information and institutions to provide the enabling environment for market exchange to take place to the benefit of poor people. Poor people often lack the capital and skills required to respond adequately to market signals, including the signal to expand productive capacity. Poverty means that poor farmers will rightly not take the risk of abandoning the production of food crops in the hope of higher returns from cash crops.

But rich countries believe the answer to the question is 'yes, poor countries *do* gain the same as rich countries'. The EU, for example, is vigorously promoting regional free trade agreements with many developing countries based on mutual opening of markets for some products. Developed countries can immediately take advantage of the market opportunities when developing countries liberalise. EU and US goods have flooded into developing countries since the AoA was signed. But developing countries can rarely take full advantage of the new opportunities when rich countries open their markets. An FAO study of the impact of the AoA in developing countries concluded that:

'While trade liberalisation [in developing countries] led to a quick increase in food imports, exports did not rise similarly or proportionately. This has implications for the pace of liberalisation for countries where supply constraints and other market entry difficulties do not allow them to take advantage of market opportunities as quickly as other suppliers are able to export to them.' [70]

Similarly, the International Trade Centre believes that with the complete abolition of rich country tariffs on textile imports, the least developed countries (LDCs), some of whom are important exporters of textiles, may not gain because of competition from non-LDC developing countries. The latter have better supply structures. Again, across the board liberalisation affects groups of countries differently.[71]

An UNCTAD agricultural trade experts' meeting described well many of the internal and external barriers facing developing countries as they try to take advantage of some of the benefits that liberalisation can bring.

Internal barriers:

- 'these countries continued to face domestic capacity limitation in the areas of production, infrastructure and research and development of technologies to improve productivity...

- 'agricultural producers, especially small-scale farmers, had also to cope with the need for investment and limited access to finances to meet incremental working capital needs either because of the non-existence of financial facilities or because of a general credit "crunch".'

External barriers:

- 'the technology and skills gap in agricultural production and quality control between developed countries and developing countries...

- 'lack of capacity and expertise in the international marketing and transport of their products...

- 'a highly oligopolistic market structure in some major commodity markets controlled by large TNCs. Certain product sectors of the world agricultural market, for instance, are highly concentrated and dominated by TNCs, which contribute up to 80 per cent of the market share in international agricultural trade. Experts expressed particular concern about this issue, stressing that such a trading environment would place small-scale farmers in developing countries at a permanent competitive disadvantage unless complementary actions were taken to strengthen their position.' [72]

Rule two: limits government regulation of services

The WTO's current services agreement is in danger of being the launch pad for offering up health, education and water services (as well as energy, transport and communication sectors) to control by TNCs. Corporate interests are clearly driving this WTO agenda, which is increasingly preventing developing countries from pursuing locally developed policies designed for their specific development needs.

What the rule says

The WTO's agreement on services (the General Agreement on Trade in Services, or GATS) encourages countries to open up their service sectors to foreign suppliers by abolishing restrictions on their access to domestic markets. GATS reduces governments' ability to regulate such access and obliges governments to give the same treatment to foreign companies as they give to domestic companies.

However, current rules do allow countries to *choose* which sectors they open up and there is no formal obligation to do so. Most commitments hitherto have been made in tourism, hotels and restaurants, and computer-related services, and the current agreement appears to exclude services provided by governments. The main danger with GATS is not its current practice but the WTO's built-in agenda of accelerating liberalisation. The GATS framework might in future expand into social sectors like health care, education and water. The danger is that an expanded and revised GATS might threaten developing countries' ability to provide services to meet the needs of poor people. [75]

About one-fifth of international trade is trade in services – a global market worth $1,350 billion with an annual growth rate of six per cent in the 1990s. Services can be defined as anything that can be bought and sold, but not picked up and carried away – telephone calls, tourism, health care and banking are all examples of services which can be traded between countries. This trade is dominated by the rich countries – the share of the least developed countries in the global trade in services is 0.42 per cent. [76] Services account for 60 per cent of global foreign direct investment, much of which is connected with privatisation of state entities. [77]

> 'The overarching objective of the global business community in the coming negotiations should be to both broaden and deepen countries' GATS liberalisation commitments.
> A contestable, competitive market in every sector and in every WTO member country is the ultimate goal.'
>
> Robert Vastine, President, US Coalition of Service Industries [73]

GATS has, in the words of the WTO Secretariat, 'a built-in commitment to continuous liberalisation through periodic negotiations'. It is also 'the world's first multilateral agreement on investment, since it covers not just cross-border trade but every possible means of supplying a service, including the right to set up a commercial presence in the export market'.[78] The GATS agreement extends 'into areas never before recognised as trade policy' in the words of Renato Ruggiero, the former WTO Director General.[79] The commitments undertaken in GATS 'have the effect of protecting liberalisation policies, regardless of their underlying rationale, from slippages and reversals', the WTO Secretariat has noted.[80]

GATS as a pure extension of corporate interests

'An active services industry involvement in the negotiations is crucial to target the EU's negotiating objectives towards priorities for business. The GATS is not just something that exists between governments. It is first and foremost an instrument for the benefit of business.'

European Commission [74]

GATS owes its existence to pressure from services companies and governments with major services export sectors – especially the US, but also Japan, the EU and Canada.[81] The head of the WTO's Services Division has said that 'without the enormous pressure generated by the American financial services sector... there would have been no services agreement'.[82] The UK Government has said that GATS is a key priority because the government has a 'vital economic interest in seeing services markets liberalised around the world' since 'the UK is among the world's top services exporters, second only to the US in 1997'.[83]

Business coalitions on both sides of the Atlantic have appeared to have little trouble in turning elected politicians into corporate lobbyists. The US Coalition of Service Industries (CSI) has led international business efforts to shape GATS and directly influence the positions of the former US Trade Representative, Charlene Barshevsky, for example at the Singapore ministerial conference in 1996 where a deal on telecommunications was pushed through. The European Services Forum (ESF) has played a similar role in Europe under a mission to 'support and encourage the movement to liberalise service sector markets throughout the world and to remove trade and investment barriers for the European services sector'. A senior EU official, Robert Madelin, once wrote to the ESF saying that 'we would like to encourage all European service industries to continue cooperating actively with us to develop the solid and detailed common negotiating position that we wish to present in Geneva'.[84] He also asked for more information on corporate priorities for 'liberalisation' of 'construction, education, environmental, health and social services, and audiovisual services' and to indicate which barriers 'are most disturbing'.[85]

The former EU Trade Commissioner, Leon Brittan welcomed corporate involvement in the negotiating process:

> 'I am very pleased to see how quickly and enthusiastically the different services sectors have organised themselves to provide business input for the GATS 2000 negotiations. Our negotiating priorities need to be rooted in the real concerns of business and we will be paying very close attention indeed to the negotiating priorities that the ESN [European Services Network] identifies.' [86]

Lord Brittan of Spennithorne moved on from being a Vice-President of the European Commission and EU Trade Commissioner to be appointed chairperson of the LOTIS (Liberalisation of Trade in Services) Group of International Financial Services, London (IFSL). IFSL was recently launched to promote the UK financial services industry and to work for the removal of barriers to trade in services. In a speech in early 2001, Lord Brittan said:

> 'There was a time when international trade negotiations in the GATT rounds were very much left to government officials. The Uruguay Round began to change that, in particular because trade in services posed more complex problems when it came to liberalisation. Private sector views on issues and priorities became important inputs for government negotiators. I recognised this myself when I was EU Commissioner responsible for trade negotiations and I invited business leaders to become more involved. The European Services Forum has proved to be a most successful vehicle for this dialogue... In the UK, IFSL's LOTIS structure has done similarly good work over many years in representing financial sector views... Internationally, I appreciated the input of the Financial Leaders Group in the run-up to and during the final stages of the World Trade Organisation agreement on financial services in 1997. All this demonstrates how important it is for companies to be involved at the most senior level...
>
> 'The business voice must make itself heard above the noise being generated from other sources threatening the ongoing health of the system. First, there are the attacks being mounted by some influential non-governmental organisations against globalisation, the international institutions and the WTO in particular. It is tempting to dismiss them as misguided and leave it at that. But the more responsible and serious minded of those organisations have staked a claim in the international debate and we cannot afford to ignore them. What we have to do is to take the debate on and win it. I do not think we have to be defensive about this. The business arguments are strong – provided they are

heard... Against the 'NGO challenge' [we should] take up the cudgels, make the business case, demonstrate convincingly that for developing countries to liberalise is of advantage to them and their populations. Show that the solutions advocated by some NGOs will harm growth and employment here and overseas. Find ways of gaining the media limelight to counter the campaigns being conducted by NGOs on and off the streets... What is the UK looking for in the new round? In general, greater commitment to liberalise in all the modes of supply for tradable services where the UK has a strong interest.' [87]

During the Uruguay Round, EU negotiators concluded that GATS would be of little benefit to developing countries.[88] Yet rich countries are currently actively pushing to significantly expand GATS and negotiations began in early 2000 with a view to reaching a new agreement by December 2002. US government policy is clear:

'The mandate of the negotiations is ambitious: to remove restrictions on trade in services and provide effective market access, subject to specified limitations. Our challenge is to accomplish significant removal of these restrictions across all services sectors, addressing measures currently subject to GATS disciplines and potentially measures not currently subject to GATS disciplines.' [89]

The EU and US have been co-operating closely to ensure that negotiations advance quickly. A particular danger for developing countries is that there is considerable consensus among the Quad group (US, Canada, EU and Japan) as to what they want.[90] Many corporate lobby groups have developed sophisticated sector-specific market access and policy reform objectives.[91] WTO officials are gearing up to deflect NGO and other criticism of the plans for an expanded GATS.[92] There is already in place a considerable global NGO campaign to help prevent the future expansion of GATS into the area of government services, undermining the public provision of services in North and South.[93]

According to the EU website, the services sector 'is central to the future of the world economy and an increasingly competitive tool for EU businesses'. The EU 'is the world leader in this field' and 'leads in the drive to liberalise trade in services worldwide and remove barriers to a truly global market in services'. The GATS negotiations 'should create even greater market opening, enable developing countries to participate more and cover important new sectors. Given the importance of GATS to business, the European Commission launched initiatives such as the 'GATS 2000', which helped prepare for the services negotiations which commenced in the WTO in January 2000. The gathering also launched the 'European Services Forum': a consultation process that enables European services industries to inform the Commission of their expectations for these GATS negotiations.'[94]

Rich countries insist that they wish to safeguard the interests of developing countries in the GATS negotiations. Publicly, the US wants GATS to ensure that WTO members 'retain the right to regulate to meet national policy objectives, consistent with existing or potential new GATS disciplines'. Least developed countries 'should be free to choose their participation in any plurilateral or multilateral GATS initiatives'.[95] And the UK government says it has 'no intention whatsoever of offering to privatise public health care or education under the GATS 2000 negotiations'.[96] Although GATS encompasses all services, many government officials believe that it makes an exception for public services like health or education 'supplied in the exercise of governmental authority' (article 1.3b). However, the agreement defines these areas so narrowly – as 'any service which is supplied neither on a commercial basis, nor in competition with one or more service suppliers' (article 1.3c) – that the exception could be meaningless if subject to a dispute settlement procedure case at the WTO.[97]

In the GATS negotiations, governments are increasingly coming under pressure to open up more and more sectors and to take on commitments which future governments cannot reverse.[98] It may become more difficult for developing countries to protect the current *voluntary* nature of agreements on services.[99] An expanded GATS may progressively open up key sectors such as health, education and water to control by foreign companies, who might marginalise the needs of the poor in their own self-interest. This fear is well-founded in the light of growing pressure on developing countries from other global bodies like the World Bank to privatise and deregulate their public services.

TNCs are specifically identifying public services as targets for competition. The potential market is huge: global expenditures on water services exceed $1 trillion, education exceeds $2 trillion and health care exceeds $3.5 trillion. According to Maude Barlow, a Director of the International Forum on Globalisation, these sectors have been targeted by TNCs 'who are aiming at nothing less than the complete dismantling of public services by subjecting them to the rules of international competition and the discipline of the WTO'. The WTO's Services Division has recently hired a private company to document world-wide policies that 'discriminate against foreign education providers'.[100] The chair of the US Coalition of Service Industries submitted in a report to the US Congress in 1999 that one of the objectives of the GATS negotiations should be to encourage privatisation of health care systems, allowing for complete foreign ownership of health facilities.[101]

A taste of the future?
Services 'liberalisation' undermining public health

Sweden has for many years restricted the direct advertising of spirits, wine and strong beer on public health grounds. However, in a ruling in March 2001, the European Court of Justice found this policy to be 'an obstacle to the free movement of services within the EU and, therefore, contravened the EU's founding treaty'.[102] The danger is that an expanded GATS will similarly pay little heed to public health and that national governments will be required to place their obligations to free trade first.

In recent years developing countries have seen a massive increase in the advertising of tobacco products as the market for cigarettes in rich countries declines and with emerging economies seen as key markets. A number of developing countries – such as South Africa – have attempted to restrict these adverts, basing the ban on public health grounds. It is possible that this legislation might come under threat if the GATS agreement is expanded in the coming years.

Concerns about poverty have not seriously figured in the shaping of the GATS agreement. Developing countries have continually asked for impact assessments to be conducted, as required under Article XIX of the GATS agreement. But little heed is being paid to this call because the developed countries are not interested in slowing down the negotiations.[103] Few developing countries had much idea what impact the GATS agreement would have when they signed it, but they are combining to argue for caution in the future. One group of African countries, for example, has called for future GATS negotiations to recognise fully that 'such factors as national policy objectives and individual levels of development can be taken into account for opening fewer sectors, liberalising fewer types of transactions and attaching conditions'.[104]

Underlying the GATS agreement is the false assumption that progressive liberalisation of services will inevitably benefit everyone, both rich and poor. This is recognised even by an unlikely source: Andrew Buxton, the chairman of the European Services Forum (and former chairman of Barclays Bank). Although the ESF is at the forefront of the push for increased liberalisation, Buxton once noted in a speech that 'there may of course be good reasons for barriers, particularly in the developing world where cultural and social conditions should be taken into account before a programme of unrestricted liberalisation is undertaken'.[105]

Rule three: limits regulation of foreign investment

The WTO's existing investment agreement is likely to prevent the poorest countries from sufficiently developing their own industries. But rich countries want to establish a new, strong investment agreement to promote unfettered access to developing country markets for their own companies. Policies that have successfully reduced poverty in the past will no longer be available to developing countries in the future.

What the rule forbids

The Agreement on Trade-related Investment Measures (TRIMs) covers conditions on investment that are related to trade in goods. It bans laws, policies or administrative regulations that favour domestic over foreign capital inputs. These include:

- local content policies – where governments require a corporation to use or purchase domestic products

- trade balancing measures – where governments impose restrictions on the import of capital goods by corporations to reflect the level of exports

- foreign exchange balancing requirements – where a corporation's permitted imports are tied to the value of its exports so that there is a net foreign exchange earning.[107]

Least developed countries have been given until 2002 to end these policies; other developing countries were given until 2000. Countries can be exempted if they are able to show that they are experiencing overall balance of payments problems. This would allow them to prohibit imports in favour of domestic goods. However, in order to invoke this exception, developing countries need to demonstrate that a variety of particular conditions prevail and have to consult with other WTO members in a formal process.

Then there are further restrictions on the use of this exemption; for example, action taken simply to protect domestic production is not allowed. Developing countries are also coming under pressure to revoke this exemption and have to make ever stronger cases for using it. Former Indian Ambassador to the GATT, Bhagirath Lal Das, notes that 'some developing countries which have lately faced balance of payments difficulties have thought of taking these measures, but have met with severe resistance in the WTO'.[108]

Though many developing countries have small industrial sectors, others have achieved large reductions in poverty through promoting industrial development. The key has generally been the successful development of *domestic* industries, which many governments have prioritised over simply encouraging foreign investment. They have imposed requirements on foreign investors to buy a certain proportion of their inputs locally. However, since this restricts their ability to trade internationally, these potentially useful development measures are now banned under the TRIMs agreement.

After the Asian financial crisis in 1998, many Asian countries argued that abolishing some of their investment policies under TRIMs would have serious consequences for domestic industry. The Philippines estimated that ending local content requirements and other policies would cost about 10,000 jobs in its car parts industry – a quarter of the workforce in that sector.[109] By ruling out these and other policies, the TRIMs agreement prevents developing countries from pursuing policies which have been very successful in promoting industrialisation in the past. According to a report from UNCTAD, the TRIMs agreement 'could limit attempts to build up domestic capacity'.[110]

> *'The TRIMs agreement, by outlawing trade-balancing and local content policies, effectively eliminates the use of trade policy for industrialisation and development.'*
>
> Walden Bello, Professor of Sociology at the University of the Philippines and Director of the NGO Focus on the Global South [106]

Many developing countries are now voicing their opposition to the TRIMs agreement as well as to a new WTO agreement on investment that could replace it. Trade negotiators from 27 African countries, meeting in June 2001, called for a review of the TRIMs agreement.[111] Shortly before the WTO ministerial conference in Seattle, the Indian Government circulated proposals on behalf of 11 other developing countries arguing for a substantial revision of TRIMs, noting that 'there is a need to review provisions in the Agreement on TRIMs which come in the way of acceleration of economic growth in developing countries and deny these countries the means to maintain balance of payments stability'. It also notes that developing countries should be exempted from the ban on the use of local content measures.[112]

Foreign investment is a key to establishing industry in countries that have no domestic industrial base. But equally, regulation of foreign investment has often been a useful tool for countries with emerging industrial sectors. Otherwise, unregulated foreign investment risks having a negative effect, driving out local investors and undermining local producers. One academic study for UNCTAD shows that foreign investment plays a more beneficial role in stimulating the domestic economy where governments impose regulations than where regulations have been largely abolished.[113]

The myth of Foreign Direct Investment (FDI) as a development panacea

Direct investment by foreign companies is able to help poor countries by supporting the production of goods and services for export, by replacing imported goods and services or by developing infrastructure facilities which can encourage further investment flows. It can help countries gain access to new technologies and support the development of local industries through backward and forward linkages. Investment by TNCs can create jobs in companies linked to their operations, and because wages are spent locally, they can boost overall demand, stimulating growth and job expansion.

But FDI must not be seen as a panacea for developing countries. First, foreign investment often fails to benefit the poor directly. Only a small proportion is invested in the small enterprise sector, for example, which is the main source of new jobs and income for the poor.[114] As the Development Assistance Committee of the OECD has noted, 'private resources generally do not flow directly to some key sectors of priority need, such as health and education'. Poverty often remains widespread in countries which have received large

A bill of rights for TNCs – the Multilateral Agreement on Investment (MAI)

The rich OECD countries recently attempted – in the negotiations on the Multilateral Agreement on Investment (MAI) – to push through an international agreement that would give equal treatment to foreign investors and ban all kinds of government regulations such as technology transfer requirements, restrictions on repatriation of profits, controls on foreign exchange flows and nationalisation. The worst aspect was that the MAI would have allowed TNCs to sue governments for legislation they might have enacted that resulted in 'limitations of profit'.

The UK's Department of Trade and Industry was one of the strongest proponents of the treaty, arguing that the UK could not afford special measures to protect workers, consumers and the environment because countries with lower standards would out-compete it.[120] The MAI was stopped partly due to a campaign by NGOs in the South and North, who argue that governments need to regulate foreign investment to ensure that it contributes to rather than undermines development efforts.

amounts of FDI, as investment and growth have often been concentrated in a few urban areas.[115]

Second, a UN study shows that, dollar-for-dollar, domestic investment is often a better generator of jobs, revenues and linkages to other firms than foreign investment.[116] According to the UN's Industrial Development Organisation, although FDI is vital for development, 'in the final analysis it is the domestic investment, domestic policies and domestic entrepreneurial skills that are ultimately decisive in industrial development'.[117]

Third, as UNCTAD points out, one lesson of the Asian financial crisis is surely that excessive reliance on foreign resources and markets leaves countries more vulnerable to external shocks. UNCTAD calls for greater attention to '*domestic* sources of growth, such as rising wage shares and higher social spending'. This includes 'a major role for public investment and the involvement of a developmental state, with new policy agendas.' [118]

In summary, foreign investment is no magic bullet for developing countries. In most cases, encouraging foreign investment will need to be balanced with encouraging domestic investment. In some cases, strategies to encourage domestic investment will need to be expressly prioritised over attracting foreign investment. Foreign investment also needs to be regulated by governments to work in the interests of the poor. There also needs to be an international framework in place that prevents TNCs being able to play weak countries off against each other by introducing the most lax regulations.

Rich countries are currently exerting their muscle to go beyond the TRIMs agreement to replace the failed Multilateral Agreement on Investment (MAI, see box). The Japanese government still describes the TRIMs agreement as a 'first step' towards achieving a MAI-type agreement. A recent European Commission proposal for a WTO agreement on investment was similar to the MAI and would have amounted to little more than a bill of rights for transnational corporations.[119] The Commission is currently proposing a more limited agreement on investment that would only cover foreign direct investment (not other forms of investment such as portfolio investment) and allow some flexibility for developing countries. However, the government of India in particular remains opposed to such an agreement.

For many developing countries industrial development forms the cornerstone of their development objectives. Whether through agricultural processing, development of new high-tech industries, or specialisation in textiles, they aim to expand domestic production, and thus increase added value. This expands and widens consumer choice and increases the benefits of trade. For these countries the option of introducing a variety of industrial and investment policies to suit their national purposes is vitally important. It is surely quite wrong that rich countries should seek to make agreements that prevent them from doing this.

Rule four: limits the use of subsidies for agriculture

WTO rules prevent developing countries from being able sufficiently to support their agriculture through subsidies, while the EU and US both spend huge sums of taxpayers' money on much bigger subsidies themselves. The reduction of subsidies in developing countries is often having severe effects on small farmers.

What the rule forbids

The thrust of the WTO agreements is to reduce and finally eliminate domestic subsidies[121] to agriculture. WTO members were required to notify the WTO of the level of their domestic support to agriculture in each year from 1995-2004, progressively reducing it and being forbidden from increasing it. Rich countries were required to reduce their total levels of domestic support by 20 per cent over six years, and developing countries by 13.3 per cent over ten years.

There are some safeguards in the agreement. Importantly, the least developed countries are exempt from reduction commitments. For other developing countries, some types of subsidies are also exempted. But while many types of subsidy used by developing countries – such as for land improvement – are now banned, many used by developed countries – such as for research and development and crop insurance – have been preserved.[122] Even where developing countries want to make use of exemptions, they have to demonstrate that they will not have more than minimal 'trade-distorting' effects, or provide price support to producers.[123]

However, at the same time, the EU and the US are pouring taxpayers' money into developing their agricultural sectors, in practices endorsed by the WTO. In 1999, OECD countries paid a total of $362 billion to their farmers – nearly ten times the aid they granted to developing countries. Every person in the UK pays over £50 per year to UK farmers, while only four per cent of the population in the UK actually farm. No other sector gets this size of subsidy.

Contrary to popular myth, most support to agriculture in rich countries does not go to help small farmers. Half of all EU support under the Common Agricultural Policy (CAP) goes to the richest 17 per cent of farmers.[124] And 70 per cent of the subsidies go to the largest 25 per cent of farms.[125] Each year the UK receives around £3 billion in subsidies, 80 per cent of which goes to the richest 20 per cent of farmers. The Duke of Westminster, Britain's richest man with an estimated wealth of £4 billion, has received £3 million in taxpayers' subsidies.[126] The richest farmers have higher incomes than the average wage in the European Union – meaning that agricultural support results in a transfer from those on low incomes to those on high incomes, widening inequalities.

These huge subsidies mean that farmers in rich countries produce much more than they would otherwise – and their over-production is often dumped on world markets. Hard bargaining in the Agreement on Agriculture ensured that rich countries were able to keep most of the payments they make to farmers, though some have to be phased out slowly over several years. At the Seattle WTO Ministerial meeting, the EU showed itself unwilling to agree to any major reduction in its subsidies under the Common Agricultural Policy. Indeed, the exceptions and special clauses in the agreement have allowed the EU and the US to *increase* rather than reduce the overall support they give to farmers since the Uruguay Round was agreed. In contrast, very few exemptions and special clauses were created for policies of interest to the developing world.

Since they signed the AoA, governments in developing and least developed countries have been prevented from increasing the level of their support to farmers above the level they declared to the WTO, even though they started from much lower levels than rich countries in the North. As a result:

- a country like Congo, which registered that it gave no support to its agricultural sector, is now prevented from ever increasing support above minimal levels, and is denied the use of measures which have allowed the EU and US to develop and maintain their farming sectors;[127]

- similarly, in the past Egypt gave no support to wheat production. This was a calculated decision in the light of large food aid shipments, which masked a potentially high food import bill. Food aid has now reduced, so the assumption upon

Christian Aid/S Cytrynowicz

Agriculture is not always a commercial venture, but an intricate sociocultural activity.

Zambia: the price of removing subsidies and liberalisation

By the mid-1980s, economic reforms were clearly needed in Zambia. Unemployment was high and rising, inflation was out of control and hurting the poor and the state-owned copper mines were inefficiently run, draining the economy of badly-needed resources. However, the reforms introduced under the World Bank/IMF were often poorly implemented and some of them hurt many groups of people hard. Social subsidies were partially removed in 1986, leading to an increase in the price of the nation's staple food, mealie meal. In turn, this provoked the worst urban unrest in the country's post-colonial history. From the early 1990s the Zambian government vigorously implemented economic reforms that included the abolition of consumer and producer subsidies, trade liberalisation and cutbacks in public expenditure. The parastatal maize marketing agency was abolished and prices left to the market. The result was catastrophic – rising food insecurity in urban areas due to the abolition of subsidies, high rates of inflation and massive unemployment. Increasing food insecurity has seen the emergence of new coping strategies which have included a reduction in the size and frequency of meals, reduced consumption of animal proteins, begging, stealing and prostitution.[130]

which this calculation was made no longer holds. The FAO has calculated that in order to raise Egypt's food self-sufficiency to 60 per cent from its 1994/5 level of 48 per cent, it would need to support wheat growers beyond the level now allowed under the AoA. To increase its food security, Egypt would therefore have to violate WTO rules.[128]

One of the key sticking-points in the negotiations on China's entry into the WTO was US government insistence that China should reduce its agricultural subsidies. This was despite the fact that, as one American academic put it, Chinese subsidies are already 'extremely low, way under the level of the US and Europe'.[129]

The UNCTAD Secretariat has specifically called for removing the issue of domestic subsidies for agriculture (and import control, as noted earlier) from the WTO disciplines. This is especially important 'where a significant percentage of the population is not only dependent on the agriculture sector for its livelihood, but also surviving just near the poverty line'. 'In such countries', it continues, 'a purely market-oriented approach may not be able to deliver the goods':

'It is a basic objective of government policies in agrarian developing countries to ensure food security and to allow the population to have sufficient food to meet its nutritional requirements. It is thus clear that issues related to food security are sensitive issues, and countries where a large part of the population is dependent on this sector would therefore like to have a certain degree of autonomy and flexibility in determining their domestic agricultural policies.' [131]

We are not arguing that agricultural subsidies are *always* the best option for developing countries. They can be costly and inefficient. But developing countries must retain the option of choosing such policies when they are likely to work in the interests of the poor. Poor farmers in developing countries, who are barely supported by their governments, are competing in international trade against rich farmers who often receive massive subsidies from their governments. The result is lack of development in agriculture where it matters most – in poor countries – and at the same time in rich countries a huge waste of resources on agricultural subsidies.

Should agricultural subsidies be included in the WTO at all?

Many developing countries are insisting that measures needed to promote and protect their national food security should be exempt from WTO rules. The WTO's justification for including subsidies in the agreements is essentially that subsidies have 'trade-distorting' and 'anti-competitive' effects. But, as Dot Keet of the Alternative Information and Development Centre in South Africa has pointed out, 'these commercial interests cannot take precedence over the necessity for countries to protect their own basic food security against the vagaries of international markets, the stockpiling of products, and price manipulations by commodity brokers and the like'.[133] The importance of food security to the world's poor people means that agricultural produce cannot simply be treated like any other tradeable commodities. We say that either the WTO agreement on subsidies should be rewritten to provide for full flexibility for developing countries or the whole issue should be taken out of the WTO altogether.

The need for protection: UNCTAD's view

'In many developing countries, agriculture is not a commercial venture, but an activity that has intricate sociocultural and environmental links and connotations. The small farmers involved have no way of withstanding large-scale international competition. They need protection if large-scale unemployment and the spread of poverty in these countries are to be limited. They should be allowed flexibility [in the WTO rules] regarding import restraint and domestic subsidy in order to protect and support household subsistence farming and small-scale farming.' [132]

Rule five: limits the use of subsidies for industry

Recent industrialisers have supported domestic industries by providing subsidies or other incentives to particular companies. But many subsidies of use to developing countries are now banned under the WTO rules, while many of use to rich countries are still allowed. This agreement is depriving developing countries of potentially important tools to promote their own development.

What the rule forbids

The WTO's Agreement on Subsidies and Countervailing Measures (ASCM) prevents governments from providing subsidies to encourage the use of domestic over imported goods ('import substitution subsidies'). Least developed countries were given until 2003 to implement this, other developing countries until 2000. UNCTAD expresses its alarm that:

> 'the ASCM bans exactly the type of subsidies primarily used by developing countries (while allowing subsidies preferably used by developed countries such as subsidies granted for research, regional development or for the adoption of environmental standards).' [135]

This creates a 'safe haven' for some of the subsidies used by rich governments, and 'represents a grave imbalance in the agreement'.[136] If these domestic subsidies have adverse effects on another WTO member, action can be taken in the WTO against the country providing the subsidy.[137]

The agreement on subsidies is a good example of the weird world of the WTO. It recognises that 'subsidies may play an important role in economic development programmes of developing country members' [138] – and then banned many types of such subsidies.

One United Nations report urged that least developed countries should 'promote firm-level competitiveness and provide infant industry with protection policies as may be deemed necessary and appropriate'.[139] Protecting infant industry is a mechanism that should be 'extended beyond the earliest stages of manufacturing and include nourishing more advanced competitive industries

> 'In most least developed countries, there are no safeguards to protect fragile industries from abusive competition, and this has resulted in the closure of many domestic industries, worsening the situation of unemployment.'
>
> UN General Assembly report [134]

through appropriate protection and support'. [140] Ironically in earlier years it was none other than the World Bank itself that urged developing countries to follow the import-substitution route to industrialisation.

Firms in developing countries often lack the efficiencies of large-scale operations, the availability of technology and finance, and other advantages which
their competitors in developed countries have. Subsidies can therefore be
important in encouraging diversification, upgrading of production and entry
into new markets.[141] The growth and survival of small and medium-sized
companies in developing countries requires national and international policies
that allow them to compete at home and abroad. UNCTAD argues that this
is especially true since such companies 'excel at job creation, and job creation
is key to reducing poverty'.[142] One of the problems with the liberalisation policies under structural adjustment programmes was that these 'SAPs have not
allowed domestic industries in LDCs enough time to prepare themselves for
international competition.' [143]

One study for UNCTAD calling for infant-industry protection argues that
the result of pressure from the WTO and the World Bank 'to liberalise their
industries prematurely and/or sharply' has been in many countries 'the destruction of their existing industries without any significant replacement; the
outcome has been severe unemployment, lower income, social deprivation and
marginalisation'. The study notes that 'across the board trade liberalisation
cannot be a substitute for a trade and industrial policy.' [144]

The fall in investment in the cotton sector, for example, has been an important contributor to the decline of cotton industries in least developed countries.
Government support and funding has largely been withdrawn, particularly for
research on improved varieties. The private sector has also failed to invest significantly in improved irrigation and modern farming methods. This decline was
brought about by the fall in cotton prices over the past decade and by the
constraints imposed by structural adjustment and market liberalisation.[145]

Some measures which helped to bring prosperity and a thriving industrial
sector to East Asia are now outlawed. Current rules have, according to
UNCTAD, 'circumscribed the scope in most developing countries for repli-
cating some of the policy measures' which contributed to growth in East Asia.
'If existing multilateral rules are indeed impeding the learning and upgrading
process in the industrial sectors of developing countries, then a re-examination
is called for.' [146]

Taoufik Ben Abdallah of ENDA Tiers Monde, Senegal – a Christian Aid
partner – explains the impact in Africa of the combination of removal of subsidies and cheap imports:

'The dismantling of customs barriers together with the end of public
subsidies to national enterprises was supposed to foster competition
between local products and imports, and lower the costs of production.
But in the absence of a supply of high quality goods produced in suffi-

cient quantity, this policy led to the closing of some local enterprises – putting thousands of people out of work – and to massive importation of cheap goods from abroad.

'The African markets that one can visit in urban areas often give the impression of being simply branches of Asian or European supermarkets. A whole socioeconomic stratum lives off the importation of products that are sold at prices that defy all competition. This leaves little room for African industries to develop, or create jobs.

'The lowering of tariff barriers when not compensated by other fiscal resources weakens the state's capacities, especially its capacity to respond to social needs. Without protection, what can African countries do when faced with enterprises producing on a global scale, with very high levels of productivity and very low costs?' [147]

Subsidies in rich countries

While insisting that developing countries cut back subsidies to their industries, rich countries fought hard in the Uruguay Round to ensure that the subsidies they use were not banned under the WTO rules. They employ a variety of industrial subsidies. The UK's Department of Trade and Industry pays around £1 billion a year in aid to industries such as steel, shipbuilding and aerospace, regional assistance, venture capital funds and other small business schemes.[148] Blocking imports from developing countries to protect domestic industry is a form of support which has received most public attention. But there are many others, among them export credits and tied aid (aid conditional on developing countries procuring good and services from the 'donor' country, and thus a subsidy to companies) – and the large regional development funds supported by the European Commission and individual EU member states.

Rule six: blocks exports from developing countries

Developing countries have been pressed to open their economies to imports, often at huge cost to the poor and their economies. But WTO rules enable rich countries to keep many of their own markets closed, to protect their own producers, thus preventing poor countries from securing much-needed extra income. Rich countries are also employing various devious means to keep out exports from developing countries, using legal loopholes to undermine the poor.

What the rule says

The WTO reinforces a situation in which developing countries are unfairly denied access to rich country markets. It allows continuing high tariff barriers for some key agricultural exports of developing countries as well as for processed goods. The WTO rules have introduced new mechanisms which rich countries are using to keep out developing country exports. 'Sanitary and Phytosanitary Measures' allow rich countries to restrict imports on health grounds. Anti-dumping measures are used by the richer countries to protect their producers against cheaper produce imported from developing countries.

'While export development is important to many least developed countries and net food importing developing countries, the implementation of the Uruguay Round agreements has not visibly improved their market access opportunities.'

UNCTAD experts meeting [149]

In less than 50 years, governments have reduced average tariffs from 40 per cent to 4 per cent, and the volume of trade has increased to the point where more than $17 billion worth of goods and services is traded every day. Yet rich countries still use high tariffs to prevent many developing country exports from entering their markets. UNCTAD estimates that by 2005 developing countries could export $700 billion more goods each year if rich countries opened their markets.[150] But there is evidence that despite promising to reduce their tariff barriers as part of the Uruguay Round agreements, rich countries have actually increased them, especially on some key exports of developing countries.[151] Rich countries' trade barriers are especially serious for the least developed countries since nearly 75 per cent of their exports go to them.

- UNCTAD estimates that rich countries' tariff barriers on agricultural exports cost developing countries around $20 billion a year.[152]

- According to the World Bank, if the 'Quad' (US, Japan, Canada and the EU) abolished peak tariffs on exports from the 49 least developed countries, the latter would earn an extra $2.5 billion a year, equivalent to 11 per cent of their current export earnings.[153]

- In the US and Japan more than half of all exports from the least developed countries face some type of border protection.[154] Of the rich countries, only New Zealand allows exports from the least developed countries to enter its market duty-free.[155]

- On average, rich country tariffs on manufactured imports from poor countries are four times higher than those on imports from other rich countries.[156]

- The WTO rules do little to discourage tariff escalation, where rich countries maintain much higher import tariffs on imports of *processed* commodities than of raw materials. This deprives developing countries of revenue and deters them from diversifying their exports away from a dependence on raw materials, which is generally recognised as part of a development strategy. It is especially damaging to developing countries since trade in processed products has been growing at the fastest rate in world agricultural trade in recent years.[157]

Raising barriers for processed goods 'is the most insidious of the ways to increase tariffs', according to John Cuddy of UNCTAD:

> 'It increases the tariff the more you process the good, so it keeps the least developed countries in the place of producing commodities, which are subject to wide price fluctuations rather than getting the added value from processing the commodities... It is scandalous for these rich countries to deny the least developed countries some trade benefits.' [158]

A joint UNCTAD/WTO study shows that tariffs on some developing countries' major export products, such as sugar, tobacco, cotton and processed food, are frequently levied at the highest peak rates, exceeding 100 per cent.[159] For Bangladesh, tariff escalation is a major barrier to increasing trade in higher value products. Tariffs escalate in rich country markets as the level of processing is increased for jute, tea and shrimps, which make up Bangladesh's three major agricultural export crops.[160] EU trade rules also make it much easier for developing countries to sell cocoa to Europe than chocolate bars. Cocoa enters the European market with no tariff, but the duty on chocolate can be as much as 27 per cent.[161]

The market access rules for the rich world are plainly unfair and must be changed in favour of poor countries. But that is only a start. The benefits of increased access for poor countries into rich country markets will be very limited without other changes to give poor countries the power to trade successfully.

- First, many countries will not be able to take advantage of lower tariffs because supply-side restrictions prevent them from competing effectively in world markets in the short to medium term. These include poor infrastructure, ineffective

The EBA: Everything But Arms...
or Everything But the Answer?

The EU's flagship for demonstrating its seriousness about improving the least developed countries' trade position is the 'Everything but Arms' (EBA) initiative. This provides duty-free market access into the EU for all exports – except arms – from the least developed countries. But domestic and corporate lobbies have successfully diluted this promise. Import duties will continue on sugar and rice until 2009 and on bananas until 2006. The Commission's capitulation to pressure calls into question its commitment to genuinely open markets.

The EBA is a welcome step towards the removal of unfair protection by rich countries. But it is a much smaller step than might initially be thought. An academic study commissioned by Oxfam shows that the 'static' gains (meaning at current levels of exports) of the EBA to poor countries would be a minuscule €7 million. It is likely that there will be more 'dynamic' gains (when countries increase exports to take advantage of improved market access) but the extent of these is hard to predict.

Moreover, for one key commodity, sugar, any gain for exporters from the least developed countries will be 'absolutely proportional' to the losses of exporters from other developing countries (who will lose market share). The gains to the least developed countries from the EBA are likely to be so low because only €95 million of exports on 11 different commodities is actually affected.[162] The EU is not offering duty-free market access for the €1.2 *billion* exports from the *non*-least developed developing countries on these 11 items, which would be far more beneficial to those exporters.

A danger of the EBA is if it offers a carrot to developing countries to open their markets further. The EU's Trade Commissioner, Pascal Lamy, said – mainly in reference to the GATS negotiations: 'If we want to improve our hard won access to foreign markets then we can't keep our protected sectors out of the sunlight. We have to be open to negotiating them all if we are going to have the material for the big deal. In the US and the EU, that means some pain in some sectors but gain in many others, and I think we both know that we are going to have to bite the bullet to get what we want'.[163]

institutions, lack of capital, skills-shortages, and an inability to respond quickly to new market opportunities.

- Second, blunt strategies to increase exports do not necessarily help the poor, or poor producers. The evidence shows the opposite can happen. In Ghana, for example, expanding cocoa production for export took up increasing amounts of land that pushed women farmers onto marginal land with steep slopes and low fertility soil.[164] In some East Asian countries, increases in exports produced growth and increasing wealth for the middle class, but many of the poor were bypassed and gaps between rich and poor widened.

- Third, increasing exports globally can risk creating severe environmental damage through eroding the natural resources of countries, sometimes earning high revenues for exporters but further impoverishing local communities. Transportation of traded goods is one of the fastest growing sources of greenhouse gas emissions that contribute to climate change.[165]

- Fourth, poor *people* do not necessarily benefit from poor *countries'* exports. A range of domestic policies needs to be promoted to ensure the poor benefit from increases in economic growth. This is, of course, a fundamental question, and relates to the trade rules more widely.

Beware of the rich bearing gifts

Developing countries would be wise to remain sceptical about the wider commitment of the rich world to negotiate deals in the interests of the world's poor. Promises by the rich countries to abolish quotas and tariffs on imports of textiles encouraged many developing countries to agree to negotiate intellectual property, services and investment as part of the Uruguay Round. The latter went ahead, while the former is taking a very long time to be implemented. Equally, rich countries' agreement to implement the Marrakech Decision to compensate poor countries for food price rises was the only reason many countries signed up to the Agreement on Agriculture. The AoA went ahead, while the Marrakech Decision remains unimplemented, as explained below. These examples do not demonstrate good faith.

Broken promises[166] – the 'Marrakech Decision'

Developing countries are often threatened with trade sanctions if they fail to implement rules that benefit the rich countries. At the same time, rules that would benefit developing countries have often been implemented grudgingly and slowly, if at all. A good example is the 'Marrakech Decision', which rich countries promised but have never implemented.

The 'Marrakech Decision' was signed by 120 countries in April 1994. Developed countries agreed to provide compensation to least developed countries and net food importing developing countries (NFIDCs), through increased food aid and short term financial and technical assistance, if these countries experienced negative effects as a result of the implementation of the Agreement on Agriculture (AoA). Although the decision represented a formal commitment by governments, it was separate from the main body of the AoA and was never given an operational structure, specific commitments, or any precise definitions.

The WTO Ministerial Conference renewed the Decision, recommending that rich countries increase financial and technical assistance through their aid programmes. But since the signing of the AoA, food aid and technical assistance to developing countries has actually fallen.[168] When world food prices rose during 1995 and 1996, rather than increasing aid, food aid shipments fell to record low levels. Rich countries refused to accept any link with the WTO agreement and were more responsive to the stocks and price situation of donor countries then the actual food security needs of the developing countries they are supposed to be assisting.[169]

> *'On the things that interest us, there are no deadlines – only on the things that benefit them, like patenting regimes.'*
> African trade minister, Geneva, October 2000 [167]

The FAO estimates that higher world prices, and decreased supply of subsidised exports, has in general lead to a 22 per cent rise in food import bills since 1993/4. In 1995/8 the value of food imports increased by 168 per cent in India and more then doubled in Brazil. Despite the fact that there was a fall in world prices in 1997/8, food import bills did not decrease because of increases in import volume, the reduction in food aid, and a fall in the price concessions that least developed and net food importing developing countries used to receive.

The FAO has presented evidence of this negative impact to the WTO, and urged that the Marrakech Decision be implemented. Egypt, India, the Southern African Development Community (SADC), and the Organisation for African Unity have also all called upon the WTO to revise and·implement the Marrakech Decision. However, the WTO Secretariat has refused to assess the impact of the Uruguay Round on food import bills on the grounds of the complexity and political sensitivity of the research. Meanwhile, no rich country is proactively supporting its implementation either.[170] So, in the words of the UN Food and Agriculture Organisation, 'to date, there has not been any concrete benefit stemming from the Decision'.[171]

Hiding behind 'health reasons'

Rich countries are currently using even more devious measures to block exports from developing countries.

The first of these is the Sanitary and Phytosanitary (SPS) Measures agreement, which sets the conditions under which one country can ban imports from another on health grounds. Any ban has to be justified by scientific evidence. But there are growing fears that the SPS agreement is being used unfairly to restrict imports from developing countries. One recent study concluded that SPS measures are now seen by developing countries as the most important impediment to agricultural and food exports to the EU.[172] There is also evidence that rich countries are applying SPS measures more stringently on some developing countries' exports than they are on exports from other rich countries.[173] Developing countries are barely represented on the main bodies which set international standards in this area (only seven per cent of the representatives on the Codex Alimentarus, the most important standard-setting body, come from Africa [174]). One African delegate to the WTO told Christian Aid how his country is being 'trapped by SPS', and can't export.[175] The WTO has failed to address this problem and failed to provide equitable ways to impose SPS measures.

Devious measure no.1: health fears as an excuse for blocking imports?

Even though they have agreed, in the WTO, to abide by the findings of the international bodies, rich countries can also impose standards that are stricter than those set by the international bodies. If challenged, they have to show that these are justifiable given the scientific evidence. In reality most developing countries do not have the resources to mount effective scientific challenges to import restrictions. The EU has recently imposed very high standards on the imports of nuts and dried fruits, for example, which will have severe consequences for many countries. The World Bank estimates that the new safety standard will, at best, save less than two lives in every billion (the EU's total population is about half a billion people). The cost to producers in the least developed countries is over $700 million per year.[176]

One product likely to be affected is Brazil nuts from Bolivia. Bolivia is the main exporter of Brazil nuts in the world, and nut exports provide the main source of income for one of the poorest regions in the country. According to the Bolivian government, the Brazil nut industry gives people living in the north of the country 'access to food, provisions and supplies for everyday existence which have given them a more dignified standard of living'.[177] The Bolivian government says that the new restrictions will cause the collapse of the Brazil nut industry, and the loss of most of the income of some of the poorest people in Bolivia. The restrictions seem more about protecting EU nut producers than protecting the health of European consumers.[178]

Devious measure no.2: a protectionist 'method of harassment'

A second way that rich countries are finding to block developing countries' exports is using 'anti-dumping' and 'countervailing' measures. This involves rich countries using the WTO process to initiate investigations into imports that, they claim, are under-cutting their domestic producers.

UNCTAD believes that anti-dumping and countervailing measures have been 'hijacked for protectionist purposes' and are primarily designed to 'protect sensitive domestic industries from increased imports'. Since the WTO agreements came into force, developing countries have become even greater targets of these actions, accounting for 38 per cent of all anti-dumping actions and 50 per cent of all countervailing investigations. Developed countries are responsible for most of these actions, and UNCTAD argue that most are launched by the developed countries knowing that they will not win the case. Rather, according to UNCTAD, they are 'a method of harassment' since even initiating an investigation can produce the desired effect – a reduction in exports, since importers 'are scared off and seek alternative sources of supply'. And TNCs are using the laws to protect their own interests. 'Contrary to the myth of anti-dumping laws defending the public interest, reality shows that a few large firms are behind a high proportion of complaints. Anti-dumping measures are part of their corporate strategy.'

Companies from developing countries are especially vulnerable to these actions as infant entrants into new markets. Although some developing countries are now using these measures themselves, it is much harder for them to do so, given the great financial and legal resources required.[179] It can cost over half a million dollars for exporters to prove that they have been exporting fairly, rather than dumping – a price well beyond the means of most companies and governments in developing countries.[180]

In March 2001, the WTO's appellate body ruled that some of the arcane methods used by the EU to determine whether imports are being dumped on EU markets violated WTO rules. This was the first ruling of its kind, and it has yet to show whether it will significantly prevent these harassment measures.[181]

When rich countries converted their protection measures into tariffs, as the WTO's Agreement on Agriculture required them to do, they set initial levels much higher than their previous non-tariff barriers. In effect this gave them the potential to increase protection of their agricultural sectors. The calculation of initial tariffs and subsidies was also done in aggregate form, which has allowed rich countries to make reductions to the letter of their AoA commitments without entering into the spirit of significantly opening their markets. They have been able to make major commitments only on 'non-sensitive' products and not on many of the most important agricultural exports of developing countries.

Do as we say, not as we do: blocking imports of textiles

The Agreement on Textiles and Clothing (ATC) illustrates another form of hypocrisy involving the world's powerful states. Exports of textiles are hugely important for developing countries, accounting for nearly 20 per cent of their total exports of manufactured goods and 25 per cent of all exports of the least developed countries.[182] More than half of these exports go to the industrialised countries.[183] But in order to protect their own producers industrialised countries have restricted imports. Under the Uruguay Round countries must reduce the quantitative restrictions they place on imports of textiles. The developed countries had ten years (until 2005) to eliminate their quantitative restrictions and there was no obligation to reduce tariffs in the meantime, while their average tariffs on textiles were more than twice the average tariffs for other manufactured goods.[184] They committed to smaller reductions on textiles imports than other goods – the average EU tariff for manufactured goods fell by 37 per cent, but for textiles the fall was only 17 per cent.[185] This means that textiles exporters were still discriminated against in EU markets, compared to exporters of other products.

Christian Aid/Achinto

Textiles account for 25 per cent of all exports of the least developed countries.

Yet, half way through the ten year period, the EU has only reduced tariffs affecting a minuscule four per cent of textiles imports – which means that 96 per cent of all textiles imported into the EU face the same restrictions as they did before the EU promised to liberalise. According to UNCTAD, rich countries have 'respected the letter, but not the spirit of the Agreement on Textiles and Clothing, with the result that developing textile exporting countries have not obtained the expected benefits from the ATC'.[186]

In addition, rich countries are imposing new restrictions, supposedly as short-term measures to allow their industries to adjust, but in reality further limiting exports from developing countries. Both the EU and the US have imposed very high tariffs on particular goods, supposedly as 'transitional safeguards'. They have also accused developing countries, for example India, of 'dumping' products on their markets, for example India. Each time the EU has failed to prove that India was dumping textiles, it has started a new case. This has led to uncertainty and instability in India's textiles sector.[187]

Rule seven: gives business rights over knowledge and natural resources

The WTO's agreement on intellectual property is a case of massive corporate protectionism that enables TNCs to secure monopoly rights over knowledge and natural resources, and that transfers wealth from South to North. The world's poorest people are prevented, through what the UN calls a 'silent theft' of their resources, from securing adequate access to essential drugs and technology.

What the rule says

The Agreement on Trade-related Intellectual Property Rights (TRIPs) covers seven types of intellectual property: patents, copyright, trademarks, geographical indications, industrial designs, layout designs of integrated circuits and undisclosed information. On patents, TRIPs makes it obligatory on all countries to make patents available on inventions, meaning conferring exclusive rights on an invention to a patent holder.[190] TRIPs has opened the door to patenting life forms since micro-organisms – such as bacteria and viruses – must be covered by patentability.

> 'The TRIPs agreement will enable multinationals to dominate the global market even more easily.'
>
> UN Development Programme [188]

However, certain types of inventions can be excluded from patentability by countries to protect health, the environment or public order, in which case governments can provide for the use of the patent without the authorisation of the patent holder. Plants and animals are excluded. But TRIPs requires that plant *varieties* be covered by some form of effective protection, either by patents or an effective 'sui generis' (national) system. This area is controversial since it extends private control over the biological wealth and traditional knowledge of gene-rich developing countries.

Countries used to be able to decide how long they would grant patents for. Now, all WTO member countries have to implement laws that protect patents for 20 years, and must show that they are going to enforce patents rigorously. This means that, in almost all cases, companies have exclusive rights over new products for much longer than they used to – at a time when the pace of change in technological development is accelerating. If countries fail to implement laws protecting intellectual property, or if their laws are too weak, they can be taken to the WTO dispute settlement body. WTO members had to implement intellectual property laws by January 2000. Least developed countries are allowed until 2005. For many developing countries, this is the first time they have implemented any kind of property rights agreement.[191]

> 'The picture painted by developed countries is that TRIPs are a magical bridge to technology transfer. There is no evidence for this. They are more to protect the interests of big companies like the pharmaceutical companies.'
>
> African delegate to the WTO, October 2000 [189]

As the pace of technological change speeds up, and the profits for those who have a monopoly on knowledge continue to increase, poor countries and poor people need to have access to the most up-to-date knowledge if they are to participate fairly in the global economy. However, international rule making in this area is leading to the control of knowledge by a global elite.

The Agreement on Trade-related Intellectual Property Rights (TRIPs) poses two major threats to developing countries – expropriating their natural resources and reducing their access to knowledge and technology.

Expropriating natural resources – or biopiracy

TRIPs allows companies from one country to patent the natural resources of another. A list follows of some indigenous resources from developing countries which have been patented by TNCs and others from rich countries.

- *Sangre de drago:* a medicine plant from the Amazon, patented by the US pharmaceutical company Shaman, which as a result has already raised millions of dollars on US capital markets.
- *Neem:* a tree well-known in Asia for both medicinal and agricultural uses for centuries. It has been the subject of dozens of patents, including some taken out by Monsanto for the wax and oil from the tree, known for their insecticide and fungicidal uses.

Christian Aid/Achinto

Spiralling drug costs have made medicines inaccessible and unaffordable to large numbers of poor people.

- *Snakegourd:* a medicinal plant from China, has been patented by New York University, on the grounds that it may provide treatment for the HIV virus. The university stands to make millions from selling the treatment to a company for commercial development.

- *Kava:* a plant grown in several Pacific islands, has been patented by French company L'Oreal, on the basis that it may provide a treatment for hair loss.

- *Barbasco:* another Amazonian plant, has been patented by a UK academic, who hopes to sell it to UK pharmaceutical companies Zeneca or Glaxo-Wellcome, as a muscle relaxant.[192]

- *Cocoa:* Mars UK took out two patents on genes from a West African cocoa plant thought to be responsible for the distinctive flavour associated with cocoa from this region. If made artificially, this could undermine the livelihoods of thousands of people in Ghana who are dependent on the cocoa industry and devastate the economy.[193]

Evidence from NGOs and others suggests that TRIPs is likely to displace a number of local plant varieties with hybrids, reduce farmers' access to affordable seeds (reducing their food security), make local agriculture dependent on imported inputs and enable foreign biotechnology companies to control local species. Local plant-breeding is essential for adapting seeds to the ecosystem and maintaining biodiversity – but the 1.4 billion rural people relying on farm-saved seed could see their interests marginalised.[194] By declaring natural resources to be subject to private patenting, TRIPs in effect legalises biopiracy of common resources and the traditional knowledge on which generations of farmers in developing countries have often drawn.

UN agencies warn against the threat from TRIPs. A report by the UN's Subcommission on the Promotion and Protection of Human Rights maintains that patenting under TRIPs 'represents outright piracy and appropriation of nature's bounty which has been designated for the whole of humanity and not for a privileged and technologically advanced few'.[195] According to the UN's Development Programme, pharmaceutical companies have for many years been sampling plant material and documenting their traditional medicinal uses. 'Without the consent of local people, this knowledge has been used to develop highly profitable drugs.' Moreover:

> 'New patent laws pay scant attention to the knowledge of indigenous people… These laws ignore cultural diversity in creating and sharing innovations – and diversity in views on what can and should be owned, from plant varieties to human life. *The result is a silent theft of centuries of knowledge from developing to developed countries.'*

This could have very damaging effects on agriculture:

> 'With increasing control and homogenisation of the market by major agribusinesses, the competitiveness of alternative varieties [of seeds] and the scope for producing alternative crops will most likely decline, depleting local genetic diversity.' [196]

The scale of legalised theft is staggering. A Canadian-based research institute, in a report for the UN's Development Programme (UNDP), estimated that even before the implementation of TRIPs, companies in industrialised countries benefited by about $4.5 billion a year from their patents on natural resources from developing countries.[197] UNDP estimates that even if just a two per cent royalty were charged on genetic resources that had been developed by local innovators in developing countries, then rich countries would owe more than $300 million in unpaid royalties for farmers' crop seeds and more than $5 billion in unpaid royalties for medicinal plants. 'But this rate is low,' states the UNDP, 'because negotiations are on an uneven footing.' [198]

But under TRIPs, instead of a net flow of royalties into the developing countries, the reverse will happen. One estimate is that, in implementing TRIPs, India will have to transfer up to $800 million per year and Brazil up to $1 billion per year to TNCs under pharmaceutical patents alone. Another

Does TRIPs violate international human rights law?

This is the judgement of the UN's Subcommission on the Promotion and Protection of Human Rights:

'In a resolution on the Trade-related Aspects of Intellectual Property Rights (TRIPs) agreement of the World Trade Organisation, the Subcommission charged that implementation of the agreement did not adequately reflect the fundamental nature and indivisibility of all human rights, including the right of everyone to enjoy the benefits of scientific progress and its applications, the right to health, the right to food and the right to self-determination, and said there were apparent conflicts between the intellectual property rights regime embodied in the TRIPs agreement and international human rights law. It requested the World Trade Organisation and the Council on TRIPs during its ongoing review of the TRIPs agreement to take fully into account existing state obligations under international human rights instruments.'[202]

estimate from Africa, based on World Bank data, is that TRIPs royalties could amount to five per cent of world trade and may treble developing countries' debt repayments. Even many mainstream economists fear that there will be initial losses for developing countries under TRIPs and that many poor countries will gain little or nothing from the agreement.[199]

Companies from rich countries hold 97 per cent of patents worldwide and 80 per cent of patents in developing countries. In 1995, half of all royalties and license fees paid in the world went to companies in the United States.[200] It is much harder for companies in developing countries to take out patents – it can cost $1 million to do so on a plant or gene, for example.[201] This is far beyond the resources available to small companies in developing countries – and may be too expensive even for larger ones.

Reducing access to technology and knowledge

The increased protection of intellectual property rights under TRIPs is likely to make it more costly and complex for developing countries to gain access to new or existing science and technology. Transfer of technology is crucial for developing countries, which tend to develop less technology domestically and be more dependent on external sources. Only 0.4 per cent of world expenditure on research and development (R&D) occurs in Africa, compared to 74 per cent in OECD countries.[203] For this reason, either increased domestic spending on R&D, or increased transfer of technology developed elsewhere through licensing or other arrangements, are of great importance to developing countries. However, TRIPs boosts the increasing privatisation of knowledge, with a decline of publicly-funded research and increase in patents under the exclusive control of private companies. At the same time, a small number of international companies control the global market across all knowledge-intensive industries.[204]

UNCTAD described the TRIPs agreement as 'a premature strengthening of the intellectual property system… that favours monopolistically controlled innovation over broad-based diffusion' of cutting-edge technology.[205] The UN's Development Programme has stated that, with TRIPs:

> 'The privatisation and concentration of technology are going too far… Poor people and poor countries risk being pushed to the margin in this proprietary regime controlling the world's knowledge… From new drugs to better seeds, the best of the new technologies are priced for those who can pay. For poor people, they remain far out of reach. Tighter property rights raise the price of technology transfer, blocking developing countries from the dynamic knowledge sectors. The TRIPs agreement will enable multinationals to dominate the global market even more easily.' [206]

When the agreement was negotiated, rich countries tried to persuade developing countries that TRIPs would make the transfer of technology from North to South easier, as greater security from patents would make companies in industrialised countries more confident about distributing technology in the South, knowing that they would be safe from copying. The TRIPs agreement states that:

> 'The protection and enforcement of intellectual property rights should contribute to the promotion of technological innovation and to the transfer and dissemination of technology, to the mutual advantage of producers and users of technological knowledge, and in a manner conducive to social and economic welfare, and to a balance of rights and obligations.' [207]

Before TRIPs, most countries that developed their own industries did so by copying and developing innovations from elsewhere. But now, according to the UN's Development Programme, 'tighter control [of intellectual property] under the TRIPs agreement has closed off old opportunities and increased the costs of access to new technologies.' [208] Prior to the TRIPs agreement, countries such as China, Egypt and India allowed patents on pharmaceutical processes but not final products. This enabled the development of domestic industries by producing mainly generic drugs similar to but far cheaper than the original brand names. Now that TRIPs requires 20-year patents on both processes and products, countries are obliged to change their patenting laws, 'making such opportunities impossible in the future', according to the UNDP. 'Countries can choose to require patent holders to give licences to competitors – but the process is long and the fees may be prohibitive.' [209]

In rich countries, too, copying was essential in allowing domestic firms to become competitive on international markets. In order to protect their own industries, and allow them to copy ideas from other companies, France did not introduce product patents for pharmaceuticals until 1960, Germany until 1968 and Switzerland until 1977.[210] Today, these countries are home to some of the world's largest pharmaceutical companies – for example, Aventis in France, Bayer in Germany and Hoffman La Roche in Switzerland. Once again a WTO agreement is preventing developing countries from pursuing policies which have been highly successful in the past.

The TRIPs agreement is a clear-cut case of the exercise of corporate power. The main pressure for the inclusion of intellectual property rights in the Uruguay Round came from US and European TNCs. Proposals made by these TNCs became the basis of US government submissions to the Uruguay Round negotiations, which in turn became the basis of the TRIPs agreement. The WTO was the favoured forum since TNCs could ensure that all countries could if necessary be brought into line on intellectual property rights under the dispute settlement mechanism.[211]

Rich country governments, especially the US, have been pressurising developing countries to strengthen patent regimes since the early 1980s. In 1988, the US government levied 100 per cent tariffs on $39 million of imports from Brazil in retaliation for the latter's copying of patented drugs – Brazil backed down, eventually passing legislation in 1996 creating pharmaceutical product patents. In 1990, the US withdrew trade benefits to Thailand because of dissatisfaction with its lack of protection for pharmaceuticals. Throughout the 1990s the threat of the US retaliation weapon forced several developing countries to change their patent laws. But according to one academic study, the TRIPs agreement signed in 1994, and coming into effect in 1995, 'satisfied most of the interests of industry.' [212]

Rich countries are now pushing to enforce the rights their companies have gained under the TRIPs agreement. By February 2001, seven cases involving TRIPs had been brought to the WTO's dispute settlement body, by rich countries arguing that developing countries had failed to implement the agreement properly. All of these relate in one way or another to patents on medicines.

TRIPs, pharmaceuticals and public health

One of the biggest fears among NGOs from South and North is that TRIPs will increase the price of necessary new medicines, adding to the financial burden of desperately hard-pressed health services in developing countries. Poorer countries find it very difficult to take advantage of safeguards written into the TRIPs agreement.

In addition there have been instances where bilateral pressure has been brought to bear on poor countries to adopt national laws that are stronger than TRIPs – so called TRIPs-plus. The United States, protecting its domestic industry, is prepared to use bilateral pressure through the WTO disputes settlement facility, and unilateral economic sanctions through the government's 301 Priority Watch List, against countries that it believes offer inadequate patent protection.

The cost of patent protection is escalating. Patents are becoming ever more complicated, covering every aspect of manufacture and presentation. Some medicines are protected by several hundred separate patents. So-called 'ever-greening' – where new patents based on minimal improvements are filed on products as their original patents expire – favours rich companies with know-how and resources. And only rich governments can afford to play the game: the United States of America spends approximately one billion dollars on its own patents office.

TRIPs raises three key health concerns:

1 Price

The price of drugs is the most important issue raised by TRIPs. At present poor countries already pay more for branded drugs than rich ones. But the agreement will reduce the competition that the big drug companies face from generic alternatives.

The prices of some vital drugs – for HIV/AIDS for example – have tumbled to remarkably low levels since countries with the capacity to copy branded drugs have done so. Brazil, as part of its national AIDS strategy, makes its own antiretroviral AIDS drug cocktails. It has a constitutional duty to treat AIDS patients. Brazil has been able to afford treatment; as a consequence the rate of infection has fallen dramatically, and hospitalisations have dropped. The Indian manufacturer Cipla is able to offer AIDS combination therapies for about $300 per patient per year compared to $10,000 in those countries where the patent system operates.

These elements of competition will be closed off for all new drugs produced after 1996 (it is estimated that there are currently in the pipeline 130 new drugs relevant to public health that will qualify for the new extended patents). The system that applied before 1995 allowed developing countries to supply many of their own domestic needs and export affordable drugs to poorer countries.

2 Transfer of technology and production

Further development of domestic production of pharmaceuticals and technology transfer may stall in developing countries after TRIPs becomes universal and mandatory. Although technology transfer is encouraged under TRIPs, there is no obligation to make sure this happens. At present about a dozen middle-income developing countries are able to produce generic drugs, that is, drugs that have run the length of their patent protection. Some also produce the bulk active ingredients from which final dosage forms are made – but these too will be patented for the full 20 year period. And some countries such as India, China and Brazil have the capacity to copy patented drugs using reverse engineering – developing new processes through working back from the product to achieve an alternative production technique. The existence of alternatives to branded drugs means that, at present, there is price competition. This will increasingly be less and less the case.

3 Drug treatments for poor country diseases

Very few drugs are being developed for the diseases which primarily or exclusively affect poor countries. There have been no new drugs for tuberculosis for 40 years, for example. The most promising treatments for malaria today are based on artemether, the active ingredient of a Chinese medicinal plant known for centuries. Crippling diseases such as Lymphatic Filariasis (elephantiasis), Human African Trypanosomiasis (sleeping sickness) and others have been ignored by global pharmaceuticals companies because commercial incentives have been lacking. TRIPs does nothing to change this situation.

Supporters of the WTO argue that sufficient safeguards were negotiated during the Uruguay Round to ensure that public health needs can override the TRIPs rules where necessary. There are provisions in TRIPs that allow for compulsory licensing (overriding the patent) of products on the basis of national public health needs (article 31), and the facility to 'shop around' for the cheapest products available in different countries (parallel importation) is also allowed. However, it is clear that developing countries are finding these provisions difficult to implement. They have so far been used only by the United States and the European Union. No developing country has yet used compulsory licensing of any product for public health.

It is encouraging that these concerns are being increasingly widely debated. Northern NGOs, led initially by the Médecins sans Frontières Access Campaign, are working in partnership with governments and NGOs in the South.

An increasingly forceful momentum has developed which could move from narrow issues of trade and intellectual property to the wider goal of upgrading public health in developing countries.

Currently two views prevail. The first assumes that TRIPs will stay, but that measures like voluntary price reductions, subsidies, a system of tiered pricing, public private initiatives, donations and as a last resort compulsory licensing will sufficiently protect the interests of poor countries. The second insists that TRIPs is fundamentally flawed, and demands that it is changed to take into consideration health and development indicators. This is Christian Aid's view, and increasingly the view of developing countries.

Geographical indications

Geographical indications fall under the TRIPs agreement, and are defined as 'indications which identify a good as originating in the territory of a Member, or a region or locality in that territory, where a given quality, reputation or other characteristic of the good is essentially attributable to its geographical origin.' [213] Wines and spirits are key products covered by these rules, and the WTO is committed to 'the establishment of a multilateral system of notification and registration of geographical indications for wines eligible for protection in those Members participating in the system.' [214]

The effect on developing countries can be very negative. The EU recently entered into a bilateral free trade agreement with South Africa. Wine and spirit producers in Europe wanted South Africa to phase out the use of the names of 'port' and 'sherry' for South Africa's fortified wines and 'ouzo' and 'grappa' for South African spirits. South African producers have been using these names for nearly 200 years, but the EU argued that they refer to specific locations in Portugal, Spain, Greece and Italy and should therefore be used exclusively by these countries. South Africa was forced to accept the phasing-out of these terms in international markets within a five year period, and over ten years on the domestic market or else risk the entire trade deal.

The livelihoods of a large number of workers in the Western Cape are at risk. Although the EU offered assistance to restructure the industry, this 'aid' will only reach South Africa once substantial progress has been made on the phasing out of the terms. Help for local communities may take years to realise.

The EU now wants to increase the status of geographical indications to a higher order of rights than trademarks. Such protectionist policies only decrease the ability of developing countries to find a foothold in the global economy. According to the managing director of Distell, a South African distilling company, 'the philosophy of exerting pressure to gain economic advantage is seemingly deeply embedded in the developed world and contrasts glaringly with public statements on the need to create fair structures in world trade that will assist developing countries to outgrow their economic dependency on older, more established economies.' [215]

How TRIPs undermines development in India

Christian Aid's partners in India believe that TRIPs is reshaping the economy of India in the interests of large corporations while poor people are being deprived of basic necessities like health care, and are forced to change the agricultural practices of centuries. Mira Shiva of the Voluntary Health Association of India (VHAI) says TNCs have been trying to boost their profits from the sales of medicines in India for over 30 years, and in the process have undermined the health rights of Indian people:

'TNCs have tried to undermine India's Patent Act of 1970 which was designed after 20 years of democratic debate to ensure people had access to affordable medicine. Excluding product patents and allowing only process patents was the main mechanism which allowed low cost generic drugs to be produced. Even before the completion of the Uruguay Round, the TNCs used the Special 301 clauses of the US Trade Act with threats of unilateral trade sanctions to force India to change its patent laws. They then persuaded the US government to start a dispute in the WTO which forced India to amend its patent laws to grant Exclusive Marketing Rights (EMRs) for pharmaceutical companies.

'Cipla, an Indian company, can today offer low cost generic HIV/AIDS drugs because of the process patents clauses in our Patent Act. The imposition of product patents through TRIPs will not just deny access to medicines to Indians, but also to the poor in other Third World countries. Already, spiralling drug costs have made medicines inaccessible and unaffordable to large numbers of poor people. Globalisation of drug prices without globalisation of incomes will mean further deprivation of access to medicines by many.'

It is not only low-cost sales of medicines that are threatened by TRIPs. Companies are using new patent rights to shape India's future health care system. Dr Shiva says:

'Seventy per cent of Indian health care still depends on indigenous medical systems such as Ayurveda, Siddha and Unani. Hundreds of indigenous plants and their medical uses are being patented in an epidemic of "biopiracy". *Phyllanthus Niruri* has been used by the poorest women in India as a cure for jaundice. It has been patented by an American company for the treatment of hepatitis. Turmeric, a proven antibiotic in indigenous medical systems, has been patented. Neem, the village pharmacy, used for dental care, skin infections, contraception, and for its bio-pesticide properties has had all its uses in indigenous medicine patented.

'Since a patent is a claim to invention and a right to exclude, biopiracy patents perpetrate double injustice to the poor – first by claiming their collective, cumulative knowledge as an invention of TNCs or Western scientists, then by denying them rights to use products they have relied on for centuries.' [216]

Other areas of the Indian economy will be affected by TRIPs. Agriculture, a key sector for many of India's poorest people, is threatened. In September 1997, the US patent and trademark office granted a patent on Basmati Rice Lines and Grains to a US agribusiness corporation, RiceTech Inc. Basmati, highly prized for its unique aroma and flavour, is one of the most superior varieties of rice grown in India. The patent covers the genetic lines from varieties developed by farmers. If enforced, farmers will not be able to grow rice strains developed by them and their forefathers without paying royalty to RiceTech. RiceTech's basmati also cuts into the Indian and Pakistani export market. The US is one of the biggest importers of Indian basmati. If RiceTech is allowed to market its rice there under the name basmati, and at a price cheaper than the Indian varieties, Indian rice exports will be drastically affected. [217]

Civil society organisations in India are resisting these changes. The Campaign Against Biopiracy is a network of Indian NGOs campaigning against foreign companies' patents on Indian natural resources. Nineteen organisations signed a letter to the US ambassador in Delhi protesting at the basmati rice patent. Other organisations are campaigning on the health impacts of TRIPs in India while farmers' organisations worldwide are protesting against the way multinational agribusinesses use TRIPs to secure profits at the expense of poor farmers. These groups are part of an increasing global campaign to stop TRIPs before it is too late.

4 Priorities of the powerful

The world's powerful governments justify the WTO trade agreements by saying that they will work in the interests of the poor. The priorities of 'making globalisation work for the poor' and promoting a 'development round' in trade negotiations are routine phrases in the speeches of trade ministers from rich countries. So if the global trade rules are not benefiting a large proportion of the world's poor people, what has gone wrong? Have honest intentions failed in implementation – or are there other, unspoken, priorities at work?

Rich countries' priorities

The more ambitious free traders want a global economy where businesses are able freely to enter all markets and countries. They want liberalisation to cover newer areas like government procurement, investment and services. In the words of the former WTO Director General, Peter Sutherland, the organisation's key goal following the Uruguay Round is to extend liberalisation to 'most aspects of *domestic* policy-making affecting international [trade and investment]'.[220]

The former World Bank economist and Clinton administration official Lawrence Summers defined the purpose of global trade policy as to 'lock in' gains and 'ensure viable investment opportunities for OECD companies'.[221] This vision of the future is embodied in the WTO's emphasis on 'progressive liberalisation'.

> '*The dynamic behind the WTO process has been the export interests of major enterprises in the advanced trading countries.*'
>
> Chief Trade Economist of the World Bank [218]

If unchecked, this process will reduce poor countries' ability to choose the best development path to address poverty, and leave them with fewer tools to intervene to make markets work better or help eradicate poverty. If left to the laws of the market, it will be the powerful who are able to gain the most.

It needs to be stressed that *promoting* such liberalisation is not the same as '*leaving* everything to the market' but requires massive intervention by governments, as the writing of the WTO agreements shows. As some analysts have pointed out, 'free trade' itself, far from being a natural state of affairs, has been brought about by major government intervention.[222] This irony shows that the powerful are promoting a quite deliberate agenda, and one that amounts to corporate protectionism.

Rich countries' basic priority is to open markets around the world to their exports. This strategy was famously described by Carla Hills, the former US Trade Representative, as using a 'crowbar' to open markets 'so that our private sector can take advantage of them'.[223] Similarly, William Daley, US Commerce Secretary, speaking after the WTO ministerial meeting in Seattle, noted that 'in trade negotiations every time there's an attempt to launch a new round it isn't always successful. But eventually they will be successful and we'll have a chance to sell more products'.[224] The new US President, George W. Bush, has said that 'the goal is to launch a new and ambitious round of multilateral negotiations focused solely on opening markets.'[225] He has said that 'we would work aggressively to open markets for US products and producers'[226] and that 'we will negotiate open trade to find new markets for American products, from movies to electronics, to Californian farm produce.'[227] Opening up global food markets has been a special focus. His election campaign statement contains this promise:

> *'It is our goal to open markets, both regionally and globally.'*
>
> Joint statement by George W. Bush and Tony Blair, 23 February 2001 [219]

> 'With 96 per cent of the world's population outside the US, Governor Bush recognises that the future prosperity of America's farmers depends on expanding markets overseas. He is committed to free trade and will work to tear down barriers everywhere and will use every available tool to combat unfair trade practices.' [228]

The EU and liberalisation

European Union priorities are, at root, very similar. A fundamental EU objective is to assist in the 'smooth and gradual integration of developing countries into the world economy'. The EU believes that 'open national markets and market oriented policy approaches are fundamental in order to strengthen macroeconomic stability and the efficiency of national economies.' In a position paper on the least developed countries – as elsewhere in EU policy statements – no alternatives to trade 'liberalisation' are put forward despite the recognition that 'while increasing trade and investment flows have been beneficial to emerging economies, marginalisation of LDCs persists'.[229] As the UN's Development Programme notes, the poorest countries are often already deeply dependent on trade, with sub-Saharan Africa's exports accounting for nearly a third of its GDP.[230]

The EU's fundamental commitment to liberalisation sits alongside commitments by EU policy-makers to make trade work in the interests of the poor. The EU Trade Commissioner Pascal Lamy concedes that 'freer trade... is only part of the development equation' and that it is vital 'to make special and differential treatment more operational to effectively meet African countries' needs'.[231] But the fundamental belief is clear: 'the process of globalisation and, more specifically trade liberalisation, if correctly employed can and will be good for development if, and this is an important if, these forces are harnessed correctly.'

European Commission policy-makers – who negotiate the EU's policies on behalf of all its members – are particular leading champions of liberalisation in services and investment. EU Trade Commissioner Pascal Lamy told the US Chamber of Commerce:

'Let me briefly turn to examine the fundamental interests of the EU and US. We share a similar percentage of world trade (around 20 per cent). Our shares of both inward and outward flows of FDI are much higher even than that. So we are both tightly bound up with the global economy and its future. But this is not just a manifestation of power and influence, but of reliance. We both rely heavily on trade and investment flows – with each other, and in third country markets. Consider briefly that we have similar leading edge industries such as telecommunications and financial services, we both need to help traditional sectors such as textiles adjust and find new markets, and we both look after our agricultural sectors to a remarkably similar extent. But each of these sectors is deeply reliant on trade.'

He stressed the importance to the EU and US of global trade agreements: 'We both have the potential, and the incentive, to deploy leverage – whether that is in Geneva, in a regional trade agreement, or in a bilateral deal. But even if we can both behave as rather vulgar landlords from time to time, that is because we both have the fundamental interests of the landlords in the system: in other words, we both have an incentive not just to be power brokers, but to respect the system, to nurture it, and to safeguard it.'[232]

Lamy also refers to the EU's 'very strong *offensive* interests in services, and we must push them forward.[233] Also for the EU, services are central. We are number one in the world: 26 per cent of world trade. Services account for two thirds of EU GNP. Against this background, just 25 per cent of our total exports are services: so there is a gap between the importance of trade in services within our economy and its importance in terms of our trade. We of course want to reduce this gap.'[234] Though GATS, he said, 'was a breakthrough in bringing services within the scope of the world trading system, further negotiations on market opening are now essential for the European economy. We make no apology for that.'[235]

On agricultural trade, the EU could be a much better ally to developing countries. The EU has pushed hard to open developing country markets but its commitment to liberalisation is tempered by its own domestic agriculture policies that involve massive domestic support. Compared with the US, the EU could be a much stronger advocate for developing countries having greater flexibility in promoting their agricultural sectors, especially in the areas of domestic support and import protection. But this positive potential has yet to be translated into practice. The EU shares responsibility with the US for the current unfairness of the WTO rules.

The UK government's two voices

Almost all major UK policy statements and speeches on trade refer to the need to make trade work in ways which reflect the needs of developing countries. In Tony Blair's words:

> 'One of the key requirements for faster progress is that developing countries themselves must lead the process of reform. For too long, some donors and international institutions have dictated to governments of the poor, imposing policies which may appear impeccable on paper, but which are ill-suited to Africa's conditions.'
>
> Article with Thabo Mbeki in *Guardian Weekly*, 21-27 June 2001

But there are contradictions and inconsistencies in the UK government's position, and sometimes it seems that it is speaking with two conflicting voices. The UK is one of the world's major champions of free trade, and has since Seattle led the push by the EU to extend liberalisation into areas like government procurement, investment and competition policy as well as trade.[236] Tony Blair told the 50th anniversary of the GATT in 1998 that 'Britain has been a wholehearted supporter of free trade since the GATT's establishment. We remain an unabashed champion of free trade today.' He noted that 'we need to extend trade liberalisation... We must send this clear message: that protectionism does *not* bring prosperity'.[237] Former Trade Secretary Stephen Byers stated that 'protectionism anywhere is a threat to prosperity everywhere.'[238] Another former Trade Secretary, Margaret Beckett, said that:

> 'A key objective for my department... is to continue developing the conditions at home and abroad in which British business can thrive. Open markets and free trade are key elements of that environment and British businesses need to be able to trade throughout the world's markets as easily as they can in home markets without facing high tariffs, discriminatory regulations or unnecessarily burdensome procedures.'[239]

The Department for International Development shares the general government commitment to liberalisation, and overall, the UK government supports the strategy of most rich countries in effectively promoting the 'one-size-fits-all' economic model for developing countries. But working within that model, the UK government is arguably one of the more progressive rich country voices, and argues strongly for the need for capacity building, WTO reform and allowing developing countries to have a more powerful voice in the negotiations.

This progressive perspective finds an echo in its Globalisation White Paper. The government argues against naïve reliance on free-market ideology. It describes as flawed the 'belief in the minimalist state and unregulated market forces which failed to secure economic growth and led to increases in inequality in the world.' It concedes that 'it is not inevitable that globalisation will work for the poor – nor that it works against them. This depends on the policies that governments and international institutions pursue.' No economic policy forced on developing countries from the outside will work: 'That is why it is so important to devise economic strategies that recognise and respect countries' specific needs and circumstances and to promote sustainable and inclusive economic and social development that spreads its benefits to all sections of society.' [240]

The White Paper argues that to benefit from globalisation, developing countries need 'effective systems of government and action against corruption; they need respect for human rights and to promote security, safety and justice for all… and they need to make markets work better for poor people.' So opening up of markets is part, but part only of the solution for developing countries: '*a necessary – though not sufficient condition for national prosperity*'. And the paper calls for fairness in world trade: 'Trade rules must not be used to impose unfair standards on developing countries or to discriminate unfairly against their exports.' So on these issues, the British government speaks with two voices: one is sensitive to the complex needs of developing countries – the other one is ideologically committed to a simplistic free-market model of development.

Trade

On the positive side, the UK government is a leading champion of ending rich countries' agricultural subsidies [241] and of rich countries opening up their markets by reducing their tariff barriers to exports from developing countries.[242] It is opposed to the use of anti-dumping measures as a disguised form of protection.[243] It also supports the WTO's commitment to achieving the International Development Targets, and urges the WTO to see trade as a means not as an end in itself.[244] Although it defends the role of the WTO as an 'organisation which takes decisions on the basis of consensus',[245] it is also committed to reforming it to give developing countries a greater say.

The negative side relates to the UK's total commitment to liberalisation in all areas of the global economy. The UK government wants to 'reduce the barriers

to trade' everywhere [246] and believes that 'trade openness, especially import liberalisation' is always the best policy.[247] It is also opposed to countries pursuing
protectionist policies [248] and appears to believe in 'export-led' development in all
cases.[249] It believes that agriculture should be 'liberalised' in all countries [250] and
is opposed to the use of 'all forms of trade-distorting subsidies'.[251]

Investment

The government supports the negotiation of a multilateral investment agreement at the WTO [252] that gives equal treatment to foreign and domestic firms.
However it insists that governments should be able to set their own health,
social and environmental standards.[253] Such an agreement would allow governments to target support to particular sectors or enterprises but only 'where such
support is available to both domestic and foreign investors'. It should also allow
governments to restrict foreign investment only 'in sensitive sectors'.[254] This
commitment to equal treatment for foreign firms sits uncomfortably with the
government's positive recognition that 'foreign investment does not substitute
for domestic investment but it can complement it'.[255]

Intellectual property rights

The government is a strong supporter of intellectual property protection and
of the TRIPs agreement.[256] It defends the agreement by saying that it does not
restrict the cost or availability of essential drugs and seeds, or reduce poor
people's access to them, and argues that there is sufficient flexibility built into
the agreement. However it acknowledges that 'the precise details of IPR regimes
need to be tailored to the particular circumstances of individual countries' and
it expressed satisfaction at the conclusion of the South African HIV/AIDS
drugs case.[257] But in general the only difficulty the government appears to
recognise is on developing countries' ability to implement the agreement on
time, and it has offered help with implementation.[258] Other than that, it only
acknowledges 'concerns' – for example that developing countries are losing out
because TRIPs does not cover traditional knowledge or access to indigenous
genetic resources, or that TNCs may be able to patent plants and animals.[259]
It is setting up a commission on intellectual property rights to investigate how
intellectual property rights can 'best be designed to benefit developing countries within the context of international agreements, including TRIPs'.[260]

The 'one-size-fits-all' approach

An enthusiastic complete commitment to liberalisation puts the UK government firmly in the camp of those in effect pressing for the 'one-size-fits-all' economic model. But the government also says it supports 'detailed discussions on possible changes to agreements to accommodate developing country concerns'.[261] It believes it is 'important to design economic strategies that recognise and respect countries' specific needs and circumstances.' [262] The Government has explicitly acknowledged that many factors in poor country economies prevent more open markets from working *now* for poor people. These are welcome and crucial acknowledgments by the government, of key importance to Christian Aid. But from the evidence before us, they do not appear to be implemented in practice. These sensible reservations are much less visible than the commitment to liberalisation.

In practice, the Government's main thrust seems overwhelmingly to be with the speed of liberalisation, rather than to question its appropriateness or relevance to solving today's problems of poverty. Take the question of whether the developing countries should be able to restrict capital flows into their countries. This is a vital issue following the East Asian financial crisis when rapid capital movements destroyed whole economies. The UK favours 'a more country-specific approach' to restricting these inflows. But its concern is with the '*speed of liberalisation*', not the fact of it. Government policy does not appear to allow for the possibility of supporting developing countries which do not want to 'liberalise' in the first place.[263]

Most developing countries are opposed to the inclusion of new issues in trade discussions. A group of trade negotiators from 27 African countries, for example, have expressed their opposition to including investment, competition policy and government procurement – among others – in a new round of negotiations.[264] But the UK still strongly advocates the inclusion of these issues in a new round. In general the government's strong support for reforming the WTO (making it more transparent and allowing developing countries a greater say) appears to be driven by a desire to secure a commitment from the developing countries to accepting the WTO agenda and better implementing its agreements.[265]

It is perhaps worth contrasting the enthusiasm of the British Government's attitude to liberalisation with that of UNCTAD, the United Nations agency set up to give specialist advice on trade and development:

> 'Agricultural liberalisation has often not been associated with a strengthening of output price incentives owing to falling world prices for export commodities, the removal of subsidies on food crops and imperfect

marketing systems… Financial liberalisation has led to high and unstable interest rates, widespread insolvencies and a rapid accumulation of public domestic debt… Trade liberalisation, where formal sector enterprises have weak technological and managerial capabilities, has often undermined domestic industry… There is also growing evidence that economic liberalisation does not deliver developmental integration into the world economy for countries which are more remote from the core growth areas of the world economy and with geographical constraints on access to international trade.' [266]

Government and business links

Rich country priorities are shaped forcibly by the growing ability of transnational corporations to influence the policies of rich country governments. This increasingly swamps the voices of other citizens' groups in industrialised countries. Pascal Lamy, for example, once told a meeting of trade ministers that something had to be done about government regulations on foreign investment because 'our enterprises have led us to act'.[267] He also asked the Transatlantic Business Dialogue – a corporate lobby group: 'If I can make one suggestion, focus and prioritise your recommendations so that we can concentrate our energies on the issues most important for you.' [268]

At crucial moments big companies have themselves driven forward the trade agenda. In 1993, when the Uruguay Round seemed to be stalled, 14 powerful European companies had a meeting with the French Prime Minister, who was seen to be a key player holding up progress in the talks. The architect of this meeting later asked, modestly: 'was this the turning point? France was arguably the decisive player and, contrary to all expectations, a deal was in fact signed just three months later.' [269] Large companies influenced the drafting and negotiating of Uruguay Round deals from the beginning. The US company Cargill, one of the biggest four food producers in the world and which controls half of global trade in grains, was heavily involved in the preparations for the US negotiating position on agriculture – some commentators have claimed that the company wrote the first draft of the US position.[270]

TNCs were also involved in the drafting and negotiation of agreements on intellectual property rights and services. According to the *Corporate Europe Observatory*, intellectual property rights were put on the agenda of trade talks by a committee of thirteen major companies including General Motors and Monsanto, following lobbying of governments.[271] Ninety-six out of the 111 members of the US delegation negotiating on intellectual property rights were from the private sector.[272] In the preparations for the Seattle ministerial meeting, businesses were even offered special opportunities to meet key negotiators in return for donations to cover the costs of the summit.[273]

A business coalition called the Intellectual Property Committee – with IBM, Du Pont, General Electric, Merck and Pfizer as members – has boasted in its own literature that its 'close association with the US Trade Representative and [the Department of] Commerce has permitted the IPC to shape the US proposals and negotiating positions during the course of the [GATT] negotiations'.[274] The current US Trade Representative continues to put pressure on Latin American countries to agree to patent laws under TRIPs. His criticisms of Argentina and Brazil reportedly 'closely echo briefing documents supplied by' the US corporate lobby group, the Pharmaceutical Research and Manufacturers Association (PhRMA). But as one US Congressman said: 'the PhRMA doesn't need to lobby. The industry is in the White House already'.[275]

The extent of lobbying by individual businesses and corporate lobby groups is large, and has been exposed in particular by *Corporate Europe Observatory*.[276] In Europe, corporate lobby groups such as the European Round Table of Industrialists, the European Services Forum, the Transatlantic Business Dialogue and UNICE (the Europe-wide employers' confederation) have been extremely active in publishing and lobbying for their concerns to be adopted by EU (and WTO) decision-makers. The evidence suggests that they have been very successful in shaping EU negotiating priorities, especially concerning the services and investment agreements and on the fundamental push to liberalise markets around the world. At root, the design of many of the WTO agreements reflect the central priorities of EU- and US-based lobbyists. At the very least, it can be said that their priorities have shaped the WTO agreements to a far greater extent than the concerns of citizens' groups in the industrialised world or pro-poor voices in developing countries.

Close personal links exist between senior officials from rich country governments and big business. Many US delegation leaders in the Uruguay Round were either business leaders or had strong business links. One came from the giant food TNC, Cargill, and another, the former US Trade Representative Carla Hills, has close links with the tobacco industry. Another former US Trade Representative, Clayton Yeutter, played a key role in initiating the Uruguay Round and was given a directorship of the Caterpillar company after negotiating the elimination of EU tariffs on construction equipment. US business groups were active in initiating the Uruguay Round, were often consulted in negotiations and were generally happy with its outcomes.[277]

WTO Director Generals have subsequently taken up positions in private companies that have benefited from WTO agreements. Arthur Dunkel, chair of the GATT from 1980 to 1993 became chair of the Trade and Investment working group of the International Chamber of Commerce, a WTO dispute mechanism panellist, and a board member of Nestlé, a company actively pushing for liberalisation in food markets. His successor Peter Sutherland, who was chair of the GATT from 1993/5, became chair of BP (which benefited, as did other oil companies, from the WTO decision that the US Clean Air Act was incompatible with WTO rules) and an associate with Goldman Sachs (which stands to benefit from services liberalisation).[278]

Christian Aid is dismayed to see trade and development ministries in rich countries failing to tackle the challenge to democratic decision-making represented by the rise of corporate lobbying in the WTO process. Governments must be free to reverse the current 'corporate protectionism' which favours the profits of the few over the needs of the many.

Does the WTO actually believe its own ideology?

WTO officials regularly cite studies claiming that trade liberalisation improves growth and ultimately reduces poverty. But a reading of WTO documents suggests some WTO officials are highly ambivalent, at best, as to whether trade liberalisation really reduces poverty, or promotes growth. One senior WTO secretariat official said that it might sometimes be the case that 'LDCs would be better advised to devote their scarce resources and domestic political capital to changing policies that will raise the share of investment in GDP and maintaining macroeconomic stability, *than to engaging in trade liberalisation.*'

WTO analyses show that success in trade liberalisation depends on a host of other policy changes, for example: 'trade liberalisation in an unstable macroeconomic context is self-defeating'; 'although trade liberalisation and reform are necessary for generating resources and growth for poverty reduction, they may not work unless they receive support from complementary policy areas (macroeconomic, regulatory and structural policies)'; 'countries will not be well-poised to take advantage of the potential benefits of trade liberalisation... unless they simultaneously take steps to reduce costs and enhance the efficiency of infrastructure sectors... and otherwise establish incentives for innovation, the creation of efficient management structures and productivity improvement.' Where policies have failed, 'the absence of companion policies is the principal reason for a reversal of trade liberalisation.'

Even for WTO officials, liberalisation is not a magic bullet that will promote development, but is meant to be part of a wider package of reforms. By attaching so many qualifications as to whether trade liberalisation can succeed, WTO officials undermine their own basic policy of pressing for it to be implemented everywhere.[279]

The theory of liberalisation

Many proponents of liberalisation present a false dichotomy – free trade and liberalisation *or* protectionism. They suggest that if you are not in favour of complete free trade and the unfettered liberalisation of all markets *now*, you must be supportive of the discredited policy of protectionism. Christian Aid would support free trade and liberalisation if we believed there was firm evidence that such a framework provided the best chance for eradicating poverty across all poor countries, and if poor people themselves believed this offered the best opportunities for development. But we simply do not believe there is evidence to support the general case for free trade and liberalisation. Indeed we agree with the British government that many conditions in the real world throw into question the blind applicability of this theoretical model.

Yet this does not mean that liberalisation *never* benefits poor people. Some poor people clearly gain, and even more gain in the short term. But in today's highly unequal world where big companies and rich countries dominate the international economy, liberalisation can lock developing countries into structural poverty, rather than offering a fast exit from it. Currently, they are being forced to make policies as if they faced a free global market, often with disastrous results. According to one study, trade liberalisation in Mauritius led to a massive rise in employment in the new export industries, with most new jobs going to women. We believe that developing countries must be able to retain the option to pursue policies of their own choice. We will continue to work with local partners to make sure that the voices of poor people help to shape and influence trade policies.[280]

Trade and competition theory suggests that countries and companies should specialise in those goods that can be produced relatively more cheaply than elsewhere. So, for example, if Ghana can produce cocoa more cheaply than the UK, but the UK can produce tractors more cheaply than Ghana, then the UK should specialise in producing tractors and import the cocoa it needs from Ghana. If the UK were to try and produce cocoa, it would produce less cocoa than it could buy from Ghana if it invested the same resources in producing tractors for trade. So through use of comparative advantage, trade is supposed to lead to a higher level of production and consumption for everybody.

According to this theory, in order to gain from their comparative advantage, governments should:

- reduce direct barriers to trade such as import or export tariffs

- reduce indirect barriers to trade such as quality controls, employment laws, or health and safety standards

- not attempt to direct the market by discriminating in favour of or against certain types of companies.

But does the pure theory hold water?

- This theory has lots to say about efficiency but not much about social goals like equality. The market might lead to more efficient use of resources, but they will not necessarily be distributed in ways that are fair.[281] In reality, national governments have always intervened in markets to make sure that social goals – like universal health care or education, or a minimum standard of living for everyone – are met.

- This approach is based on an idealised, not a realistic, view of the world. In reality there has never been, and never will be, a completely free market. Some actors in markets have more power than others and can dictate the price of goods or the amount that is sold. When the largest TNCs are many times bigger than the economies of entire countries, there cannot be genuine competition between TNCs and small companies within those countries.

- The theory does not say much about how countries *obtain* comparative advantage in the first place. It's not a natural phenomenon. Tractor industries do not spring up overnight. Looking at today's world, it might seem obvious that South Korea, for example, has a comparative advantage in producing electronics. But 50 years ago, South Korea was poorer than Sudan, and its main export was wigs. Competitiveness did not just happen through the free play of market forces. Instead it was nurtured by altering the incentive structure and by implementing a range of policies which over time created such competitiveness. In the same way countries do not automatically move up the value chain of production. They have to work hard to increase value added and to expand capacity and range. This reduces the risks which come from a narrow production base. History also shows that it is the strongest countries that promote free trade, since they are better able to compete in global markets.

The myth that countries are poor because they have not liberalised enough

The argument is often made that the reason why the poorest countries have not benefited from free trade is that they have not liberalised *enough*.[282] However, WTO officials note that least developed countries 'have taken significant steps in autonomous liberalisation', reducing their average tariffs from 45 per cent in the late 1980s to around 20 per cent now.[283] IMF data show that trade liberalisation has proceeded further in the least developed countries than it has in other developing countries. Thirty-seven per cent of least developed countries had average import tariff rates below 20 per cent, coupled with no or minor non-tariff barriers, while only 23 per cent of the 78 developing countries sampled had this degree of openness. In a sample of 45 least developed countries, only nine maintained strict controls on remittances of dividends and profits and capital repatriation. Twenty-seven had a free regime, guaranteeing such transfers, while nine had a relatively free regime.[284]

According to UNCTAD, many least developed countries have 'significantly liberalised' their foreign investment regimes, with many now eliminating discrimination between foreign and domestic investors, allowing profit repatriation and protection against expropriation. In Senegal, for example, there are no restrictions on the transfer or repatriation of capital and income in convertible foreign exchange, while Tanzania has abolished foreign exchange restrictions. Countries like Nepal, Zambia and Uganda have changed legislation to allow foreign investors to participate in privatisation programmes.[285] Of 32 least developed countries in Africa, 26 had a liberal or relatively liberal regime for the repatriation of dividends and capital.[286]

The same goes for agriculture, where radical liberalisation has often failed to raise the living standards of the poorest rural producers. The government of Kenya told the WTO's Committee on Agriculture:

> 'At the end of our sixth year of the implementation of the Agreement on Agriculture, the agricultural sector in Kenya is already more liberalised than what was committed as the final bound level in 2004. It is substantially more liberalised in terms of support to domestic farmers and exporters than most high-income developed country members. All of this is despite the fact that Kenya's future development critically depends on the income and the employment from the agricultural sector, while the agricultural sector in high-income developed countries accounts for less than two per cent of their GDP and less than seven per cent of their total employment. In Kenya, almost half of the rural population lives below the national poverty line, where over 60 per cent of the total population live on less than $2 a day. Could such facts fail to strike as a structural imbalance built in the Agreement on Agriculture?'[287]

Ideas that have worked in the past...

History shows that some of the countries which have most successfully reduced poverty have pursued policies which are very different from those prescribed under the liberalisation model. Many would now be banned under the WTO agreements. Successful recent examples of poverty reduction include the East Asian economies. Taiwan's exports increased a hundred-fold between 1965 and

1987, with very little unemployment, virtually 100 per cent literacy and the fairest income distribution in the world. Poverty reduction has been spectacular.[288] To reduce poverty, the government used a whole range of policies to direct the economy and increase growth while ensuring that the benefits were widely distributed. East Asian countries pursued different policies at different times (another key lesson), but they share some key elements.

- *Preference for domestic companies*

  The East Asian countries tended to prioritise domestic industries on the grounds that for long-term industrial development, domestic capability in management, finance and technology was more important than the short-term benefits offered by TNCs.[289] East Asian companies allowed foreign investment, but within the context of strict rules framed within national parameters. Measures included restricting investment to joint ventures with domestic companies (in South Korea), and tax incentives for use of local inputs, export performance and activities in certain sectors (Taiwan). In East Asia, the amount of foreign investment has tended to be well below the international average for TNC investment in the economy,[290] but several East Asian firms have grown to the extent that the region now exports capital to other countries, such as the UK.

- *Protection from competition*

  East Asian countries often protected their domestic industries – but for limited periods and with clear performance requirements. The key was combining protection for new industries with policies to promote exports, ensuring that those industries were able to compete internationally after a certain period.[291] Selective and conditional policies of trade protection and liberalisation contributed to the planned development of domestic companies. This was combined with intense market competition between domestic companies.

- *The state in the economy*

  As well as active regulation, the state in several East Asian countries has had a role in owning companies and financing investment. In Taiwan, the state established its own companies in new sectors, handing them over to the private sector once established.[292] Governments have also been major providers of finance for new industries, as in South Korea. Though this sometimes involved massive corruption, the East Asian experience overall suggests that an effective state can be a beneficial actor in the economy, directing the market towards quite specific ends rather than leaving individual companies to decide their priorities on the basis of the short-term drive for profits.

The point is not that these policies can be held up as an alternative model – or ideology – to be pursued in all cases. It cannot be assumed that what 'worked' for the East Asian countries in the 1970s and 1980s will work for all countries in the changed world of the current century. Indeed, policies of protectionism in many poor countries have in some cases in the past not benefited the poor at all, and been very costly to implement. But the conclusion from these negative experiences should not be to rule out such policies forever.

Christian Aid believes that policies such as domestic protection initiatives, which have in the past made major inroads into poverty, should be considered in working out how best to eradicate poverty today. The East Asian experience provides powerful evidence for the view that developing countries need to be able to retain the option of pursuing different policies from the currently dominant model. They must not be strait-jacketed into any single 'one-size-fits-all' ideology. The evidence for this is even stronger when we look at what the impact of the currently dominant model has actually been.

> *'The manner in which Malaysia was able to recover from the East Asian financial crisis has a great deal to do with the policies they adopted, in defiance of the prevalent prescriptions. In some parts of the world, advocacy of free market principles does not include a surrender of some basic concepts of a "welfare state".*
>
> M.D. Abdul Jalil, Bangladeshi Minister of Commerce [293]

... And ideas that have not worked: the experience of 'liberalisation'

In the 1980s and 1990s, most developing countries were pressed to liberalise their economies in return for loans from the IMF and World Bank under structural adjustment programmes (SAPs). SAPs invariably involved liberalisation of international trade and domestic markets, privatisation, reductions in government spending on health and education, and a range of other policies based on minimal government intervention in markets. In addition shorter-term stabilisation programmes were introduced to curb inflation and create macroeconomic stability. Much has been written about the varying impacts of these policies. Although SAPs benefited some groups of people and contributed to overall growth in some countries, in many countries SAPs failed to reduce poverty and in many cases exacerbated it. This is not altogether surprising since SAPs were never specifically designed to reduce poverty.

The World Bank's own figures suggest that many of the countries in Africa with the highest growth rates in the 1980s and 1990s were those that had shown the least enthusiasm for adjustment policies.[295] UNCTAD states that the improvement in economic growth for least developed countries undertaking SAPs in the late 1980s and 1990s was 'on average, slight'. Average real GDP per capita was declining by 1.4 per cent in the three years before the programmes were initiated, was stagnant in the three years after initiation and then declined by 1.1 per cent in the next three years.[296]

> 'During the 1990s there has been an accelerating process of economic liberalisation in many least developed countries. However, overall progress in increasing real incomes, reducing poverty and moving towards various international targets for human and social development has been disappointingly slow, except for a few of them... The efficacy of the economic reforms on which so many lives and livelihoods now hang, is, and must remain, an act of faith.'
>
> UNCTAD [294]

The experiences of many particular groups of poor people paint an even bleaker picture of the effects of liberalisation under SAPs. Farmers in many countries saw prices collapse as private monopolies replaced state monopolies, and industries were wiped out by the competition from imports.[297] Consumers often saw prices rise as subsidies ended and private monopolies reaped the benefits of liberalisation. In Mozambique, prices tripled in the first year of the adjustment programme.[298]

There is no clear evidence that liberalisation policies have helped rather than harmed developing countries' position in world trade by encouraging particular sectors to develop competitive advantage. Most developing countries have not been able to diversify their exports and break out of their dependence on a few low value exports. Though the value of trade between the low income countries (excluding China and India) has tripled in the last 20 years, their

The Ugandan experience

'In terms of the evolution of Structural Adjustment Policies in Africa, we are willing to agree that considerable success has been achieved in liberalising our economies and putting our budgetary policies on a sounder footing. However, when you look at the balance of payments of most African countries, progress has not been translated into dramatic improvement in our trade performance. We need a fresh effort to look at this problem... Most LDC countries have been encouraged to pursue export policies that are claimed to be consistent with their static comparative advantage based on an abundance of natural resources and unskilled labour. However, this strategy has not succeeded.'

Kweronda Ruhemba, Minister in the Office of the President, Uganda[299]

Globalisation and human rights?

A report by the UN's Subcommission on the Promotion and Protection of Human Rights argued that unfettered free market policies can conflict with basic human rights:

'The negative impact of globalisation – especially on vulnerable sections of the community – results in the violation of a plethora of rights guaranteed by the [United Nations] Covenants. In particular, the enjoyment of the fundamental aspects of the right to life, freedom from cruel, inhuman or degrading treatment, freedom from servitude, the right to equality and non-discrimination, the right to an adequate standard of living (including the right to adequate food, clothing and housing), the right to maintain a high standard of physical and mental health and the right to work accompanied by the right to just and fair conditions of labour, freedom of association and assembly and the right to collective bargaining, have been severely impaired. Developing states are, more often than not, compelled by the dynamic of globalisation to take measures that negatively impact on the enjoyment of those rights. The result is that states cannot fulfil their international human rights obligations, even if they are desirous of improving the human rights situation in their countries. The critical question is the following: Can international economic forces that are engineered by both state and private actors be unleashed on humanity in a manner that ignores international human rights law?

'International economic relations and the policies that drive those relations cannot in the name of laissez-faire economics be exceptions to the international rule of law... While states and multilaterals are directly obliged to comply with those principles, they are also obliged to ensure that private economic actors within their jurisdictions do not act in a fashion that abuses and blatantly violates those rights.' [30]

share of world trade has halved over the same period. At the same time big TNCs which produce and trade high-value products have seen their markets expand and their profits soar. As a result, inequalities between the richest and poorest countries have risen.

Given past experience with SAPs, it is worrying to see many broadly similar policies being promoted through the WTO agreements. Appendix II provides analysis from UNCTAD experts on the combined impacts of SAPs and the WTO agreements on agriculture in five countries. The WTO's Secretary General believes that 'the best vehicle' for pursuing trade liberalisation in developing countries currently is 'the development vehicle of the PRSPs, developed by the

Christian Aid/Paul Lowe/Magnum

Are their rights to adequate food, clothing and housing being eroded by globalisation?

World Bank and the IMF' [300] (the PRSPs or Poverty Reduction Strategy Papers process is the successor to SAPs). WTO officials argue that by including trade policy in the PRSPs, 'countries may be induced into integrating their economies within the world economy' and that progress in this area 'would be rewarded by access to a higher level of assistance' from the World Bank. [301]

The cashew crisis in Tanzania and Mozambique – how liberalisation can fail the poor

Tanzania

The people of Mlundelunde village in Mtwara, South Eastern Tanzania, were not expecting visitors from Christian Aid. But the planned journey to a village further afield was prevented by the impassable roads, a common problem in rural Tanzania in the rainy season.

Despite the unexpected presence of their guests, they were only too eager to talk about cashews. In fact, it is hard to find anyone in Mtwara who does not have something to say about the cashew nut. Cashews are the main cash crop of the region and the economy is entirely dependent on getting a good price for the harvest. Cashews are not processed in Tanzania, but are sent to countries like India for processing and packaging before they are sold to European and American consumers.

This year the news is not good. The price for raw cashews being offered to

Tanzanian farmers has fallen to as little as one quarter of the price they received last year. The effect on the economy is devastating. The local government will not meet their budget for the provision of local services and many farmers will struggle to survive.

Bashiri Hasani, one of the farmers in Mlundelunde village told Christian Aid:

'The whole economy is affected by the fall in the price of raw cashews. We have lots of debts we can't pay because we buy the sulphur powder on credit. Many of us are unable to pay our labourers because of the poor cashew price. Many of us can't afford the school fees for our children. We had planned to build proper houses out of bricks in the village but now we can't afford to.'

The story is an all too familiar one for countries like Tanzania and people like Bashiri. Individuals are dependent on just one or two cash crops for all their yearly income, and countries are dependent on the same crops for their export earnings. They are the victims of huge fluctuations in price and an unstable market dominated by a few transnational trading companies, leaving cashew farmers and the entire economy in a desperately vulnerable situation.

'It would be much better if we could process the cashews in Tanzania', says Hashim Millanzi, a fellow farmer. 'The price would be constant, the market would be more secure and it would create jobs.'

The people of Mlundelunde village know the situation cannot continue as it is. But they also know that the international trading system is not on their side. The frustration facing farmers like Bashiri and Hashim is compounded by the sight of Tanzania's dormant cashew processing factories. The factories are a remnant from Tanzania's previous attempt to process cashews internally.

The venture was successful for a while but was beset with some of the same problems that face Tanzania now. Rather than contributing to the development of industry in Tanzania, qualified engineers like Mr Chinkambi are employed to check over empty factories and rusting machinery. 'I feel bitter about the fact the factory is empty. I worked here while it was open and it was a thriving factory. It is sad to see it empty and closed,' he said.

For Tanzania to develop its own cashew processing industry, it needs to attract investment. The Tanzanian government is working hard to try and attract investors to revive the factories. It estimates the processing industry could generate 10,000 jobs, in addition to providing a more stable income for the cashew farmers and helping to develop the local infrastructure. But it is proving difficult to get the investment needed. Unless investors can be guaranteed some form of government help it is not an attractive proposition. And due to liberalisation policies, countries like Tanzania are not able to offer companies the sort of protection they need.

Mozambique

The experience of Tanzania's neighbour, Mozambique, shows that investment in local processing can often need protection if it is going to succeed. Mozambique is also a big cashew grower and has tried to develop its processing industry. As part of structural adjustment, the Mozambican government was told to privatise the cashew industry. Companies were bought up by mainly local investors, many of whom wanted to develop Mozambique's cashew processing industry and increase export earnings for the country.

However, the new owners were frustrated by another of the World Bank's dictates. They had hoped the protection state-owned factories had enjoyed would continue, and that they could develop the processing industry with a steady supply of raw cashew from Mozambique's thousands of cashew farmers. But this was not to be. As well as privatising the factories, the World Bank decreed that Mozambique had to liberalise its trade in raw cashews, and encourage cashew farmers to export the raw product. The result was the loss of raw materials for the newly privatised factories, the closure of Mozambique's cashew processing industry, the loss of 10,000 jobs and no increase in the price paid to cashew farmers for the raw cashews.

After a protracted five-year battle with the World Bank, in January 2001 Mozambique won the right to impose an 18 per cent export duty on unprocessed raw cashews. It was finally acknowledged that the cashew farmers actually gained a better price for their raw cashews when the local processing industry was thriving and exports of the raw product were restricted. Liberalisation did not work for the cashew farmers of Mozambique, or for the new investors into Mozambique's industry. However, careful strategic intervention by government did.

The same is true for Tanzania. It makes economic and social sense for Tanzania to develop a cashew processing industry. An international trading system that was designed to benefit poor countries and poor people would make this easier, not put obstacles in the way of development. Current policies frustrate the ambitions of local investors to develop industries based on products that African countries are already producing. What chance then, for Bashiri and the farmers of Mlundelunde village?

The WTO, fairness and democracy

Trade is not only about economics. It should also be underpinned by moral concerns. In the prevailing world economy, rich and poor do not compete on equal terms: the benefits of trade accrue disproportionately to the rich. Christian Aid's view is not that we need a world trading system which enables rich and poor to compete on equal terms. Instead we believe that in an unequal world it is our responsibility to create a global trading system which explicitly and deliberately favours those who are currently severely disadvantaged, one which gives priority to resolving the problems of acute poverty *before* it begins to create systems based on fairness and equality of outcome.

We thus believe that there is a moral imperative to put the poor first. Currently this does not happen. Poor people from developing countries play no role in WTO discussions. The unrepresentative nature of some developing country governments is partly to blame; but so too is the very nature of the WTO as a centralised global institution dominated by rich countries. Overall, the WTO represents a great challenge to democratic decision-making and to the demand for simple justice for poor people in poor countries.

> 'The way the WTO works is like putting an adult in a boxing ring with a child. It's like pitching Manchester United against an unknown Zimbabwean football team. The WTO assumes all countries are equal – but they are not. The WTO should be helping to make countries more equal.'[303]
>
> Christian Aid partner in Zimbabwe

1 Undermining national policy choices

Global trade rules inevitably involve some necessary pooling of national sovereignty. But the current rules lock developing countries into 'one-size-fits-all' policies which fundamentally undermine national democratic policy-making. This is especially serious in areas like food security, where the removal of policy options such as adequate protection against cheap imports can directly threaten the lives of many poor people. Christian Aid's view is that, in a world where hundreds of millions of people have inadequate access to food, these policy areas should not be subject to restrictive global rule-making.

Yet WTO officials have praised the power of global agreements to restrict national policy choices, saying that policy makers 'have found themselves in international agreements, implicit or explicit that provide a check on their policy'.[304] The WTO Secretariat has described one of the benefits of GATS as helping to 'overcome domestic resistance to change'.[305] There was a similar endorsement for an academic study which suggested that participating in an international agreement can enable developing countries to undertake domestic reforms 'that might otherwise be successfully resisted by interest groups'. Trade negotiations may help to mobilise groups of consumers, 'who will benefit from increased trade', while 'offsetting the influence of organised producers and workers who compete with imports'.[306] The very nature and global remit of the WTO represent a challenge to democracy.

The importance of reforming governance

The seriousness with which developing country governments seek to reduce poverty varies from country to country, ranging from a country like Sudan – at war with much of its own people – to Uganda and Mozambique, where concerted government efforts have made major improvements to people's lives. Changing the trade rules alone will not eradicate poverty. Poor *people* do not necessarily benefit from increased exports or from policies of protection against cheap imports, just as they do not necessarily benefit from economic growth. For poor people to gain, domestic political and economic policies must focus on their specific needs, and governments need sufficient resources, capacity and will to implement their policies. Their impact must to be closely monitored, not least by poor groups themselves.

Thus, Christian Aid clearly recognises that changes in trade rules need to be matched by changes in domestic policies in developing countries. We believe that developing country governments need to be given much more flexibility to pursue their own policies, and in formulating and monitoring those policies the interests of the poor must be at centre stage. Civil society groups in these countries should lead in the struggle to press their governments to adopt pro-poor policies.

As this report shows, a number of developing countries accept the thrust of WTO agreements and current initiatives because they have little choice in accepting faits accomplis. Many developing country governments clearly do not articulate the needs of the poor in their activities at the WTO. The key point is that poor *people* need to play as big a role as possible in deciding policies that affect them, and the chances of this are greater if national rather than global institutions are the prime movers in creating those policies. As a global institution, it is hard to see how the WTO could ever properly reflect the concerns of poor people *better than* democratic, locally based, community and national structures.

Clearly governance issues lie at the heart of both trade and national development policies. There is no magic bullet for improving governance in developing countries. A range of factors needs to be addressed: corruption, lack of transparency and accountability, poor information networks and democratic processes, weak institutions, and the absence of effective legislation. Decision-makers in rich countries often choose to stress domestic factors, but the international pressures exacerbating poor governance in developing countries are critical and should not be overlooked. It is likely that the unthinking imposition of rigid global trade rules on poor and weak governments could undermine national governance because it reduces the prospect of implementing nationally-owned, transparent policies working in the interests of poor people. To argue that inflexible global trade rules are better for the poor because some developing country governments are anti-poor or corrupt makes no sense. In both cases, the poor lose out.

2 Domination by rich countries

Although the WTO in theory operates by consensus, and some developing countries are increasingly making their voices heard, the reality is that decision-making is dominated by the powerful countries and the poorest continue to be marginalised. Other organisations like UNCTAD, the UN's main trade body, have been somewhat emasculated and elbowed aside, and opposition to many WTO agreements expressed by various UN agencies has been ignored.

The consensus rule in the WTO means that in practice it is much easier for developing countries to oppose a measure than to propose one. So their influence is seriously limited. [307] As with each new issue developing countries give in to, the WTO rules move in the direction set by the developed countries and

An Indian perspective on the 'level playing field'

Former Indian Ambassador to the GATT Bhagirath Lal Das sums up the position of developing countries:

'The developing countries are in a very weak position. This weakness is manifested in various ways, some of which can be well identified. For example:

a   the developing countries have been getting less than equal treatment in several areas,

b   they have been making significant concessions to major developed countries without getting much in return from them,

c   several important provisions of special and differential treatment of developing countries have not been properly implemented,

d   the subjects and areas of interest to the developing countries have been consistently ignored and not attended to,

e   in the working of the dispute settlement process, important interpretations are evolving which have the potentiality to constrain their production and export prospects,

f   big loopholes and traps have been left in some agreements which could have possible adverse impacts on the developing countries etc.' [310]

further away from promoting the priorities of the developing countries. [308] One senior WTO official admitted to Christian Aid that 'periodically the large players will focus on an issue and go for it, and the rest get swept aside. Other countries are simply not equipped to defend their interests.' [309]

Representation is a key factor. Half of all the least developed countries that are members of the WTO do not have any representation in Geneva. It is expensive to maintain a permanent representative in Geneva, the UK government estimates its mission costs around $900,000 per year (not including the costs of office buildings). [311] Those developing and least developed countries that do have some representation in Geneva often will have only one person who is responsible for negotiations in the WTO, when there can be more than 40 meetings a week on subjects ranging from air transport to competition policy, environmental agreements to industrial tariffs. One African delegate expressed his frustration as the only representative of his country at the WTO:

> 'My own impression is that we are just playing games. On average, there are three or four meetings a day on different issues, all starting at the same time. It's just not workable. You get what you put in. If they have 100 people working, and you have one, they are 100 times ahead of you.' [312]

Finally, it is much harder for developing countries to use the WTO's dispute settlement mechanism weapon. Legal costs are often prohibitive. Another key handicap is the fear of reprisals against developing countries by rich countries, should the former institute proceedings against them.

Problems with the dispute settlement mechanism

The Dispute Settlement Understanding (DSU), created by the Uruguay Round, makes the WTO unique among global institutions in having a coercive enforcement mechanism. The existence of the DSU persuaded many developing countries that the WTO would be an improvement on the General Agreement on Tariffs and Trade (GATT), since powerful countries could be made subject to the rules. But in practice the DSU has proved to be less than even-handed.

- The disputes are taken up by small panels of legal experts who are appointed partly because of their adherence to the assumptions of the neo-liberal theories underpinning the WTO.

- The WTO secretariat plays a key role in establishing the panels, and its legal department is quite interventionist, blurring the separation of the executive and the judiciary.

- In some cases, panels have made controversial rulings based on political judgements, such as accepting the US maintenance of its much-criticised 301 trade laws which enable the US to take unilateral action to press other countries to open their markets.

- Rich countries have brought many cases against developing countries which have tended cumulatively to expand the power and rights of industrialised countries – especially the US – and increase the obligations of developing countries. [313]

3 Agreements behind closed doors

Though not a formal institution, the Quad group of countries – the USA, Canada, Japan and the European Union – regularly act together within the WTO. Meeting informally – often in a floating restaurant called The Pirate on Lake Geneva – they will agree positions or make deals before the main WTO sessions. This means that WTO negotiations are dominated by the compromises agreed between the major powers, rather than by the interests of the majority of WTO members. Other meetings are restricted 'Green Room' discussions, which are only open to selected countries. The effect is to exclude from key talks representatives of the majority of the world's population. Even Charlene Barshefsky, the US Trade Representative, acknowledged during the Seattle ministerial meeting in 1999 that:

> 'The process… was a rather exclusionary one. All meetings were held between 20 and 30 key countries… And that meant 100 countries – 100 – were never in the room… This led to an extraordinarily bad feeling that they were left out of the process and that the results… had been dictated to them by the 25 or 30 privileged countries in the room.' [314]

At Seattle, many developing countries were furious at their exclusion from crucial discussions. The African delegates reported bluntly that 'there is no transparency in the proceedings and African countries are being marginalised and generally excluded on issues of vital importance for our peoples and their future'.[315] Developing countries were able to prevent an agreement at Seattle by announcing that they would not join the consensus. But in terms of getting their concerns onto the agenda and positively promoting their interests in the WTO, little has changed since then. Most decisions are still made in informal meetings of a few important players, and other countries are presented with ready-made deals. According to a representative of the Philippines, the domination of negotiations by rich countries meant that, in agriculture, developing countries ended up signing up to agreements 'which address the problems which they did not have'.[316]

4 The use of threats

The richest countries exercise their power both explicitly and implicitly, when countries 'persuade' others to agree with them. Aileen Kwa, of the NGO Focus on the Global South, writes that:

> 'What commonly happens when a developing country refuses to buckle down from a position which is in opposition to key countries, for example the US, is that the US administration would ring up the capital (contacting, for example, the Minister of Trade or the President) in that country to complain that a delegate is "not behaving". Threats of cuts in aid are delivered, or even simply, that the next shipment of shirts to the US would be held up at the port. One government representative has even reported that his US colleague at the WTO would then inform him (even before he has heard from his capital) that his position would have to change and that he would be hearing about that shortly from the capital.' [317]

In 1998 it was revealed that US Vice President Al Gore had bullied the South African government with threats of sanctions if it bought cheaper generic alternatives to brand-name AIDS drugs – this was despite the fact that South Africa had the right to do so under the TRIPs agreement.[318]

In Christian Aid's view reform is needed to the WTO and to the way global trade rules operate. The priority is not so much to strengthen the WTO, but to shift its strategic purpose and focus. We are calling for the needs of poor people, especially from the poorest countries, to be placed centre-stage. Decisions on international trade must make it easier for democratic developing country governments to enact trade policies that are in the best interests of their own poor people. The WTO must help to set effective rules, structures and mechanisms which will create an international framework for trade which makes tangible progress in fulfilling the world community's commitment to eradicating global poverty. It is within this context that global world trade needs to be framed.

5 Transnational corporations and the need for regulation

Private sector companies and large transnational corporations (TNCs) in particular, are the biggest winners from globalisation. They have huge power across the global economy, and are steadily increasing their influence over the lives and livelihoods of hundreds of millions of people. But ensuring that these corporations work more in the interests of the poor, and that at the very least their activities do not hurt poor people, is not currently on the agenda of the WTO, the UK government or other rich countries. Currently, rich country governments and the TNCs themselves only promote *voluntary* codes of conduct and *self*-regulation.

Policy-makers largely ignore the global regulation of TNCs as they pursue their business objectives beyond national boundaries. While the private sector is obliged under international law to promote international human rights, development and environmental standards, no effective enforcement mechanism exists to ensure compliance. The governance of global business is therefore perhaps the most pressing problem of globalisation. An effective rules-based system for TNC activities is crucial to enhance and confirm the positive role that the foreign private sector can play in development.

Pros and cons of TNCs

It is too easy to overlook the diversity of TNCs, and to ignore the positive influence they could, and sometimes do, have. Not all TNCs are large – any company operating in more than one national market can be categorised as a TNC. And not all TNCs are from OECD countries. According to UNCTAD the top 50 multinational corporations from developing countries held $105 billion of foreign assets in 1997, the last year for which figures are available.[319]

TNCs can make a positive contribution to the economic development of host countries in a number of ways.

- They can bring *new technologies and processes* which raise productivity levels above those of national firms. This in turn can lead to knowledge and technology transfer which improves the overall productivity of the host economy.

- They can enhance, deepen and facilitate *international specialisation*, for example through development of backward and forward linkages, and can accelerate progress up and across the value chain of production.

- They can help to stimulate *the expansion of competitive domestic production*.

- *Research and development* spending can be higher, strengthening the innovation capacity and competitiveness of host countries.

- *Salaries can be higher* than in comparative domestic sectors, leading to improved standards of living, and in turn increased opportunities for the next generation in terms of better health and education.

- *Jobs can be created* (often the main reason to attract TNCs in the first place). The number of jobs in TNC affiliates often increases faster than those in national companies.

- *Revenue generation* for public expenditure. Companies pay taxes, rents and rates which allow national governments to pay for public and other works.

- *Higher labour standards.* TNCs often bring higher labour standards than those found in national companies facilities.

- *Higher environmental standards.* TNCs can bring cleaner and more advanced technologies which reduce damage to the environment. Best practice can spread to national companies, reducing the overall impact of economic growth on the environment.

A 1999 OECD report states that TNC operations in OECD countries can lead to all these good results.[320] It also finds that in OECD countries with strict regulation and implementation of rules, TNC operations are at their best. Global regulation of TNCs would require them to operate these standards throughout the world.

In recent years many TNCs have sought to become 'good citizens', and argue that they play a positive role in furthering human rights and good governance. But it would be naïve to believe that all TNCs will deliver all these different benefits without some form of active regulation and the pressure of public opinion. Like any other businesses, TNCs are also driven by the need to make profits, expand market share and, if public companies, ensure adequate returns to shareholders. It is not part of their remit to reduce poverty or promote development, though these may be by-products of their activities. The opposite often happens, for instance when TNCs put pressure on governments to demand tax holidays, or set up export processing zones with lower labour and environmental standards, or remove requirements to source inputs from domestic producers, or lower job security and minimum wage levels in return for investment made in the country.

NGOs have charted the negative impact of TNCs over many years. But there are several reasons why it is urgent to refocus attention on their role today.

- *Under globalisation, a number of TNCs now have unprecedented power and influence in the global economy.*
  Of the world's 100 largest 'economies', 51 are TNCs and only 49 are nation states. Global commodity markets are almost all controlled by a small number of TNCs. Never in human history has a small number of private corporations wielded so much power.

- *Policies of liberalisation in developing countries increasingly open up national economies to the influence of transnational capital.*
  Thus the reach of TNCs into domestic markets of developing countries has been greatly extended under globalisation, and this has been helped by the WTO rules as well as structural adjustment policies.

- *With greater public scrutiny of TNCs, many now systematically portray themselves as acting ethically and as upholders of 'corporate social responsibility'.*
  Highly-effective corporate PR spin may even suggest that TNCs are motivated more by promoting the public good, than private profit. Yet the reality for the people affected is often quite different – and lacking PR resources, their voices are not heard.

There is a danger in exaggerating the role of TNCs by either demonising them as responsible for all the ills of the developing world (which is plainly untrue) or conversely believing that only minor reform is needed to tackle their downsides. There is also a danger of assuming that all TNCs have the same level of ethical commitment, or conversely that widely reported abuses by individual TNCs reflect the practice of all TNCs. Christian Aid's concern is with the unaccountable power of the world's largest TNCs, which command huge wealth and influence over the global economy. The world's top 200 TNCs have combined sales equivalent to more than one quarter of world GDP – this is larger than the combined economies of all countries except the biggest ten and 18 times the combined annual income of the poorest 1.2 billion people living in absolute poverty.[322] We believe that there is a particular need for national and global regulation of these corporations as part of a new approach to globalisation, one that seriously addresses its very real harsh impacts on the poor by articulating and implementing pro-poor economic policies.

It is wrong that growth in the power of TNCs over recent years has not been matched by an increasing ability to hold them to account. The workers, families and communities most negatively affected by their activities are largely powerless against the vast financial, economic and political resources corporations have at their disposal. Legally binding frameworks and enforcement mechanisms are needed to make companies accountable to governments and to the local people whose lives they sometimes harm.

Regulation is only part of the answer

This chapter addresses the need for the international community to implement legally-binding regulation on TNCs. But our starting point is the need for economic policies which work in the interests of the poor. All over the world, Christian Aid partners are coping with the adverse effects of globalisation, are challenging authorities to change policies, and are sometimes shaping and implementing alternatives themselves. TNCs may – or may not – figure in these efforts. *Regulation* of TNCs can only be part of the answer.

The current global economic paradigm could be described as TNC-led globalisation. It is the result of policy choices, not natural inevitability. Regulation may mitigate the worst behaviour and activities of TNCs without challenging the fundamental reason why, in many cases, the poor are kept poor: an international system and set of rules which blatantly disregard the poor. Proposals for regulation must be placed within this wider context: one where private corporations have accumulated vast financial wealth, often translated into political and global economic power. In this situation, inequalities are widening, poverty is deepening in many places and large groups of people, especially poor people, cannot influence the decisions that affect their lives.

'If it were true that globalisation was about the unregulated power of cynical multinational corporations coercing governments and playing off one country against another – then I would be the first to call a halt.'

Stephen Byers, UK Secretary of State for Trade and Industry, Seattle, 30 November 1999

Subjecting TNCs to democratic control is an obvious, badly needed, immediate first step. Legally-binding regulation of TNCs at national and global levels would help to make trade fairer and work more in the interests of the poor. TNC-led globalisation is not necessarily the most appropriate response for all countries in all situations. This assumption needs to be vigorously challenged.

How TNCs can undermine the poor

TNCs have grown as trade, financial flows and investment regulations have been liberalised. This has allowed companies to reorganise themselves to exploit their growing size to achieve greater opportunities to obtain security and higher returns. For many of the larger TNCs, the recent wave of mergers and acquisitions has radically increased their overall market power and influence. Global strategies have sometimes involved moving production to developing countries, where governments often compete with each other to give foreign investors the best deal. Intense competition for investment puts pressure on countries to ease labour legislation and can create a 'race to the bottom' in standards. For example, Mexican president Vincente Fox, trying to persuade business leaders to invest in his country, once boasted that 'we have labour costs that are some of lowest in the world, given the productivity and the quality of Mexican labour'. [326]

The TNC balance-sheet:
a view from the UN Commission on Human Rights

'Transnational corporations are active in some of the most dynamic sectors of national economies, such as energy, telecommunications, information technology, electronic consumer goods, footwear and apparel, transport, banking and finance, insurance and securities trading etc. They bring new jobs, capital and technology. Some corporations make real efforts to achieve international standards by improving working conditions and raising local standards of living conditions. They also encourage their employees to do voluntary work for human rights and development. They certainly have the capacity to assert a positive influence in fostering development.

'Some transnational corporations, however, do not respect international minimum human rights standards and can thus be implicated in abuses such as employing child labourers, discriminating against certain groups of employees, failing to provide safe and healthy working conditions as well as just and favourable conditions of work, attempting to repress independent trade unions, discouraging the right to bargain collectively, limiting the broad dissemination of appropriate technology and intellectual property, dumping toxic wastes, etc. Some of these abuses disproportionately affect children, minorities and women who work in unsafe and poorly paid production jobs, as well as indigenous communities and other vulnerable groups.

'Extraction industries in particular tend to be associated with serious human rights problems, mainly because they may not be able to select their locality and may feel compelled to work closely with repressive host Governments. There is also a growing body of evidence linking extraction industry activities to environmental and human health impacts. Export processing zones are also associated with some of the worst abuses of human rights as some workers do not enjoy healthy and safe working environments.' [321]

Basic facts about TNCs

Definition A TNC is a company that owns or has a controlling interest in a subsidiary enterprise in one or more countries other than where the parent company is registered. As with any company they have a fiduciary duty to maximise profit for their shareholders.

Ownership A TNC can be publicly or privately owned or a mixture of the two.

Number Over the last 30 years, the number and size of TNCs has increased dramatically. In 1970, there were 7,000 TNCs, while today there are 63,000 parent companies operating with about 690,000 subsidiaries in almost all sectors, countries, industries and economic activities in the world.[323] Though most of the largest TNCs are based in the rich countries, there has been a marked expansion in the size and number of TNCs from especially the richer developing countries.

Size Many TNCs are bigger than most countries in which they operate. In 1998, the annual turnover of BP was larger than the GDP of all the least developed countries combined.[324] In 2000, British Telecom's profits of $4.883 billion were greater than the GNP of Senegal. Cargill, one of the world's top four food producers, has a greater sales turnover in coffee than the GDP of most of Africa's coffee growing countries. Almost all the largest TNCs in the chemical, petroleum, car, pharmaceutical, electric equipment and electronics industries are based in developed countries. The foreign affiliates of the world's largest 100 TNCs employ six million people and have foreign sales of $2 trillion.[325] Only 29 of the world's largest 500 corporations are based in developing countries, 21 of them in newly industrialising countries of East Asia. Only one is based in Africa. The top 25 TNCs from developing countries have total foreign sales worth more than $400 billion.

Importance The world's largest TNCs – almost all of them based in rich countries – are the principal drivers of international production and trade. More than a third of all global trade takes place between TNCs; 70 per cent of all trade involves at least one TNC.

Accountability Companies are only legally accountable to their shareholders for their financial performance. Accounts are presented yearly by means of an annual report. There is no formal requirement to present the impact of their activities overseas, nor do annual reports have to include information on social issues, human rights or environmental impact.

Globalisation Previously, the bulk of global production occurred within national boundaries, but in the last few decades international trade and production has become increasingly globalised and corporate activity has diversified and multiplied. This means that many TNCs have their headquarters located in one country, where they are registered, their sourcing or production networks in one or more other countries, and their share listings on several stock exchanges.

The mobility of capital means that TNCs can increasingly move freely around the globe in search of the least restrictive conditions in which to operate and sell to make profits. Fundamental rights such as the freedom to organise and adequate health and safety conditions can be compromised. TNCs can play countries off against each other or take advantage of weak or absent national governance.

Under TNC-led globalisation, the evolution of the world economy continues to be driven by expanding inequalities in wealth both between and within most countries. Income differentials are generally widening, skewing wealth distribution towards the middle classes and the rich. The result is that markets, products and services are increasingly focused on supplying the needs of these powerful and dominant consumers. The global trends towards reducing taxes means the system also fails to redistribute sufficient resources to poor people to enable most of them to meet immediate needs and enable them to engage in markets. Hundreds of millions of poor people do not gain from the global economy because they are partially or wholly excluded from markets. They need to be helped by national investment and growth policies which are more explicitly pro-poor. But as TNCs' share and control of global economic activity increases, developing countries have to make more and more concessions to them, skewing national development priorities to the demands of TNC-driven global markets.

Christian Aid/Sophia Evans

TNCs can crowd out indigenous and small-scale companies.

Export processing zones (EPZs)

EPZs are set up specifically to attract foreign investors and provide the links in global production networks. They are deregulated industrial zones in which imported materials undergo some degree of processing before being exported again, for example the manufacture of garments or assembling of electronic components. EPZs offer special financial incentives such as tax holidays, duty free exports and imports, and abundant and relatively cheap labour. They often have a separate system of law, exempting investors from some national legislation. As developing countries have increasingly adopted export-orientated industrialisation, EPZs have become a main component of development strategy in many countries. There are now around 2,000 zones, several hundred in China alone.

EPZs also offer TNCs access into Southern markets. A recent report by the UN's International Labour Office (ILO) found that market access ranked as the most important consideration in influencing choice of 'export platform', along with the availability of skilled human resources. Market access is important because companies can capitalise on the preferential access granted to certain countries in terms of trade agreements and on the speed with which the market can be reached. For example, in Costa Rica companies in EPZs sell up to 40 per cent of their output in the local market.

For developing countries, EPZs are meant to earn much-needed foreign exchange, raise standards of living by providing jobs, introduce new technology, and provide backward and forward links to improve local enterprises. It is hoped in some cases that EPZs can kickstart the economy as a whole. EPZs are often sold to the governments of developing countries as ways of creating employment, modernising the economy, improving competitiveness and integrating the country into international trade. However, according to ILO, the

Transfer pricing

A recent study by Oxfam estimated that the total revenue lost to governments through transfer pricing is between $50-$200 billion every year, at least $50 billion of which is attributable to tax havens alone. This is roughly equivalent to the total annual aid flows to developing countries.[327] Through transfer pricing a company can set up offshore accounts and 'paper companies' through which most financial transactions occur, without having to pay as much in taxes. Internal accounting and costing is adjusted to minimise company costs and maximise profits. An estimated 80 per cent of international payments for technology royalties and fees is made on an inter-company basis.[328]

incentive structure of most zones has limited the potential of this strategy to promote local economic development. The cost of securing the extra revenue is high, incentives given to foreign companies are not performance related and tariff and duty exemptions limit the knock-on effects on the local economy.

Nine ways that TNCs harm poor people

TNCs have huge power which can work to the benefit of poor people in developing countries – or equally to their detriment. These are some of the ways TNC activity can damage the interests of poor people.

1 Undermining local companies

TNCs can dominate markets by crowding out or swallowing up indigenous and small-scale companies. This stifles competition and jeopardises the livelihoods of small producers. No WTO rules exist to outlaw restrictive business practices, market abuses or moves towards the development of monopolies. And new TNC jobs can often be at the expense of old jobs, especially in domestic companies.

2 Repatriating profit

TNC activities can provide an important source of revenue for a developing country. But because of legal changes to favour foreign capital, an increasing share of the profits generated by TNCs in host domestic markets can be repatriated to home countries, sometimes up to 100 per cent. (The WTO has in effect supported this trend in the GATS agreement, where Article XI states that a member shall not apply restrictions on international transfers and payments for current transactions relating to the sectors it has opened up, except in special circumstances such as balance of payments problems.) Developing countries also lose potential revenue through creative accounting practices which seek to minimise tax payments by boosting and declaring higher returns in low-tax economies. There is evidence of massive fraud and tax avoidance by some TNCs, such as through transfer pricing.

3 Securing political influence

Globally, coordinated corporate lobbying can secure significant changes in WTO agreements. Nationally TNCs are rapidly increasing their financial contribution to political campaigns. For example, US drugs companies alone reportedly contributed $24.4 million to US political parties in the 2000 election.[329] And companies operating overseas can fund local politicians to ensure a favourable environment for their operations and to counter local resistance to their activities. This can easily translate into corruption. There is increasing evidence of some TNCs using their resources to pay bribes or other forms of inducement to create a dominant market position, for instance to gain access to land illegally.

4 Undermining democratic decision-making

The sheer economic power of TNCs can translate into political influence over national governments, especially those struggling to develop, but also those in the North. Political and economic decisions by elected governments are increasingly made to provide favourable environments for the investment and marketing needs of TNCs. Governments compete to offer preferential terms to them, due to the perceived need to remain internationally competitive.

This is particularly the case in developing countries. In the Philippines, for example, recent changes in regulations mean that much of the economy is now dominated by TNCs in whose interests the laws have been altered (see case study, page 163). In 1995 it was revealed that the Australian mining TNC, BHP, had drafted legislation with the government of Papua New Guinea which forced inadequate compensation upon landowners whose land was being polluted by the company's gold mine. The legislation also criminalised any further attempt to pursue legal action. The government allowed BHP the right of veto over the legislation before it could be passed by the parliament.

5 Exploiting labour

TNCs provide an important source of direct and indirect employment. The largest 200 TNCs provided 18.8 million jobs in 1995, or 3 per cent of the world's labour force.[330] TNCs often pay higher wages than local employers and through 'demonstration effects' can encourage other, domestic employers to pay at a fair rate. They can encourage wider skills training, which can increase mobility of labour.

But for decades some TNCs have also been exposed as providers of sub-poverty wages and users of child labour. Recent findings from a survey of more than 4,000 Nike workers in Indonesia reported that 56 per cent had witnessed supervisors verbally abusing co-workers and 24 per cent witnessed either sexual harassment or physical abuse. While 96 per cent said the wage was above the national minimum wage they said this was not enough to match the increasing cost of living.[331] Some TNCs are also 'footloose' – providing jobs to achieve short-term advantage and profits and then closing down when market conditions change. The social and cultural dislocation caused by these 'in/out' investments can be profound and long-lasting.

6 Degrading the environment

By definition, extractive industries – such as oil and mining – affect and can threaten the environment. But they are not the only ones. A recent study of 22 computer companies based in rich countries showed that they had moved half of their manufacturing and assembly operations, involving highly toxic materials, to the South. Bayer, the German chemical giant already fined in the US for health and safety regulations, is currently taking advantage of the lax pollution legislation in Brazil. A study conducted by Greenpeace shows the company is releasing toxic chemicals that pose a grave danger to both the environment and human health.[332]

7 Corporate complicity in human rights violations

TNCs are sometimes complicit in human rights violations. High-profile recent examples include activities in Nigeria, Colombia, Burma and Sudan. In these cases, indigenous peoples have been particularly victimised by oil and mining companies. TNCs often lend credibility and legitimacy to oppressive regimes, and the revenues they secure provide a financial lifeline to the government, directly enabling it to pursue policies that undermine human rights. This is currently the case with foreign, including UK companies, active in Sudan (see case study, page 176).

8 Threatening livelihoods

TNCs encroach on people's land rights as they have sought to develop their commercial activities, threatening and in some cases destroying the livelihoods and even the lives of poor people. Indigenous people are particular victims (see case study on the Philippines, page 163). Many TNCs promote themselves as 'corporate citizens' but the reality often shows a disregard of the citizenship of people in the communities affected by their activities.

9 Unaccountable to local people

TNCs are legally accountable to their shareholders for the financial performance of the company, not to the host countries in which they operate. Additionally, workers affected by TNCs' activities frequently find it difficult to pursue cases in the courts. This is not just because of a lack of funds, but also because of lack of clarity over the applicability of local laws to foreign corporations.

Thor Chemicals: restructuring to avoid responsibility

Thor Chemicals is a British-owned company that processes mercury waste. It was criticised by the UK health and safety executive for its operations in Margate, in the UK, because of the high level of mercury in the blood and urine of the employees. So Thor transferred its operations to Thor Holdings in KwaZulu-Natal, South Africa, in 1988. There it continued the same working practices, except the company employed predominantly casual and untrained workers who were laid off and replaced, or 'recycled', with new workers, when their mercury levels became too high. The mercury poisonings were discovered in 1992. Two workers died, another was disabled and many became ill as a result of mercury poisoning. A Commission of Inquiry was initiated in South Africa and found widespread exposure of the workforce and the pollution of local rivers.

The case was brought against the parent company and its chairman Desmond Cowley, in the UK courts in 1997. The UK law firm, Leigh Day and Co., represented 17 former Thor workers and the families of three dead workers. The claimants eventually received R9.4 million (£1.3 million) in damages and costs. But the company did not admit liability and settled out of court.

In 1998 fresh action was taken in the UK by 20 South Africans still working at Thor claiming compensation for ailments arising out of chronic mercury poisoning. A Medical Research Council specialist said medical examinations showed that new workers had been frequently exposed to mercury levels up to 12 times the level recognised as safe by the World Health Organisation. Instead of limiting the leakage of mercury into the environment, extracting it and protecting the workers Thor had instead 'shuffled' the workers into different posts when tests showed their mercury levels were too high.

However, by this time Thor Chemicals had 'demerged' the holding company and moved its assets to the new company Tato Holdings, in what was seen as an attempt to avoid justice by transferring assets between different corporate entities. The company Eurotrust (also the controlling interest in Thor Chemicals) had shares worth £19.5 million in Tato. Desmond Cowley's family are the main beneficiaries of Eurotrust. Thus by moving the company assets from Thor Chemicals to the new company Tato Holdings the money was successfully put beyond the reach of the claimants if the company was successfully sued. In 1998 Thor Chemicals assets plunged to £2.5 million – from £19 million in 1994 – directly threatening the compensation claim of the victims, as there was no assurance that their legal costs could be met by Thor if the case was successful.[333]

In 2000, the case went to a Court of Appeal which required Thor to lodge £400,000 with the court and produce documents regarding the demerger. The judge concluded that 'there is an arguable case, indeed a good arguable case, that in entering into the demerger Thor had the purpose of putting assets beyond the reach of future claimants'. [334] Thor's example shows how easy it is to exploit the absence of binding global regulation.

CAPE plc: workers are finding that justice comes slowly...

The UK company Cape plc was operational in the Northern Cape and Northern Province of South Africa from 1890-1979, mining asbestos directly until 1948 and then through its wholly owned subsidiary, Cape Asbestos (SA). In 1954 it was found that asbestos dust was linked to painful illnesses and deaths, and Cape's UK workers received £30 million in compensation.

Conditions in the South Africa mines were deplorable. Almost a third of all workers were children. This was justified by the company as contributing 'very largely to the material welfare of the native community – even the smallest of our juveniles regularly handing over part of their wages to their mothers'. A report by a government health inspector noted that young children routinely trampled down the asbestos which fell over them all day. Some were whipped by supervisors for failing to concentrate. The company argued that it would be uneconomical to employ adults. Even the apartheid government turned down Cape's request to employ more children, on health grounds. Workers did not have protective clothing and asbestos levels were claimed to be 30 times those of the UK.

In February 1997 the first compensation claims of South African workers, based on the parent company's negligent control of its world-wide business, began in the UK. In January 1998 Cape successfully delayed the case by applying for it to be heard in South Africa. In July the court refused this application on the grounds that the alleged breach of the company's 'duty of care' took place in England and not South Africa. In January 1999 another 2000 claims were submitted over alleged asbestos poisoning. Again Cape applied to stay the case on the basis that the emergence of such a large group changed the case entirely and appealed that the case be heard in South Africa. The court of appeal dismissed the counter appeals of the victims for leave to continue their case against Cape on the grounds that South Africa was the more appropriate forum in which the case should be heard (even though the company had stopped operating there 20 years previously). However, it was argued that the workers would not be able to obtain legal representation or assistance in South Africa. An appeal made to the House of Lords in July 2000 was successful, based on the fact that the decision to expose the workers to deadly illnesses was made in the UK, and the case will be heard in April 2002. By then it is feared that many of the workers will have died.[335]

The regulatory void

Despite the multiplicity of problems associated with TNCs, there are no binding international regulations to hold them to account for their activities both in their home country and overseas. In national legislation, TNCs are not legally responsible for the activities of their subsidiaries and are under no obligation to apply standards across all their operations. National laws, because they are national, remain wholly inadequate to address the malpractices of corporations that extend beyond national boundaries. And because national laws have focused on trying to compete successfully to attract foreign investment, it is inevitable that legislators have been persuaded to enact laws that are much less favourable to the individual national interest than could have been achieved through a more collaborative approach.

> *'There are no mechanisms for making ethical standards and human rights binding for corporations and individuals, not just governments... But multinational corporations are too important and too dominant a part of the global economy for voluntary codes to be enough.'*
>
> UN Development Programme [336]

International law in relation to TNCs is a decidedly murky area with a lack of clarity surrounding the precise ways in which TNCs could be held accountable to promoting international standards. However, although it is widely believed that only states are obliged to uphold international law, responsibility also lies with the private sector. According to the UN Commission on Human Rights:

> 'While the extant international legal framework imposes legal obligations to respect human rights mainly on states and intergovernmental organisations, it cannot be forgotten that the Universal Declaration of Human Rights calls on every individual and every organ of society to take action in order to secure the universal and effective recognition of the rights recognised by it. The Universal Declaration clearly envisions the promotion and protection of human rights as a collective effort of both society and the state; it does not restrict the task only to state action. In fact, article 29(1) declares that "everyone has duties to the community in which alone the free and full development of his personality is possible". *It is not possible for private actors whose actions have a strong impact on the enjoyment of human rights by the larger society, therefore, to absolve themselves from the duty to uphold international human rights standards.* It is even less acceptable for actors that have been created by states – such as the MLIs [multilateral institutions] and WTO – to shirk their responsibilities under international law.' [337]

TNCs are obliged to uphold international law, but a major problem arises in regard to enforcement. Host developing country governments are often unwilling to make strong demands on a company, either because of the fear of limiting foreign investment, because of corruption or because the rules prevent them from regulating foreign companies. The fact that countries must respect each other's sovereignty compounds the difficulty of enforcing national legislation of the home country when it differs from that of the host country.

Until 1993, the UN had a Centre on Transnational Corporations (UNCTC) that worked with the Commission on Transnational Corporations, an inter-governmental body charged with developing a code of conduct for TNCs. In 1998 a draft code of conduct was produced which, while voluntary, would have prohibited some TNC activities. The draft code was gradually watered down and a final version never approved, mainly due to pressure from business and the US government. In 1993, UNCTC was closed down and UNCTAD became the focal point for UN work on TNCs. UNCTAD, however, has never formally addressed the issue of TNC regulation.[338] Opposition from business and some governments to legally-binding regulation for TNCs continues, highlighting the real political obstacles there are to formulating much-needed international regulatory law.

Opposition to regulation

Many of the largest corporations and business groups continue to campaign strongly against binding regulations on business. The International Chamber of Commerce (ICC), for example, has been particularly active in the area of international environmental treaties. ICC Secretary General, Maria Cattaui, has criticised the UN Development Programme for being 'on the wrong track in calling for a mandatory code of conduct for multinationals'. Such binding rules 'would put the clock back to a bygone era… Governments in the poorer countries now compete to create a hospitable climate for foreign direct investment'.[339] The ICC's US affiliate, the US Council on International Business (USCIB), is also firmly opposed to mandatory regulation and rejects 'the notion that companies can be held responsible for the overall behaviour and policies of their subcontractors and suppliers throughout the supply chain'.[340]

While TNCs and their governments oppose regulations that impede TNC activities, they have been successful in pressing developing countries to strengthen regulations that benefit foreign direct investment (FDI). From 1991/1997, 94 per cent of a total of 750 changes in the FDI regimes of countries were in the direction of a more favourable environment for TNCs.[341] These changes included an increase in legal protection and guarantees awarded to foreign investors. More recently, limitations on profit remittances and the repatriation of capital and other transfer of funds have been relaxed significantly. The establishment of performance requirements is also now becoming less important, partly in response to WTO rules. Not all of these are necessarily harmful developments, but they leave much less room to hold TNCs accountable and in check.

When foreign companies buy up local firms overseas these companies can become subsidiaries often allowing them to secure special concessions. Mergers and acquisitions pose one of the biggest challenges not only to regulation but also to accountability, since pinning down and allocating responsibility to one company or one individual can become almost impossible. TNCs have many affiliates and can divide themselves, by shedding affiliates and subsidiaries, when negative publicity or liability threatens.

Foreign Direct Liability (FDL)

One way of attempting to hold a TNC accountable for environmental damage or human rights violations committed across borders and outside its own national boundaries is through Foreign Direct Liability (FDL). This involves suing the parent company of a TNC subsidiary or affiliate in the courts of a developed country for activities which have taken place in developing countries.

The US Alien Tortes Claims Act (ATCA) gives district courts in the US the power to hear the claims of foreign citizens for injuries caused by actions 'in

The UK government and TNCs: the failure to address regulation

The UK government is the first in the world to have established a Minister dedicated to the issue of 'corporate social responsibility', a welcome step in recognition of the importance of this issue. However, UK government policy towards TNCs appears to be weak and contradictory. The Globalisation White Paper makes no explicit mention of the harmful impacts that TNCs can have but merely praises their positive role.[342] It concedes that 'TNCs should... be subject to adequate regulation' but does not suggest what this is. Neither has the government put forward any subsequent proposals.[343] In reality, the government is putting its faith in the concept of 'corporate social responsibility' – purely *voluntary* initiatives by companies to improve their behaviour. It has said, for example, that 'the challenge is to extend responsible business practice throughout the business community and to improve the quality and coordination of *voluntary* initiatives'.[344] It has also said that 'the UK strongly supports the revised OECD Guidelines on Multinational Enterprises'.[345] Yet neither of these – voluntary initiatives or the OECD Guidelines – have the teeth necessary to regulate TNCs effectively.[346]

The other beneficiaries of globalisation: organised crime and drugs cartels

According to the UN's Development Programme, 'criminals are reaping the benefits of globalisation'. The lack of sufficient regulation of corporations and financial institutions is enabling the flourishing of the illegal drug trade and money laundering. In 1995, the illegal drug trade was estimated at eight per cent of global trade, more than the trade in motor vehicles or iron and steel. The IMF estimates money laundering to be the equivalent of two to five per cent of global GDP. Organised crime grosses around $1.5 trillion a year, 'rivalling multinational corporations as an economic power', according to UNDP.[348]

violations of the law of nations' or a treaty of the US, in a law dating back to 1789. One of the first cases, in 1997, was the Doe (representing a group of Burmese refugees) versus Unocal (the US oil giant). The court upheld the right of the Burmese to sue Unocal for alleged crimes against humanity in using a contractual partner – in this case the government of Burma – who knowingly used slave labour to build a pipeline. Government forces allegedly funded by the oil company forcefully relocated the inhabitants of the area from their villages, and then confiscated their property, forced them to work for slave wages, sexually assaulted many and killed and tortured those who resisted.[347] Currently, action is being pursued against oil giant Chevron, in a San Francisco federal court, for damages relating to the killing of two protesters by the Nigerian military.

There is no equivalent to ATCA in the UK. However, the UK has two acts that have extra-territorial effect. These are: the Child Sex Tourism Act, allowing for prosecution of British sex tourists for offences committed abroad; and the OECD Convention on anti-bribery, which the UK signed in April 2001. The legislation will give UK courts jurisdiction over UK nationals committing bribery offences abroad.

In England and Wales the law used to call parent companies to account for abuses overseas is based on their responsibility to ensure that their behaviour as investors matches the 'standards of care' expected at home. Crucial to the success of these cases has been the ability to prove that the parent companies' involvement in the day-to-day management of the overseas facility was sufficient to allow litigation under the law of negligence. But these types of legal actions are rare. In most cases different companies in the same TNC group must be treated as separate legal entities, thus making it almost impossible to hold the parent company to account. The process is costly and currently relies on law firms acting on a 'no win, no fee' basis. So far there has not been a single clear victory, although some cases have been settled out of court.

Why self-regulation and voluntary codes of conduct are not enough

Rich country governments generally advocate that business adhere to high global principles on human rights and the environment. But this contrasts with their refusal to establish mandatory regulation of company activities to ensure they abide by these principles. Currently, governments put almost all their faith in voluntary codes of conduct and self-regulation for business. For example, the UK oil company Premier Oil has been criticised for its activities in Burma where it has been shown that forced labour was used. The Foreign Office said that the company should leave Burma, but this was never enforced and the company is still operating there.

The strengths and weaknesses of voluntary codes of conduct

Self-regulation usually takes the form of codes of conduct – sets of principles or rules which establish standards for company behaviour. In the UK more than 60 per cent of the top 500 companies now have their own codes, a reflection of the fact that companies are keen to portray themselves as socially responsible upholders of ethical standards and as promoters of 'corporate social responsibility' and 'corporate citizenship'. For example, BP's code of conduct states: 'we believe that wherever we operate our activities should generate economic benefits and opportunities and our conduct should be a source of positive influence; that our relationships should be honest and open, and that we should be held accountable for our actions.' [350]

Strengths

- Adoption of codes can improve company behaviour where previously there may have been few standards at all.
- If used inclusively and transparently, codes can be used to develop 'best practice' and form a template for what can later become binding regulation.
- A code can be used to hold a company to account publicly (though not legally) if activities do not match the rhetoric.
- For civil society groups developing codes can be a pragmatic way of working *with* business to secure improvements in their activities.

Weaknesses

- Codes are voluntary and have no enforcement mechanism – the degree to which they are implemented depends entirely on a company's good will.
- Codes can often be used by companies primarily for public relations and may not make any real impact on a company's behaviour.

- Many codes do not contain reference to the most basic human rights and labour standards.
- Codes take the pressure off governments to establish effective regulation of companies to control their power and make them accountable for the impact of their activities. Codes increase the power of the corporate sector by reinforcing self-governance. By promoting codes of conduct, governments avoid having to take a heavy hand with business and they can continue to enjoy a privileged relationship.

Another weakness of codes of conduct is that in many cases they are adopted following abuses. For example, in the case of Sudan, the Canadian oil company Talisman endorsed the Canadian code of conduct for business abroad after a divestment campaign had targeted it for its complicity in human rights abuses carried out in the name of oil exploration. Likewise, the Swedish oil company Lundin adopted a code of conduct after it was complicit in the Sudanese government's forced displacement of thousands of people in the vicinity of an oil road. In these cases the adoption of codes appears to be intended to cover up negative publicity and advertise a 'caring' public image. Codes can therefore be a way of deflecting attention away from abuses already committed and helping a company evade its responsibilities, in this case from the need to address reparations for displaced peoples and suspend operations.

'The business community's aversion to binding international legal standards governing corporate operations contrasts with its strong advocacy of international law commitments applied to the obligations of governments towards foreign investors.'

UNCTAD [349]

Monitoring of codes of conduct is also an area of serious concern. Currently, most are monitored by auditors who do not have the skills needed to verify compliance accurately. For example, ascertaining whether or not a company is employing child labour in its supply chain is extremely difficult. If a company auditor cannot speak the language or gain the confidence of the workers, he or she is unable to fulfil their remit. Without detailed consultation with local people monitoring codes cannot be effective.

At present the process for establishing and adopting codes is generally untransparent and exclusive. The extent to which codes are making positive change on the ground is often unknown to the public as companies rarely report the degree of compliance and progress made in addressing problems encountered. Codes of conduct have yet to prove that they can make a meaningful difference to company activities. The elaborate rhetoric of 'corporate social responsibility' is clearly not sufficient to change corporate culture and actual company activities.

Why current international guidelines are inadequate

OECD Guidelines on Multinationals

Adopted in 1976 and revised in June 2000, these guidelines set out standards for OECD-based TNCs operating overseas. They cover areas such as core labour standards, environmental protection, human rights, compliance with anti-bribery laws, tax avoidance, the facilitation of training and creation of employment opportunities, disclosure of company information on social and financial performance, and standards for competition such as refraining from price fixing.

In practice, however, these guidelines remain weak in addressing the adverse impacts of TNCs. This is due to:

- the lack of an enforcement mechanism – compliance with the guidelines is purely voluntary
- the fact that most businesses are unaware of their existence
- the fact that the guidelines are full of loopholes in relation to implementation, one of the most significant being full exemption 'on grounds of business confidentiality'
- the fact that there is no simple procedure for the public to initiate action. In the UK, the current system of bringing information to a National Contact Point (NCP) in the Department of Trade and Industry relies on the government's own willingness to implement. Other OECD governments have tri-partite NCPs made up of governments, NGOs and unions. After adjudication by the NCP it is not clear what procedure is then taken to address the problem, nor how much disclosure will be made by the NCP of the final outcome.

Since the Guidelines were established there have been only 30 cases against corporations, only two of which were in the 1990s. This suggests that current procedures are far from effective.

European Parliament Resolution

In 1999 the European Parliament adopted a Resolution on standards for European companies operating in developing countries. It required the EU to establish binding regulation on EU-based TNCs to ensure that they comply with international law relating to protection of human rights and labour and environmental standards when operating in developing countries. Potentially the Resolution has the great strength that it standardises the many different codes in existence and thus helps establish coherence and consistency. However the EU has so far failed to do this and the Resolution has not been fully implemented.

The Resolution also requires the European Parliament to hold annual hearings where good and bad company practice can be highlighted. The EP had its first parliamentary hearing in November 2000 on labour practices in countries where Nestlé and Adidas operate, but neither of the companies attended, provoking strong public criticism. Support for the Resolution in the European Parliament is mixed and there is a clear indication of resistance from Commissioner Pascal Lamy, whose position is that the OECD Guidelines for TNCs should take precedence over the Code of Conduct.[351]

Australian Code of Conduct Bill 2000

The Australian Code of Conduct Bill was introduced to the Senate in September 2000. Although not yet adopted, it seeks to apply environmental health and safety, human rights and employment standards to Australian companies operating overseas that employ more than 100 people. The strength of these standards is that they are based on international human rights and environmental standards which Australia has already signed and ratified under the UN.

Companies must make provisions for the enforcement of these standards and report in Australia on their compliance. The Bill requires companies to make regular environmental impact assessments, to regulate working hours of employees and to adhere to International Labour Organisation core labour standards. The Bill also requires companies to report on their compliance of the standards to the Australian Securities and Investment Commission. ASIC will then produce an annual report for the Australian Parliament. The Bill also crucially requires that company directors are held accountable for the contravening of the standards. This allows anyone who suffers loss or damage as a result of company activity to bring a complaint to the Federal Court of Australia, thus allowing liability to be pursued in the Australian courts for the first time.

United Nations Global Compact

The Global Compact (GC) was launched by Kofi Annan, the UN Secretary General, in July 2000, with 500 senior corporate executives and representatives of banks, business associations, TNCs, governments, UN agencies and some NGOs. The Compact involves nine 'universal principles' based on the Universal Declaration of Human Rights, the Rio Principles on environment and development and the ILO's Fundamental Principles on Rights at Work. The GC asks companies who join to make three commitments: to publicly advocate the principles and the Global Compact; to post on their website concrete steps they have taken to respect the nine principles in their own corporate practices; and to join in partnership projects of benefit to developing countries.

While Christian Aid welcomes the Secretary General's initiative to draw attention to the need for companies to base all their activities on core principles of human rights and international law, we do not believe it is sufficient. In our view the GC is not and will not ever be an effective mechanism to stop current abuses and to ensure companies shift to a more ethical way of conducting business. There is no enforcement mechanism if companies violate any of the nine principles. And there is no indication to show how compliance will be monitored or how it will be verified. UN Assistant Secretary-General, John Ruggie, stated that 'this is not a code of conduct and the UN has neither the mandate nor the capacity to verify compliance'.[352] Rather, the Compact offers free publicity for many TNCs – such as Nike, Shell and Rio Tinto – many of which have bad reputations for violating international human rights, labour and environmental standards. This is a challenge to the integrity of the UN, since the same companies are allowed to enhance their image by displaying the UN logo if involved in a UN project.[353]

The Global Compact is hailed as a 'new partnership' between the UN and international business whose stated aim is to 'discuss how new partnerships can benefit corporations by providing access to emerging markets while helping the UN in its drive to eradicate poverty'. As part of the Global Compact deal with big business, Kofi Annan has promised to 'continue to make a strong case for free trade and open global markets',[354] describing the Compact as 'the most sensible way forward to safeguard open markets while at the same time creating a human face for the global economy'.[355] He also stated that 'from a more narrowly self-interested point of view, corporations which embrace these principles are better placed to deal more constructively with pressure from single-issue groups'.[356] But Carol Bellamy, the Director of UNICEF, has said that 'it is dangerous to assume that the goals of the private sector are somehow synonymous with those of the United Nations, because they most emphatically are not'.[357]

In response to the Global Compact an alternative Citizens' Compact has been formed which is supported by many NGOs around the world. It is also based around the nine principles but sets different guidelines for companies, NGOs and governments and stresses the need for a monitored legal framework of regulation (see box opposite).

Global Reporting Initiative

Formed in late 1997, the GRI involves leaders from business, the UN, NGOs, and accounting firms and will become a permanent organisation in 2002. The aim of the GRI is to develop globally applicable guidelines for reporting on environmental, economic and social performance in an attempt 'to explore how

Principles of the NGOs' alternative Citizens' Compact [358]

1 Multinational corporations are too important for their conduct to be left to voluntary and self-generated standards. A legal framework, including monitoring, must be developed to govern their behaviour on the world stage.

2 The United Nations will continue to develop tools to ensure universal values of environmental protection and human rights, through such mechanisms as multilateral environmental and human rights agreements, codes of marketing, and ILO conventions.

3 The United Nations recognizes the legitimate purpose of national and local legislation to protect ecosytems, human health, labour standards, and human rights. The United Nations will assist civil society and governments in enacting and implementing such legislation.

4 The UN must find ways to ensure that other intergovernmental bodies, such as the IMF, World Bank and WTO, do not depart from the principles and goals of the UN Charter.

5 United Nations agencies will advise and offer assistance to corporations wishing to understand and improve their human rights and environmental behaviour. Such assistance will not be considered a 'partnership'.

6 The United Nations does not endorse or promote products or brand names of any private corporation, and will avoid the appearance of such endorsements.

7 The United Nations will avoid any public association or financial relationship with companies with destructive practices, or products that are harmful to human health or the environment. Before entering any relationship with a corporation, the UN will thoroughly evaluate whether the objectives of that company are compatible with those of the UN. In doing so, it must set up open and transparent processes of dialogue with NGOs and community groups with expertise on those corporations' activities.

8 The United Nations and its agencies will continue to fulfil their mission with funding from governments. In cases where private corporations wish to make a donation, the money will go to programs that have no connection to commercial projects for that company.

9 The UN will act with full transparency in all its dealings with the private sector, at the conceptual, planning and implementation stages. NGOs should have access to the same information in this regard as the private sector.

corporate accountability and disclosure can be harnessed to advance progress towards sustainability'.[359] The strength of the GRI is that it encourages greater disclosure of company activities and has the potential to evaluate the impact of those activities on the ground. By requiring companies to report on a wide range of criteria relating to sustainability, it helps establish the idea that companies have social and environmental responsibilities outside their fiduciary duty to maximise profit.

The great weakness of the GRI is that sustainability and human rights are not clearly defined – nor how they are to be measured. The GRI will remain just another top-down Northern initiative until the crucial stakeholders, those people most affected by company activities in the developing world, are wholly included in such processes.

ILO Tripartite Declaration concerning multinational enterprises and social policy

In 1977 the ILO's International Labour Conference adopted the Tripartite Declaration which is a universally applicable but non-binding code covering industrial relations, conditions at work and labour standards. It establishes the rights and responsibilities of employers, governments and trade unions. However, after 20 years this has treated only seven cases, the last in 1984.

Summary: why voluntary regulation and codes of conduct are ineffective

- They are not binding or enforceable.
- There are no penalties for non-compliance.
- TNCs are not held responsible for the activities of subsidiaries based in other countries.
- Government commitment to apply standards is weak, or in the case of many Southern governments capacity and know-how is lacking.
- Existing voluntary standards, such as the OECD Guidelines, are not widely known.
- There is no independent monitoring of voluntary initiatives, verification of progress made, or requirement to measure a company's social performance.
- Civil society groups are denied a system of arbitration to defend their rights.
- UN initiatives are mostly untransparent and exclusive with little NGO or Southern involvement.

6 Trade for life: pro-poor trade alternatives and recommendations

Trade needs to stop being a tool that enables the rich to dominate the global economy and instead become a means to eradicate poverty. Global trade rules need to be rewritten in order to benefit poor people and it is an indictment of current rules that they were not designed with poverty eradication and development in mind. A genuinely pro-poor international trading system would look very different from the current one. Rather than trade being driven by a theoretical model whose impact on poor people is at best irrelevant and at worst damaging, Christian Aid advocates a system that champions diversity, protects the rights of governments and people to decide how best to develop their own economic activities, and ensures that trade is seen as a means to promote development, not pursued as an end in itself.

> 'If trade expansion is to begin benefiting the poorer developing countries, the international rules of the game must be made more fair.'
> United Nations Development Programme [361]

Christian Aid is calling on policy-makers to rewrite the global trade rules in three main areas:

1 reversing the principles upon which WTO agreements are based
2 making changes in six areas that underpin all the rules
3 rewriting the seven specific deadly rules.

1. Reversing the principles upon which WTO agreements are based

Fundamentally, the WTO is about:

- treating all countries the same (with special and differential treatment for developing countries more the exception than the norm)
- treating domestic and foreign companies the same
- minimizing regulation of the global private sector
- the primacy of inflexible global rules.

But the WTO *should* be about:

- treating rich and poor countries differently as the norm
- allowing governments to treat domestic and foreign companies differently
- effective regulation of the global private sector
- the primacy of national and local decision-making for developing countries (ie deciding policy at the lowest possible level while still tackling global problems through global rules).

Treating rich and poor countries differently

'Special and differential treatment' is accorded to developing countries in some areas and WTO Article XXXVI states that rich countries do not expect reciprocity for commitments made by them in the trade negotiations. But in practice there are few exceptions, mostly involving longer transition periods. WTO agreements expect all countries (eventually) to implement the same policies, a position that is based on the belief that all countries stand to gain equally from liberalisation. But the reality is that some countries gain and lose more than others and the instruments fail to allow individual countries to adopt the policies that are relevant to their own needs.

'What is required is nothing less than a radical review of the whole system of trade liberalisation and a critical consideration of the extent to which it is genuinely equitable and geared towards shared benefits for rich and poor countries alike.'

UN Sub-commission on the Promotion and Protection of Human Rights [360]

For that reason, trade rules should be based firmly on 'non-reciprocity' between rich and poor countries and special and differential treatment for the developing countries (which means different rules, not just longer implementation periods for the same rules).

Differential treatment should be the norm not the exception in WTO rule-making. This is a more effective strategy for all, since reductions in poverty in the poorest countries would lead to benefits for the richest countries as well.

Treating domestic and foreign companies differently

The idea of 'non-discrimination' (ie treating all companies the same) in trade agreements is based on the myth that there is no real difference between national companies and foreign investors. Experience shows that this is not the case. Trade rules which have poverty reduction as the objective would allow discrimination in favour of companies and sectors of the economy that are most effective in reducing poverty over the long term.

Regulation

The bias in WTO agreements has been to reduce the amount of government regulation as far as possible. A key element in any pro-poor trade strategy is to understand what regulation is needed to protect and support poor people. The WTO must encourage regulation that is in the interests of sustainable development and human rights.

The primacy of national and local decision-making

In the long term, current global rules seek to impose uniform economic policies on developing countries, thus undermining the diversity of options available to countries. Governments need to set their own development strategies in line with national, demo-cratically agreed priorities, which means that global rules need to be made more flexible in some areas and that some policies should not be subject to restrictive global rules at all. The need for decentralised policy-making for developing countries contrasts with the need for the much tighter (national and global) regulation of corporations.

'As a standard procedure, those proposing further liberalisation of agricultural trade should demonstrate the potential impact on poverty and food security before the proposals are considered for multilateral negotiation.'

UN Development Programme [362]

2. Making changes to six areas that underpin all the rules

The global trade rules must be rewritten:

1 To ensure their impact on the poor can be assessed, and changes made where needed

- An impact assessment of the effects of existing agreements must be urgently conducted – as WTO members promised under Article XX of the Agreement on Agriculture (and Article XIX of GATS). This must be an independent assessment of all agreements, taking evidence from a variety of groups, especially communities affected by them. No new negotiations should begin until this assessment is completed. In addition, the WTO's trade policy review mechanism could be much better used in country debates and assessments on the impact of WTO rules.

Calls on the UK government

Two hundred and sixty-two UK Members of Parliament have signed up to an 'early day motion' that calls on the government to ensure that there is an independent and thorough assessment of the likely impact of an extension of the GATS agreement. The onus is now on the government to take action in this area. [363]

- Any major new international agreements should be required to demonstrate independently a likely positive impact on poor people in the light of possible alternative policies.

- Provision needs to be made for regular, independent external monitoring of existing and new agreements. The ongoing impact of all trade rules on poor people should be continuously monitored against measurable and time-bound targets for poverty reduction. Where performance is not satisfactory, possible amendments should be routinely investigated.

2 To ensure that they explicitly contribute to the reduction of poverty

Though the WTO commits itself in the preamble to the Uruguay Round agreement to working towards sustainable development, it asserts that the way to do this is through progressive trade liberalisation. The evidence presented in this report shows that the combination of current WTO rules does not work in the best interests of poor people in developing countries.

- In its mandate, the WTO must replace its commitment to progressive liberalisation with a more specific commitment to promote trade policies and support mechanisms that help to reduce poverty and promote sustainable development. This is not so much a question of changing the wording of the mandate as of changing the basic theoretical paradigm that underpins the WTO. What is needed is a paradigm for the WTO that is less narrow than the present one and *more* open and inclusive to different countries' needs and especially to the needs of the poor.

3 To narrow the focus of the WTO to ensure that more decision-making on trade policy takes place at local and national levels, meaning closer to poor people

- The WTO's remit to promote global rules should be changed to facilitate overarching global rules only where they are strictly necessary. Global rules that impinge on national sovereignty need to be limited. In accordance with the principle of subsidiarity, more decisions on trade policy should be taken at local, national and regional levels. This makes it more likely that they will take more into account country diversity and ensure that policies are more suited to the national context (see box opposite).

- The principle that poor countries need to be treated differently as a matter of course needs to become a key tenet of all agreements, with special and differential treatment becoming the norm rather than the exception. Commitments made by countries should reflect the trade regime they *need* to contribute to poverty reduction, not an external global norm. This applies especially to agriculture, where developing country governments require much more flexibility to promote food security and to decide themselves which policy areas they make subject to WTO disciplines. [364]

- All of the restrictions on developing countries' policy-making in the seven rules need to be abolished. There should be an immediate review by a UN body of the various trade-related policies that developing countries need to be able to pursue to promote development and eradicate poverty.

4 To ensure they are decided in a fair and democratic way

- The practice of 'green room' discussions needs to end, and new criteria established to ensure that all major decisions are taken with all members participating. Informal meetings on decisive issues and informal 'non-papers' needs to be forbidden. All rule-making within the WTO must be transparent.

- Instead of consensus decision-making, which allows the powerful to dominate the WTO, a more formal one member, one vote system should be introduced. Voting should be weighted to reflect not merely economic power but also population size and other criteria.

- Capacity-building support to developing countries must be strengthened to enable them to develop institutional capacity on trade policy and law at government level. This support must enhance developing countries' ability to take independent decisions in their own national interest.

- The WTO needs to become transparent, with full disclosure of papers submitted to it and disclosure of which countries are supporting which positions as decisions are made.

- National parliaments in OECD countries, including the UK parliament, need to scrutinise government policy towards WTO issues more systematically from a sustainable development perspective, not just a national economic one.

- Trade policy review reports should become a more effective tool democratically to assess the impact of the WTO rules on different groups in society.

- The UK's International Development Select Committee should call on the UK government to present its current positions on WTO issues and also disclose all advice they have received from outside bodies, including business groups.

- In the short term, individuals leaving the WTO should be required to seek clearance from an independent body before taking up employment with a private company with interests in the WTO agreements. The WTO should also, as in the UK and other parliaments, have a full register of members' interests.

Reform or abolish the WTO?

Many voices are calling for reform of the WTO or for its abolition. But there are dangers in putting faith wholeheartedly in either approach. On one hand, the abolition of the WTO is unrealistic and there seems little point in investing energy and resources in a hopeless campaign. On the other hand, most rich countries now accept the need to reform the WTO, but within definite limits. Pascal Lamy, the EU's Development Commissioner, has called the WTO 'almost medieval in its organisation' and called for the WTO to be made more transparent and legitimate. [365] This has been echoed by the British government. This recognition of the need for change at the WTO is certainly welcome. However the motives behind this may be the need publicly to re-legitimise the WTO so that it can continue to press its liberalisation agenda. A danger of the simple reform agenda is that it may strengthen the WTO.

Strengthening the power of developing countries in the WTO will not guarantee that new global trade rules work in the interests of poor people. The central issue here is not the extent of democracy in the decision-making of the WTO but the breadth of its *remit and the authority it has over local and national decision-making*. As the analyst Dot Keet has pointed out, 'the challenge is how to defend the rights of people to pursue policies and modes of development tailored to their needs and aspirations within their own communities and national frameworks, while at the same time defining global parameters and overarching common principles that need to be observed by all'. [366]

Christian Aid believes that if poor people are to derive maximum benefits from trade, decisions must be taken as close to them as possible. A reformed, strengthened, global institution which still promotes inflexible rules will not help. Instead, more decisions on trade policy should be taken at local and national level. Restrictions on developing countries' policy-making as required by the seven rules should be abolished, and TRIPs and the issue of agricultural subsidies should be removed from the remit of the WTO. The WTO must change from being an increasingly powerful institution setting overarching rules, many of which are inappropriate to the needs of poor people.

Christian Aid urges developing countries to exert significant influence in this area since they are more able, by acting together, to block unhelpful extensions of the WTO's remit. But they should also be seeking to rein in the WTO's remit, as it currently stands, enabling them much greater flexibility to pursue policies suited to local and national circumstances. The issue of global and national governance is therefore critical. Globally, the remit and limits of the WTO's powers need to be transformed. Nationally, domestic governance structures need to work in the interests of the poor.

But while we advocate narrowing the remit of the WTO, we argue for increasing the power of the international community to hold TNCs to account through legally-binding regulation. A re-balancing of global governance therefore needs to take place to ensure that decision-making takes place at the right level. Poor people in developing countries are owed the right to an international environment that works in their favour, not one that is manifestly unjust as is currently the case.

5 To ensure they are fairly enforced so that rich countries, as well as poor countries, abide by them

- The dispute settlement mechanism needs to be significantly changed to take proper account of the needs and capacities of poor countries. The current right to impose economic sanctions is wholly unbalanced when applied to countries of vastly different economic strengths. The current bilateral nature of the system, which allows more powerful individual countries to dominate and override the weaker, must be replaced by more effective multilateral mechanisms.[367] The legal aid system established in Geneva to support cases brought by poorer countries should also be supported.

6 To address the activities of Transnational Corporations with legally binding regulation at national and global levels

All TNCs need to be made legally accountable to the communities, workers and consumers affected by their activities.

- Legislation needs to be passed in developing countries to allow people to pursue complaints against the subsidiaries/affiliates of TNCs and the parent company.

- Legislation needs to be introduced in rich countries to allow those communities to process complaints against the TNC parent company through the courts in the Northern country.

- National legislation on TNCs needs to include requirements that TNCs and their affiliates publicly disclose information on their social, environmental and human rights performance.

All TNCs need to be held accountable for abiding by internationally agreed ethical standards.

- A legally-binding global code of conduct for TNCs needs to be established requiring companies to adhere to international environmental, human rights and development standards already enshrined in international agreements. Governments in North and South would incorporate this global code of conduct into their national legislation. (Appendix III outlines a code of conduct for companies drafted by the UN Commission on Human Rights.)

- Governments should also be required to subject companies to the international laws to which they as governments are signatories, for example the Universal Declaration of Human Rights.

- A new Global Regulation Authority should be established within an existing UN organisation to monitor this code and be responsible for compliance. It would be able to conduct investigations into possible breaches of the code to submit as evidence to national courts.

The WTO agreements need to incorporate TNC regulation.

- The principle of allowing developing country governments to prescribe the precise conditions under which TNCs may operate in developing countries needs to be made an explicit part of the WTO agreements.

- All WTO agreements need to be made compatible with the required regulation of TNCs, though the WTO would not be the body to uphold such regulation.

Foreign Direct Investment needs to be made to work in the interests of the poor.

- One of the Global Regulation Authority's functions should be to work with UNCTAD to act as an independent monitor of FDI and provide advice to international investors and developing countries on how to maximise the opportunities for the poor presented by FDI.

The case for legally binding regulation of TNCs

Why legally binding?

Our analysis shows that voluntary self-regulation is not enough on its own to address the multitude of problems associated with TNC activities. Enforcement of standards can only be guaranteed where application is mandatory.

Why a shared national responsibility?

Governments ratify international standards such as the Universal Declaration of Human Rights and have a duty to protect their citizens. These obligations imply that they must also regulate companies in their jurisdiction to uphold the same standards. However in many cases it is problematic to rely completely on *host* countries to hold TNCs to account because many of these governments are weak in relation to the TNCs. Many countries are fearful they will lose their competitive advantage if they comply with international regulations. Neither

Proposal for a new Global Regulation Authority (GRA)

Christian Aid's view is that a new body is needed to oversee the regulation of transnational corporations, to ensure that their activities safeguard people's basic rights and contribute to the eradication of poverty globally. A global body should not itself legislate and police the regulation of TNCs: that should be the responsibility of governments. Such a body should not be created outside an existing institution, and one of the UN agencies is the most likely candidate to house it. The GRA is needed to play several roles.

- It would draw up and establish a code of conduct that all TNCs and their subsidiaries/affiliates would need to abide by in all their operational activities and also in their role as financial investors in other companies. This code should consist of the various core standards that are included in a variety of UN conventions, and agreements to which most governments are already signatories – such as on basic human rights, working conditions and the environment (see Appendix III). [368]
- It would also have a research and monitoring function to monitor company compliance with this code. It would respond to requests from civil society groups, communities and also companies, to investigate possible breaches of the code by TNCs.
- It could have a Citizens' Support Unit that would resource and assist organisations bringing cases in national courts.

- It would be able to conduct more detailed official investigations into cases where breaches appeared likely in order to submit these as evidence to national courts.
- Though national governments would have primary responsibility for legislation, the GRA should be empowered to make legally binding rulings against companies breaching the code in situations where governments have failed to enact sufficient national legislation.
- The GRA should also be responsible for setting minimum standards of disclosure of information on the activities of TNCs, and for monitoring TNCs' public disclosure policies. This would include a register of TNCs in each country.
- It should also monitor and sanction market abuses such as restrictive business practices, cartels and monopolies.
- The GRA should also monitor FDI and advise countries and companies on opportunities which will contribute to sustainable development and the eradication of poverty. This would mean a strengthening of the role of UNCTAD's Investment Policy Reviews, which provide government officials with a means of monitoring FDI. [369]

Setting up a GRA involves jumping a number of major political hurdles. But there is no excuse for the international community not to try – if only by devoting a fraction of the time and energy currently being devoted to the WTO agreements.

do they often have the capacity, the technical know-how or political will to enforce such regulations.

Since the bulk of TNCs' profits flow to home governments and most TNCs are domiciled in rich countries, the *home* governments need to play a key role in legislation. National laws governing competition and preventing monopolistic behaviour must be extended to include the application of standards overseas. Home governments can also use measures such as withdrawal of licences, penalties and fines to punish offending corporations.

Why global responsibility?

By itself, national regulation is not enough. Through mergers and acquisitions TNCs are often bigger and more powerful than the countries in which they operate or which seek to regulate them. A global regulatory body is needed to support and strengthen national legislation, to ensure standardisation and to establish international co-operation.

The importance of governance

Formal legislation by itself may be no magic bullet. Establishing national laws is one thing but compliance can be quite another. Developing countries may lack the resources and capacity to fully implement legislation. Governments need to establish adequately-resourced, and good, governance structures – something that needs much more support from aid programmes. Also, the current absence of these in many countries does place more responsibility on companies to be much better at regulating themselves. Self-regulation is therefore not irrelevant as a practical aid to making legally-binding regulation work – just that, as outlined in chapter 5, it is not by itself enough.

3. Rewriting the seven deadly rules

The seven deadly WTO rules identified by Christian Aid need to be rewritten:

Rule one: protect adequately against cheap food imports

Developing countries need to be able to protect themselves against cheap imports that undermine viable domestic production.

- Developing countries must be free to use tariffs to help them promote poverty-focused development. This particularly includes protection against disruption caused to domestic production by cheap imports or violent price fluctuations. This is vital in relation to agricultural imports. The Agreement on Agriculture should be rewritten to allow developing countries to prevent cheap imports undermining domestic producers and local food security, or the issue should be taken out of the WTO altogether.

- Export subsidies in rich countries should be banned under the WTO rules.

'For reasons of national security, economic and political stability, special and differential provisions giving more flexibility in agricultural trade policies must... be allowed to developing countries. Key products, especially food staples, should be exempted from liberalisation.'

Group of 11 developing countries [370]

'Developed countries should eliminate totally their domestic support and export subsidy [sic] [for agriculture] immediately, the latest by 2005.'

UNCTAD Secretariat [371]

Rule two: require no mandatory opening up of services sectors

Poor countries should not be required to open up their service sectors to foreigners without careful analysis and without their explicit agreement.

- No future services agreements should be drawn up until detailed analysis of their effects on poor people has been made, and unless all services directly affecting poor people have poverty alleviation as their priority objective.

> *'African countries should reaffirm their right to regulate the services sector.'*
>
> Trade negotiators from 27 African countries, June 2001 [372]

- There should be no further negotiations on liberalisation of services sectors in poor countries except as now on the understanding that agreements can only be made on a voluntary basis.

Rule three: ensure appropriate regulation of foreign investment

Developing countries need to be able to pursue investment policies that suit their domestic development purposes.

- The WTO agreement on investment (TRIMs) needs to be reviewed (in accordance with its article 9) and rewritten to ensure that foreign investment can be properly regulated. Domestic legislators must be able to make and enforce laws that balance the need to attract foreign companies with the need to enhance development and poverty eradication strategies.

- The ban on policies that discriminate in favour of domestic companies should be replaced by agreements that allow poor countries to choose policies which balance the promotion and regulation of domestic and foreign investment.

- A new multilateral investment agreement should not be negotiated in the WTO unless it is based explicitly on the above principles.

Rule four: ensure adequate ability for countries to promote essential national and local food security policies

Developing countries need to be able to support their agricultural sectors to maximise food security. With this in mind they must decide the extent to which they wish to open up their economies to commercial cash crop promotion.

> *'The [WTO] disciplines of import control and domestic support should not be applicable to food products in developing countries.'*
>
> UNCTAD Secretariat [373]

- Either the WTO agreement on subsidies should be rewritten so that developing countries have full flexibility to promote essential food security policies, or the issue should be taken out of the WTO altogether.

Rule five: ensure adequate ability to support domestic industry

Developing countries need to be able to promote the development, expansion and deepening of their industrial sectors to stimulate economic diversification.

- General global rules outlawing industrial subsidies and other support mechanisms need to be reversed to permit poor countries in particular to intervene in ways they deem appropriate to establish viable and competitive industries.

'There should be additional provision, if necessary, so that the subsidies used by developing countries for development, diversification and upgrading of their industry and agriculture are made non-actionable [ie legal].'

UNCTAD Secretariat [374]

Rule six: enable fair access to rich country markets

Rich countries need to remove the unfair protection against imports from the poorer countries.

- Exports from least developed countries should be able to enter rich country markets duty-free.

- Tariff peaks and tariff escalation on all processed products must be eliminated.

'Existing tariff peaks, especially on actual or potential export products of least developed countries and net food importing developing countries, should be eliminated. Tariff escalation should be eliminated with a view to enhancing product diversification.'

UNCTAD experts' meeting [375]

- There needs to be an increased burden of proof on rich countries seeking to use 'Sanitary and Phytosanitary' measures to ban imports from developing countries. Where a ban is considered, a specifically created fund should be made available for advice and action so developing countries can eliminate the possible health risks at source and resume exports as fast as possible.

- Anti-dumping rules need to be revised to prevent their use as a protectionist measure and to ensure that developing countries have equal recourse to such rules.

- Developed countries need to keep their promise to end protection of their textile markets under the agreed timescale of the Agreement on Textiles and Clothing and reduce the existing high tariffs drastically.

Rule seven: ensure adequate safeguards against biopiracy and patenting

Developing countries need to be able to secure easy access to essential drugs and technology and ensure that companies, including TNCs, are not able to monopolise natural resources for private profit.

- There is no good reason why intellectual property is being negotiated in the WTO since it bears little relation to trade. It should be taken out of the WTO and be the subject of negotiations through the UN. A new UN international panel should start by taking evidence from communities affected by patenting. This panel should make recommendations on how IPRs can promote development and poverty eradication and consider how patenting can be harnessed properly to promote development. [378]

'Intellectual property rights under the TRIP agreement need comprehensive review to redress their perverse effects undermining food security, indigenous knowledge, biosafety and access to health care.'

UN Development Programme [376]

- Until the international panel has made recommendations on the future of patenting, companies taking out new patents must be required to disclose the origin of biological materials that are the subject of new patents, and to demonstrate prior informed consent of the original holders of any knowledge or resources applied in the development of patented products.

- National, 'sui generis' systems of protection should be strengthened to protect local communities from biopiracy, and safeguard farmers' rights to save and reuse seed and promote food security.

- The ban on patenting of plants and animals should continue.

- Developing countries must have greater flexibility in overriding current patent protection, based on their own development priorities, especially in cases of public health emergencies.

'Intellectual property protection… is for most poor countries a simple tax on their use of such knowledge, constituting therefore an unrequited transfer to the rich, producing countries. We [are] turning the WTO, thanks to powerful lobbies, into a royalty-collection agency, by pretending, through continuous propaganda that our media bought into, that somehow the question was "trade related".'

Jagdish Bhagwati
Council on Foreign Relations [377]

What Southern governments should be allowed to do

A pro-poor trade strategy needs to be built around the needs of all poor people, producers and non-producers. It needs to be informed by asking how the poor can benefit most from changes in economic activity, and how they can best be protected from the negative effects of international trade. Pro-poor trade strategies require a more active role for governments, sometimes protecting their own companies and people and regulating the activities of foreign investors. Poor country governments need to be allowed to implement policies which can:

- develop the capacity to take advantage of trading opportunities

- promote the expansion of viable domestic producers in line with nationally agreed priorities.

Taking advantage of trading opportunities

Many of the world's poorest people are unable to take advantage of new opportunities for trading when they arise, for a myriad of reasons including their own low levels of production and the absence of physical infrastructure. The first crucial step is to take seriously the differences in people's capacity to trade, rather than make the mistake of assuming that opening markets will have the same effect on everybody. Poor people's capacity to trade needs to be drastically enhanced. To develop capacity to trade they need:

- an effective *transport* infrastructure, including roads and public transport facilities in rural areas and efficient and cheap freight services

- an effective *financial* infrastructure, including access to credit in rural as well as urban areas

- an effective *communications* infrastructure that provides information on market requirements such as quality and technical standards

- a broad-based *education* system, which provides widespread access to primary education and availability of secondary and tertiary education

- an effective and transparent *legal system and institutional framework,* which supports the needs of poor traders

- *transparent democratic institutions,* which deliver good governance and give voice to poor people's needs and aspirations, especially poor women.

Active government involvement is essential to create this capacity, even if the private sector delivers important parts of the infrastructure. When resources come from the private sector, government regulation must prevent companies from 'cherry picking' the most profitable areas for investment and ignoring others. When telephone services were privatised in Senegal, for example, new investors had to promise to install public telephones in half of all rural villages with over 3,000 people by the year 2000, as one of the conditions of their investment.[379] By contrast, privatisation of the banking service in Mozambique led to reductions in the number of banks serving the rural poor.[380] Governments must never step back and merely hope that the private sector will provide what they need.

Governments must also intervene to stimulate the creation of economic and social activities vital to long-term development. For the poorest countries this often means building up the capacity to process the primary products which currently form the majority of their exports. Support might include cheap credit, subsidised transport or communications, or government-sponsored training schemes for workers. International trade agreements must encourage governments in this kind of tried and tested economic intervention, not prevent them from intervention.

Support for domestic producers and service providers

For ideological trade liberalisers, protectionist policies are what dragons were to writers of medieval romance – enemies that have to be slain to allow all good and virtuous things to prevail. We must have sensible international debate, not ideology about protection. Direct and indirect support is needed to accelerate the development process and minimise the risks of external shocks. National capacity, so important in our globalising world, will be never be effectively developed in many of the poorest countries if local producers are crushed by foreign imports, producers or service providers before their capacity to compete has been built up. Direct support will often be a key tool to allow local producers and service providers to become competitive, develop export capacity and meet local needs.

However, protection is a blunt instrument and in the past has often worked against the interests of particular groups of poor people. It can involve corruption, when a government protects its own business supporters in various forms of 'crony capitalism'. And protection always incurs significant costs through distortions of the market. These costs must be met, but by whom? Poor people themselves need to be consulted if direct support policies are to benefit them, rather than privileged vested interests within the domestic economy. It is for these reasons that we believe it is preferable to frame discussion not within the negative context of protection but within the more positive framework of direct support.

Direct support is not a no-cost option for poor countries, and if governments are to adopt such policies they need to set clear criteria for beneficial protection of local producers and have answers to questions like the following.

- Direct support for what purpose? Is the main competition for domestic producers in domestic or international markets, or both?

- Direct support for how long? Given the likely growth patterns and the other government policies, how long is protection likely to be required?

- What will be required of companies in return for support they receive? Some rigorous performance requirements are needed to focus on export performance, productivity gains, or other indicators.

- How will direct support best be implemented – through tariffs on imports or exports, conditions on investment or imports by foreign companies, or by direct subsidies?

- What will direct support cost and what alternatives will be foregone if this option is chosen?

To help ensure that direct support schemes favour poor people it may be useful to have pro-poor criteria for their use defined in the WTO. This could help to avoid situations where policies are abused and further corruption. Whatever specific policies emerge, a bias in favour of *domestic* companies and enterprises may often need to be a part of a pro-poor national development and trade strategy. This is very different from the free market agenda rich governments are currently trying to push through the WTO.

Domestic producers also have a key role in the achievement of other social objectives. Where food security is concerned, it is often prudent to keep a minimum level of domestically produced food, rather than rely too much on imports. Short-term support to local producers can often be an effective way of developing enterprises which can compete in international and domestic markets. There may be good reasons to maintain protection in some sectors indefinitely, in pursuit of social goals. This has been the practice in almost all industrialised countries.

Supporting regional trade

Co-operation between countries with similar levels of development often reaps the benefits of trade without suffering the costs in terms of increased inequalities. For poor countries, intra-regional trade allows the development of mutually supportive trading links. Regional, or sub-regional, integration can offer producers the benefits of economies of scale, and can encourage new firms to become competitive in regional markets first before aiming to attain international competitiveness. [381]

Christian Aid/Gideon Mendel

Support for local farmers is key to meeting local needs.

Though official intra-regional trade is often relatively small, for poor people informal cross-border trade is often a crucial source of markets and consumer goods. The story of Señor Gabriel at the beginning of this report demonstrates the importance of informal links between northern Mozambique and Tanzania. This happened despite the lack of an all-weather road linking the two countries. If trading relations between the two countries were officially encouraged, and investment made in infrastructure, communications and transport links, then the informal links which exist could be developed and expanded to the benefit of both countries, and of poor people in them.

Regional trading arrangements should be promoted with a number of underlying principles.

- Priority should be given to relationships among relatively equal countries, where the risk of increasing existing inequalities is less and the potential gains from specialisation and mutual support are greatest.

- Regional arrangements should build on existing trade flows, particularly those which involve poor people. Informal cross-border trade should be strengthened and facilitated by regional arrangements.

- Regional trading agreements should not be seen simply as free trade agreements, but they should also involve other aspects of trade and development policy such as developing industrial capacity, supporting domestic industries, and promoting growth in sectors of benefit to poor people.

Trade for life

Developing countries should not put all their faith in international trade. Globalisation offers a long-term vision of a more integrated world in which everyone participates on a basis of equality, and each country benefits from its own comparative advantages. But the real world is one where huge inequalities exist between rich and poor countries – in provision of education, infrastructure, financial services and natural resources. The rules of international trade must recognise this fact if the long-term vision is ever to be delivered. It is naïve or Utopian to believe that there is an instant free-market fix for the most intractable problem of the world economy: the widening gulf that separates the world of rich people from the world of the poor.

Christian Aid urges the international community to take a much more sophisticated approach to the reform of the global trading system in order to deliver the benefits of economic growth and security to the poor as well as the rich. Poor people and their democratic representatives must have a central role in shaping this new world. Their governments must be free to put in place what they see as the right policies for development, even if they challenge the ideological fashions of the wealthy countries of the North. The unaccountable power of transnational corporations must be regulated if their extraordinary dynamism as wealth-creators is to work to everyone's benefit – not just to their shareholders'. Long-term sustainable development and economic growth will not just happen through the magic of a global free-market. They have to be worked for, through a painstaking process of policy-making which recognises that there are significant fundamental differences between countries at varying stages of development.

The growing gap between the limited life-chances of more than 1.3 billion people living in extreme poverty and the expanding opportunities of the rich is morally unacceptable. The current global economy, its institutions and the way it is set to expand are failing to resolve the problem of poverty for very many of the world's poor. Because they are relatively powerless, poor people in developing countries have a prior right over the rich to an international environment which works to meet their needs and to fulfil their core human rights.

It is our duty to help ensure that this happens, and that it happens fast. One major way to achieve this is to try to make global trade work better for poor people. Trade can and must make a more positive difference to the rooting-out of poverty and to the improvement of the lives and life-chances of the world's poorest people.

Christian Aid case studies

Case study one: cheap rice imports in Haiti

Two years ago, Muracin Claircin, a young rice farmer from Desarme in Haiti's Artibonite valley, sold his plot of land, left his wife and two small children and headed with three of his neighbours to the Ile de la Tortue, off Haiti's northern coast. There he paid around 1,000 dollars for a place on a boat to take him to the United States.

'I had to do this because I could no longer support my family from growing rice,' he says. After a torturous week drifting at sea without enough food or water, the captain told them they would have to turn back because the ship's compass was broken.

Although his money was not returned, Muracin was luckier than many who lose their lives trying to enter the United States illegally in unseaworthy boats. Now back in Desarme, but with no money or land, Muracin lives with his family in a tiny single-roomed house on the edge of the market. He rents a small piece of land, but barely makes enough money to make ends meet. He cannot afford to send his children to school, and is worried that if any of his family fall ill he will be unable to buy medicine.

'There's no incentive to grow rice any more,' he says. 'It's virtually impossible to make a profit.' At the first opportunity he is going to try again and join the tens of thousands of other desperate Haitians who every year risk their lives trying to enter the United States illegally.

Muracin Claircin's story is not uncommon. Over the past decade Haiti's rice farmers have had a tough time adapting to the rigours of economic liberalisation. In return for support from the World Bank and the International Monetary Fund, successive Haitian governments have had to eliminate restrictions on almost all imported goods.

Haitian farmers say this has prompted a flood of cheap, imported rice, mostly from the United States, where arable farmers are given nearly $5 billion every year in subsidies and export credit guarantees. Haitian farmers say this puts them at a competitive disadvantage. They are left with two options: to find alternative crops or abandon their land.

The Artibonite valley in central Haiti produces 80 per cent of the country's rice. For decades this lush, fertile valley has provided tens of thousands of families with a livelihood and an income. In the past the region used to attract migrant workers from all over the country. Now many of the farmers are leaving, bitter at what they see as the failure of the government to protect them from cheap, imported rice.

Fenol Leon inherited a small piece of land in the Artibonite valley when his father died a few years ago. The land has been in his family for generations, but with imported rice driving down the price of Haitian rice, he says he is making plans to go and find work in the Dominican Republic in order to earn enough money to send his four children to school. 'Unless something is done to protect us from cheap rice imports I don't think there's a future for us – we'll all be wiped out,' he warns. 'Opening the country to foreign rice has made us too dependent on imports. If things ever get difficult and there's a shortage of rice on world markets, the prices will go up and we will not be able to afford it.'

Haiti is the poorest country in the western hemisphere. According to the IMF, annual per capita income is under $US 400. Farmers who decide to sell up and abandon their land have few alternatives. Some like Muracin Claircin risk their lives going to the United States. Others head to the vast shanty towns encircling Port-au-Prince, while others cross into the neighbouring Dominican Republic. The men tend to work in the construction industry or cutting sugar cane. The women may end up employed as domestic servants, or working in the sex industry.

Few would argue that rice production in Haiti is a cost-effective or efficient process. The political turmoil of the past decade has meant that a succession of governments has either been unable, or failed, to invest in agriculture, still a vital source of income for 65 per cent of the Haitian population. In the Artibonite valley the irrigation system no longer works in many places; this has kept yields low while the cost of inputs has steadily risen. With few or no credit facilities, many farmers have been forced to turn for money to loan sharks, who charge exorbitant interest rates to pay for fertilisers.

Luckner Jean-Baptiste shares a small farm between Desarme and Verettes with his two brothers. He recalls how last year they actually lost money on their rice crop because they had to take out a loan to pay for fertiliser. 'The loan shark charged us 20 per cent interest every month. This meant we had to harvest the rice before it was ready, so we made a loss.'

But Luckner says the problem is not a just a lack of affordable credit and government investment. Cheap imports are edging farmers out of the market place and off the land. 'We want the government to reduce rice imports. We know we don't produce enough rice in Haiti to be self-sufficient, but the

Christian Aid/Leah Gordon

It is virtually impossible to make a profit from rice farming in Haiti.

imports need to be controlled so we have a better chance of selling our rice and making a decent profit.'

Trade liberalisation in Haiti began following the demise of the Duvalier regime in 1986. This was briefly interrupted between 1991 and 1994 when the United Nations imposed a trade embargo on Haiti in response to a military coup. But with the return of President Jean-Bertrand Aristide the policy of trade liberalisation continued with renewed vigour.

Under the tariff reform programme, approved in February 1995, import restrictions on agricultural commodities were virtually eliminated. Most tariffs were reduced from between 40 and 50 per cent to between zero and 15 per cent. Meanwhile, tariffs on basic products such as rice, sugar and flour were reduced to between zero and three per cent. The tariff for rice remains at three per cent. In return for opening its markets to foreign imports, Haiti received hundreds of millions of dollars in loans and aid from the World Bank and the International Monetary Fund.

The impact of these policies is clearly visible on the streets of Port-au-Prince where the city's pavements and markets are piled high with imported goods, including clothes, shoes, medicines and food. Here, a local measure, known as a marmite, of imported rice sells for just over two US dollars. The equivalent measure of Haitian rice sells for three to four dollars.

Twenty years ago Haiti was virtually self-sufficient in rice. Figures from the Ministry of Agriculture show that in 1985 Haiti produced 180,000 tons of rice.

This has now fallen to just over 100,000 tons. Meanwhile, imports from the United States have grown from 79,000 tons in 1989 to just over 215,000 tons a decade later. According to Camille Chalmers, who heads a Christian Aid supported organisation, the Platform for Development Alternatives (PAPDA), the increase in cheap imports has led to an increase in consumption. People have given up eating traditional crops grown in Haiti, in favour of cheap imported rice. Haiti now produces less than one third of the 300,000 tonnes of rice eaten in the country every year. This, he argues, has put the country in a dangerous position and highly vulnerable to fluctuations in the price and production of rice on the world's markets.

The town of Segur lies in the heart of the Artibonite valley. The local mill, which is cooperatively owned by the Movement of Organisations for the Development of Segur (MODEPS), was bought with money from Christian Aid in 1999. Farmers and traders from the surrounding area bring their rice to the mill to be processed before taking it to the local market in Pont Sondé or on to Port-au-Prince.

Edline Normil, a trader at the mill, says that when the markets in Port-au-Prince are awash with imported rice, many buyers do not make the journey to the Artibonite valley to purchase Haitian rice. On two or three occasions every month she is left with rice she cannot sell. 'When this happens either I have to pay additional transport costs to take the rice home to store it, or I have to sell it at an even lower price just to get rid of it,' she explains.

Phillippe Michel, the general secretary of MODEPS, says Edline Normil is typical of many rice traders. He admits that the situation has become critical. A friend of his and one of his cousins, both rice farmers from the neighbouring town of Villard, fell into debt and decided to go to the United States. Neither of them was heard of again; everybody on board the boat is believed to have drowned when the boat sank. Farmers he says are becoming desperate. 'You wake up one morning hungry. You've got nothing for your children to eat – what do you do? Some people have taken to the boats, others have committed suicide.'

In its most recent report on Haiti the IMF acknowledges that as rice imports have increased, domestic production has gone down substantially. It adds: 'The downward pressure on domestic price of rice has stemmed from competition from US imports.' However, it notes that the Haitian government has consistently favoured a low-tariff policy. 'In the authorities' view,' the report says, 'the loss of production reflects impediments to growth other than prices, in particular inadequate irrigation, low investment in hulling machines by traders, and land tenure issues.'

However, farmers in the Artibonite valley blame the government both for failing to provide investment and for implementing a structural adjustment policy which has opened the country to an invasion of foreign products. In the words of one farmer this policy is turning Haiti into 'a nation of refugees'. In 1996 a leaked World Bank draft strategy paper on Haiti suggested that two-thirds of the country's rural workers would be unlikely to survive the free-market measures imposed by the bank. The document concluded that farmers would be left with two possibilities: to work in the industrial sector, or to emigrate.

Camille Chalmers echoes these concerns. He maintains that the short-term advantages of cheaper rice imports for millions of Haitians are far outweighed by the social costs farmers have to pay. 'Haiti's dependency on imported goods is not only making us vulnerable to changes in global markets, we're losing our identity and self-esteem with mass migration, higher unemployment and greater poverty,' he says. In addition, farmers say that the fallout from the crisis in rice production is being passed on to their children who, unable to go to school, will burden the state with a host of social problems that it is ill-equipped to deal with.

Farmers in the Artibonite valley know that, even though imports of American rice are putting them out of business, without them millions of Haitians would starve. They believe that the government should establish a system of seasonally adjusted quotas of rice imports, so that when there is an abundance of Haitian rice, imports can be restricted. However, officials at the Ministry of Agriculture argue that such a scheme would be unworkable and would contravene agreements signed with international lending agencies which underpin Haiti's free market economy.

Rice farming is not the only agricultural sector which is being harmed by cheap imports. In recent years the country's poultry and pig farmers have had to face up to the problems of meat imports from the United States. According to the Ministry of Agriculture, hundreds of local poultry farmers have gone out of business in the last five years. Jean René Cadet, who works for the development programme of the Methodist Church in Haiti (COD), which is supported by Christian Aid, warns that meat imports are starting to threaten COD's programme to re-populate rural areas with pigs, after they were wiped out in the early 1980s following an outbreak of swine fever.

'Haiti is not going to progress while it is economically dependent on other countries,' he says. 'If we're going to move forward, then we have to build up our own capacity to produce and not be just consumers.'

Case study two: tobacco growing in Brazil

In the early morning of 14 February 2001, 42 year old Paulo Rochinski hanged himself in his new tobacco-curing barn in Parana, Brazil. His wife found him later that morning.

December and January had followed their usual pattern for Rochinski, his wife Iremar, daughters Miriam and Elisiane and son Elsio. It was the time of the tobacco harvest. 'It's always a frantic time but I came to dread it more because of what harvesting did to Paulo,' says Iremar. 'He always became terribly withdrawn and was nervous, anxious and irritable. Often he would sit for long periods of time in the evenings with his head in his hands. Then he would jump up as if to do something but instantly forget what he was going to do.'

Twenty-six years earlier Rochinski had signed his first contract with Souza Cruz, the Brazilian subsidiary of British American Tobacco. His father and brothers were also Souza Cruz farmers, and he stayed with the company until the end of his life, making him one of the company's most loyal suppliers. After his suicide, Iremar was sent a letter by Souza Cruz asking her to guarantee that all the tobacco on the farm would be delivered to the company.

Iremar blames heavy use of pesticides, including organophosphates, for his death. She believes the large debt he incurred by purchasing his new curing barn from Souza Cruz was the trigger. 'Paulo agreed to the new barn (from Souza Cruz) because he was told it was better than the old one but he was

Christian Aid/Antonio Olmos

Regulation of large tobacco companies is necessary to protect farmers.

disappointed with the way it was performing,' she says. 'It cost 12,000 Reals (US$6,000) which we have to pay back over the next six years. Souza Cruz were planning to deduct a proportion of our crop each year.'

Rochinski's suicide was not an isolated incident. His brother Marcos and his friends warned him that the pesticides he was using were affecting his health. They urged him to stop using them. But like most tobacco farmers working for the 13 companies operating in Brazil, Paulo believed the quality of his tobacco depended on using the cocktail of pesticides that was sold to him by Souza Cruz.

There are 148,627 small-scale family tobacco farms in Brazil's southernmost states of Parana, Santa Catarina and Rio Grande do Sul. In 1999 those farms produced nearly 550,000 tonnes of dried tobacco.[387] Over 300,000 tonnes of this was exported, 41 per cent (122,466 tonnes) to the European Union.[388] Tobacco earned three per cent of Brazil's export revenue, and delivered Souza Cruz profits of over US$250 million.

Brazil is the world's biggest exporter of tobacco.[389] The vast majority of Brazilian tobacco (92 per cent[390]) is grown in the south. But behind the impressive statistics is a global business which seems to fail in its responsibility towards the people who work in it. In 1998, Sousa Cruz made a profit of £177 million.[391] Christian Aid has interviewed some of the 47,500[392] 'associate growers' (contract farmers) who made these profits possible. They are not a contented workforce.

In this area of Brazil, tobacco cultivation is the only option for farmers. There is no market for alternative crops and farmers grow food only for their own consumption. So the 13 tobacco companies, including the largest, Souza Cruz, and global giants such as Philip Morris and Universal Leaf Tobacco, operate in a way which some describe as a virtual cartel, promoting the same system of farming as each other and paying the same prices for the crop.

The average size of tobacco farms in southern Brazil is less than two hectares. Farmers sign a contract to produce an agreed quantity of tobacco for sale exclusively to one company. Farmers are also sold a technical package of inputs by the tobacco company which includes seed, fertiliser, pesticides, protective clothing and spraying apparatus. Rather than paying for this in cash, which many of the farmers lack, it is offered to them as a loan to be paid off in tobacco when the crop is delivered.

Souza Cruz carefully controls its relationship with its growers in Brazil, but as contracted farmers they receive none of the benefits and security of being on the payroll. By enforcing a specific system of growing tobacco, selling farmers the inputs, holding them in debt until the crop is delivered, then grading the leaves and paying the farmers, Souza Cruz controls their livelihoods. At the same time, the company incurs none of the costs, risks or responsibilities of owning its own land, growing and curing its own tobacco and paying its own employees. Farmers take all the risks associated with cultivating tobacco and receive few of the benefits.

'If I could get out of tobacco farming tomorrow I would,' exclaims Flavio Graener, a farmer in the village of Linha Almeida, in the heart of Rio Grande do Sul. 'I only wish those Souza Cruz executives in suits would come and spend a day working in my fields. Then they'd see how hard we work and what our true value is.' Like most of Souza Cruz's 47,500 farmers, Graener does work hard. Farming tobacco is ten times more labour intensive than cultivating corn [393] and each tobacco plant has to be handled between 30 and 60 times from seedling to harvest.[394]

Like many other farmers Flavio Graener's life has been touched by tragedy. In 1994 his father-in-law, on whose farm he used to work, killed himself. Then Graener bought his own plot of land and signed his first contract with Souza Cruz. As well as borrowing the technical package each year, Graener also took out an initial loan from Souza Cruz for his curing barn. Five years later he is still paying this off.

Christian Aid's concern is that Souza Cruz fails to reward the value delivered by farmers locked into these contracts. Because farmers are not able to be present when their tobacco is graded at processing plants many miles away from their farms, they feel – rightly or wrongly – they are being fiddled. Farmers in the USA, producing comparable export grade Virginia tobacco, are paid around US$5 per kilo. In 1999, the average for Brazilian farmers was US$1 per kilo.

Sebastiao dos Santos, whose daughter committed suicide by drinking the organophosphate Chlorpyrifos, spends the first hour of every day struggling up the steep slope of his tobacco field. 'There is no such thing as BO1,' he says (BO1 is top grade tobacco), 'it doesn't exist. I always grow several arobas (bales) of perfect tobacco but when Souza Cruz grades it, I never get paid for BO1.'

On its website, Souza Cruz's parent company, British American Tobacco, makes great play of being 'a responsible company in a controversial industry'. In particular, the website points to its relationship with associate growers world-wide, citing efforts to stamp out child labour, especially its programme in Brazil: 'The Future Is Now'. On visits to farms working under contract for Souza Cruz in January 2001, Christian Aid discovered children as young as eight years of age playing a key role during normal school hours in sorting and baling cured tobacco. As a result they miss schooling, and they come into contact with nicotine and pesticides through handling the tobacco leaves.

Souza Cruz do not insist on pesticide use. But having paid around US$2,000 for the package of pesticides, seed and fertiliser, farmers will gener-ally use it. They apply pesticides in the belief that the price they are eventually paid for the tobacco will be lower if they do not. However, the UN Food and

Agriculture Organisation's code on the safe use of pesticides[395] clearly indicates that *all* farmers, and especially small-scale farmers in tropical climates, should avoid the handling and application of pesticides that require uncomfortable and expensive clothing and equipment. Southern Brazil is sub-tropical, and the temperature in the summer, when the tobacco is in the fields, regularly exceeds 40 degrees Celsius.

The code states that '... the wearing of additional protective clothing and other equipment [in tropical climates] may cause severe discomfort and even physical distress if they are made of inappropriate materials. Alternatively, because of the discomfort, operators may dispense with protective apparel and become subject to greater exposure.' Christian Aid's research indicates that although Souza Cruz sells protective clothing to its contract farmers, few either use it or know how to use it properly. Farmers often remove their gloves before removing the rest of the protective clothing so their skin comes into contact with pesticide infused fabric. Furthermore, it is only in the last year that Souza Cruz has been selling one-piece suits that offer farmers better protection when spraying with a backpack.

'I got tired of telling the instructor from Souza Cruz about the problems we were having with our health but he insisted the pesticides were not harmful, ' says Adao Cosme Peres, former tobacco farmer from Sao Mateus do Sul in Parana. Adao signed a contract to grow for Souza Cruz in 1994. But in the very first year both he and his family began to feel ill effects. 'I would vomit in the afternoons after I'd been in the fields and I would have pains in my stomach and pains in my arms and legs,' recalls Adao. 'I was dizzy too, like I'd drunk a few. My wife was also affected. She had problems with her nerves and then my son began to faint when he was working in the fields.[396] I had to carry on working, though, because I owed money to Souza Cruz to pay for the fertiliser and the pesticides.'

Adao Cosme Peres stopped farming tobacco in 1997 after three years with Souza Cruz. He still suffers from nerve problems and pains in his legs and chest. He remains convinced that his ill health is related to pesticides rather than to any congenital illness and his doctor has told him that organophosphates may be to blame. 'Both my son and I have to see specialists,' he says. 'Neither of them have been able to find any illness but we still have these symptoms.'

Peres' story is far from rare. Most farmers consulted by Christian Aid reported problems with their health. In Rio Grande do Sul, one such farmer, Jose Wanderlei da Silva, is about to take on the might of the tobacco industry. A farmer for Souza Cruz for many years, Wanderlei da Silva can now no longer walk, talk or eat. He has spent many months in hospital and has attempted suicide. What makes his case rare is that his medical records cite exposure to organophosphates as a cause of his illness. As a result, Wanderlei da Silva plans to take Souza Cruz to court and sue the company because of the damage to his health.

His lawyer, Laercio Levardosk, believes he will have a tough time. Levardosk is based in Sao Joao do Triunfo in Parana and has been involved in many cases against the tobacco industry. He is currently putting together a case for the family of a farmer who committed suicide while working for Dimon, another large company operating in Brazil. His death certificate links his depression to pesticide use. This will be the first case Levardosk has fought on health grounds.

Usually his efforts are directed at rescuing farmers from the debts they owe companies such as Souza Cruz. 'It's a situation of near slavery because the farmers have a minimal profit if the production is good,' says Levardosk. 'But if they have a bad harvest then the debt they owe to the tobacco company is rolled over to the next year. The ones I see are those who never manage to escape.' The situation of tobacco farmers in Brazil is viewed by the farmers as a form of debt bondage. In order to farm for Souza Cruz or any other tobacco company, they claim that they become debtors to the same company who will ultimately decide on the value of their tobacco.

But the most disturbing aspect of contract farming is the extraordinarily high rate of suicide. Another lawyer, Dr Leticia Rodrigues da Silva, studied records of deaths in the municipality of Venancio Aires between 1979 and 1995. Her research showed an astonishing average figure of 21.8 suicides in every 100,000.[397] On comparing this with state and federal averages for Brazil she discovered an average suicide rate for Venancio Aires more than two and a half times that of the average in Rio Grande do Sul (8.09 per 100,000 [398]) and seven times higher than that of Brazil as a whole (3.2 [399]).

'Two thirds of those who killed themselves were from tobacco farms and more than half were heads of families,' recalls Dr Rodrigues da Silva. 'This is the person who has most contact with the chemicals, does the crop spraying and would be most likely to suffer the depressive illnesses that certain groups of chemicals, organophosphates in particular, are known to cause.'

Dr Rodrigues da Silva enlisted the help of two leading agronomists from the State University in Porto Alegre and a toxicologist, Dr Lenine Carvalho, who was already studying the effects of exposure to organophosphate pesticides. They produced a report which attempted to draw the link between the high rate of suicide in Venancio Aires and the use of pesticides by the tobacco farmers. 'When the report was released in March 1996, it caused uproar among the tobacco companies,' says Rodrigues da Silva. 'It was pure empirical evidence of a very high suicide rate amongst tobacco farmers, but the companies still attempted to discredit what we were saying.'

The illnesses and suicides in tobacco farming areas should lead to the invoking of a precautionary principle. But it is not in the Brazilian authorities' interest to intervene in the tobacco industry because the government earns a large annual income from the sale of both leaf and cigarettes. Souza Cruz has an 80 per cent share of the Brazilian cigarette market. The precautionary principle does not exist. Globally, as well as in Brazil, the burden is on those who suffer injury or illness to prove that companies are responsible through shoddy or irresponsible working practices.

Christian Aid believes that the case of tobacco farmers in Brazil proves the need for greater regulation of large, global industries such as tobacco, where TNCs have direct contracts with farmers. Currently no regulation can hold companies to account for debt-bonding contract workers, for creating the economic conditions that encourage the use of child labour, or encouraging the use of and selling of toxic pesticides in a situation where people's safety cannot be guaranteed.

While tobacco as a product is successfully regulated in many developed countries, its cultivation and consumption causes increasing difficulties in developing and poor countries. Growers are at the wrong end of a production chain, which sees them bearing all of the risks of cultivation and enjoying few of the benefits. The total dependence of farmers on the tobacco companies through an annual cycle of debt further weakens their position. Farmers have no bargaining power and must accept the terms of the industry, whether these are in their interests or not.

Case study three: mining in the Philippines – where laws are stacked against the poor

Across the world extractive industries have often been responsible for undermining the basic human rights of poor people. One example is in the Philippines. Poor, marginalised communities have been confronted by the activities of large TNCs, including Canadian mining companies.

Background and overview

In the late 1980s the Philippines was one of the world's most heavily indebted countries. Under pressure from the World Bank, the Asian Development Bank and the UNDP it was pressed to liberalise its economy and in particular its mining legislation. The aim was to draw in extensive foreign investment into what was a declining sector of the Philippine economy. By 1995 the government had introduced a Mining Act, part drafted by the mining companies themselves, and at the time one of the most liberal in the world. It was also one of the most controversial.

Christian Aid/Sharon McClenaghan

Civil protest against Crew has led to the revoking of mining licences.

It promises for companies a speedy processing of mining claims and allows for 100 per cent repatriation of profits and remittance of earnings, combined with various tax holidays. The Mining Act virtually guarantees return on investments and profitability to the contractor. It supersedes all former laws on foreign equity, allowing foreign mining companies to have full control of mining projects throughout the country. The Act opened up the whole country to foreign mining companies. Few new mining projects are yet fully operational but more than 50 per cent of the entire country is now covered by mining claims. Mining is now the fastest growing sector of the economy.

Under the Mining Act all public and private land is open to mining exploration. However the Act also deals specifically with ancestral land held by indigenous people. This provision was also supposed to be strengthened by the Indigenous People's Rights Act (IPRA) of 1997 which allowed indigenous peoples to claim actual title to indigenous lands. In any case, the Mining Act stipulates that companies must gain the required 'prior informed consent' before proceeding on a project, acknowledging the rights of communities to oppose mining. Similarly, exploration and mining permits require the successful completion of an Environmental Impact Assessment (EIA), which seeks to evaluate the 'social acceptability' of the project for affected communities.

Despite the legal obligation to ensure social acceptability, in almost every case Government agencies have prioritised the needs of foreign capital over those of local communities. Many people, especially indigenous people, do not want mining companies on their land. Resistance has been fierce and sustained. Despite this, increasing numbers of applications are being granted to foreign companies by central government.

In February 2001 Christian Aid visited the Philippines to assess the impact of mining with Mindoro Assistance for Human Advancement through Linkages (MAHAL), a local partner, and other local groups. In the areas we visited of Mindoro Oriental and Zamboanga del Norte, we found that the livelihoods and cultures of poor people were being threatened and eroded, especially those of indigenous farmers, small-scale miners and fishing families. We found that the activities of mining companies are directed at dividing communities and lead to increasing conflict. In many instances we discovered that the wishes of the communities had been misrepresented and instead of 'informed consent' communities had been duped and co-opted by misinformation disseminated by company propaganda, as described in the two examples below.

Crew development in Mindoro

In 1997, Mindex, a Norwegian prospecting company, identified rich deposits of nickel on the island of Mindoro. In 1999 the company was taken over by the much bigger Crew Development Corporation, based in Vancouver. Crew's nickel project is important for both the company and the Philippine government. The Philippine Chamber of Mines sees it as one of the country's five potentially major international-class mines, and a company sponsored feasibility study has claimed it will produce amongst the cheapest nickel in the world.

But the project is highly controversial. The nickel will be produced through mining surface. From the mine the ore would be mixed with water and carried as a slurry 43 kms to Pili. The Pili plant will use a method called High Pressure Acid Leaching (HPAL) which leaches the nickel and the cobalt from the ore with concentrated sulphuric acid. The tailings – millions of tons of waste – will be neutralised with lime and dumped on the seabed. This submarine mine tailings disposal (STD) will be at a rate of 4 million tons per annum. Globally, the STD process is at an experimental and controversial method stage and is effectively banned in Canada and the USA.

The proposed nickel site is currently made up of large areas of forests, and small farms used by shifting agriculturists of the Mangyan tribes. Much of the area would be cleared for mining. This would be disastrous for an island whose forest cover has dropped from an estimated 98 per cent in the 1920s to 8 per cent. It would also be disastrous for the 12 Mangyan communities, who are one of the oldest indigenous groups in the Philippines and are well known for their peace-loving qualities. The area is also a refuge for rare wildlife.

Crew has a concession area of more than 9,700 hectares. But when Mindex owned the company, initial exploration permits, valid for two years, had been granted by the central office in Manila without the knowledge of provincial officials. When the company had later sought local endorsements for an extension of its project in December 1998, it gave out gifts of gold watches to some members of the provincial board members before a crucial meeting (see *Philippines International Review*, Vol.2, NB1, 1999). In December 2000, much to the shock of local people, and in an apparently sudden and previously unannounced decision, Crew received its Mineral Production Sharing Agreement (MPSA), a licence to operate from the Department of Environment and natural resources (DENR). The MPSA requires an environmental impact assessment to evaluate the feasibility of the project from an environmental and social perspective. It also requires the 'prior informed consent of the community'. But the MPSA was advanced regardless of the absence of an EIA and in the face of strong local resistance. The MPSA was also obtained through Crew's *subsidiary* company Aglubang Mining Corporation for 2,291 hectares. This company purchased the original exploration rights of Crew for the nominal sum of two pesos (about 2.5p). Crew part-owns four smaller subsidiary companies which it formed, all of which have separate claims on the 9,700 hectare site. Aglubang is listed on the Philippines stock exchange and shares some of the same directors as Crew.

Crew claim they have the support of local people. At a meeting with indigenous groups who belonged to the indigenous alliance KPLN and the Mangyan mission, Christian Aid found strong evidence to the contrary. The fourteen representatives of four tribes we met told us that Crew were ignoring them. They said that Crew claimed to have gained the 'prior informed consent' of local people through negotiating a memorandum of agreement (MOA) with an indigenous group of Mangyan people called Kabilogan. The Mangyan we spoke to claim that Kabilogan is a creation of the company, organised largely from amongst their temporary employees and consisting of no more than 50 Mangyan families. In addition, the inaugural meeting of the group was held on company grounds in the presence of company supervisors.

The ownership of the land is also disputed. We learnt that prior applications had been made by two local organisations of Mangyan tribes for ancestral land to be recognised in the form of a certificate of ancestral domain claim (CADC), long before the company first entered the area. This should allow them priority rights over the land and enable them to reject the mining application. But Kabilogan made another CADC application, backed this time by the government's National Commission for Indigenous People (NCIP) and some local officials on behalf of Kabilogan. This is the memorandum of agreement the company say they have obtained.

In the short term the Mangyan are being wooed with gifts and promises.

They are promised jobs and better houses as their land has been cleared. The company has given them food, promised to pay for hospital bills and to send children to school. Christian Aid was told that those in the Mangyan tribes who favour the project have been recognised by the company and appointed as paid community liaison officers who, according to one woman, 'work as spies for the company', keeping tabs on those against the project. In order to help win over those opposed to the mine, they distributed extra gifts of four cans of rice and one can of fish per year per family, leading to local conflict as the community debates whether or not to take the gifts. But it has worked in the company's favour. The same woman told us:

> 'When there were many opposed, the company set aside a budget to distribute more rice to those not in favour. The company people said it was free and all you had to do was sign for it. We were told, "if you don't sign then we won't know who is receiving the rice". Then we learnt the company went to NCIP with all the signatures and said, "look how many people are supportive of this scheme"!'

Those who are opposed have been bombarded with pro-mining publicity and promised that the negative effects of mining will be minimal. The company has offered to help facilitate other land claims for the Mangyan. But so far this has not happened and the reality is that the company is now claiming to have been given prior rights over the land the Mangyan have lived on for centuries.

In the meantime the livelihood of the Mangyan community is under threat. They currently survive by farming and selling forest products such as honey and rattan cane from which furniture is made. But the land the company badly wants for mining is the flatter riverside land which the Mangyan farm. Test pits are ruining their land as well as hampering their mobility. As one woman explained to us:

> 'We don't want the mines. The land is being destroyed. From the first exploration until now we have experienced our rivers getting flooded because of the trees cut down to make way for exploration. Test pits are being dug closer and closer together and are dangerous. The productivity of the land is affected. Some of the elders who are now receiving salaries from the company are neglecting the land.'

But the effects do not stop there. There is a threat of flooding resulting from deforestation. The proposed mining area is also a watershed. Victoria had its worst ever flood late last year in which many of the roads were impassable. As Mayor Alfredo Ortega said, 'People in Victoria will support any movement against the mine because our rivers are silting up as trees are being cut down.' The municipality also has lost faith in the company's consulting process. Last year the international consultancy firm Dames and Moore did an assessment or 'scoping' exercise for the company's Environmental Impact Assessment. But they had to leave the province after it was shown that they had forged the signature of a provincial administrator on an endorsement document. Previously, in a 1991 study, the company had stated, 'Where populations depend on existing environments for their subsistence… the direct disposal of tailings to the seas, lakes, or rivers may drastically reduce the resource base on which the populations depend.'

Other local livelihoods threatened by the project are those of the fishermen and local fruit farmers whose trade would be affected by the construction of a large processing plant in Pili. Pili is at present a baranguay in the Pinamalayan municipality surrounded by a lush green landscape, looking onto the sea. This would soon change if agricultural land is replaced with an industrial zone. There are fears of acid rain and air pollution as tonnes of sulphuric acid are used each day in a 1000 hectare site. Fishing families fear that submarine disposal of mine tailings will destroy fish-stocks.

All of the residents we spoke to in Pili were against the mining project. Out of the eight Baranguay officials only one was in favour, arguing that the project would bring much-needed local revenue and community development. Local Baranguay councillor Shirley Fronda disagrees:

> 'What will we do with the money if our island is destroyed? I worry for the people of this town. Of course I worry for myself and my children but it is for the people of Pili that I am really scared. Ninety per cent of the people in this area are fisherfolk and farmers and the mine will destroy their livelihoods.'

In Crew's pursuit of 'social acceptability', hundreds of households in the municipalities of Naujan and Pinamalayan are being sent gifts and pro-mining information. Crew have their own radio programme, and sponsor their own TV programmes and journalists all promoting the positive aspects of mining. They distribute pro-mining cartoon literature in school and even supply the electricity. The company has helped established Mindoro Public Relations Bureau, promoting the benefits of mining in the press and elsewhere.

Resistance is widespread. While the company has been making its representation in Manila, rallies organised by Mahal and Alamin have had up to 11,000 turning out to protest against the company. The provincial board of Victoria has issued a statement saying that it completely rejected the mining project and all 15 municipalities had issued a resolution of rejection. The Governor himself is resolutely opposed to it.

These protests finally seem to be making a difference. Until recently both the Philippine and Canadian Governments had been sending signals that the activities of these companies is acceptable. However, on 16 July 2001 the exploration permit was revoked, and the MPSA was cancelled for Aglubang. While Crew has outstanding claims on another approximately 7,500 hectares, this is the first signal that the Philippine government is taking concerns about the mine seriously.

Crew has helped raise 15 per cent of international capital, part of which funds its mining activities in the Philippines, through the UK firm DWA Capital plc, formerly David Williamson Associates.

TVI in Zamboanga Peninsula in Canatuan

Despite a long history of local protest, the Canadian mining company TVI Pacific of Calgary have been in Canatuan in the Zamboangan peninsula of the island of Mindanao since 1994. Canatuan is a mountain area, the trail only accessible on the back of a motorbike or four-wheel drive. Movement in and out is severely restricted. TVI have already acquired an MPSA, having bought the rights off a local Filipino company, Benguet Corporation, and from a former small-scale miner.

Like the Mangyan, the indigenous Subanen people have been struggling to have their ancestral land recognised for many years. In 1989 they applied for a Forest stewardship agreement, which

> 'We do not want TVI or any commercial mining on our land.'
>
> Onsino Mato, Secretary of Siocon Subanen Association Inc (SSAI)

was granted to them in 1991. In 1992 they filed their land claim, which was only granted in 1997, not long after IPRA came into law. However one year previously in 1996 the DENR had already granted TVI an MPSA and the rights to mine, thus leading to confusion over who has the right to the land.

The Subanen share the land with small-scale miners who previously were active in mining and selling their gold rich tailings to small mining companies. But their livelihoods are threatened by the company as they are now prohibited from operating on what they see as their own land. The Philippines has a long tradition of small-scale mining, which once accounted for 50 per cent of the country's gold production and the employment of over 200,000 people, mostly from indigenous and poor rural communities. The current estimate of small-scale miners greatly exceeds this figure.

Since TVI entered the area communities have faced direct and indirect intimidation by the company. As exploration started, local resistance increased and the company introduced heavy policing of the area. TVI hired its own security company, numbering up to 100 men and trained by the Philippine military. Checkpoints were set up in 1994 and in 1997 the blockade began. The road out of the village was closed and controlled by the company's armed checkpoints, meaning movement became severely restricted. This developed into a complete blockade on the movement of goods in and out of the area, including food, in an attempt to prevent mine tailings belonging to the small-scale miners being taken off the site. It was also reported that two-inch-long barbed metal spikes were hidden on the foot trails in the surrounding areas of the road blocks, by company employees, in order to stop those trying to dodge the checkpoints.

In 1999 a number of peaceful pickets were mounted by the Subanen, through their indigenous people's community organisation the SSAI, when they formed a human barricade to defend their ancestral land from the entry of company equipment. This was broken up violently by company security, reinforced by military personnel and Onsino Mato, the leader of the SSAI, who was illegally detained. The security firm are accused by the Subanen of assault, intimidation and extortion.

The history of TVI in Canatuan is one of intimidation and harassment, and violation of the Mining Act as well as IPRA. Local groups have done all they can to register their protest and hold the company accountable for its actions. They have appealed to local and national government. In November 2000, a church-sponsored delegation even visited Canada to protest about their treatment at the hands of the company, as well as to inform the Ontario Securities and Exchange Commission about the company's activities.

Since then, the company has acknowledged that there are significant problems with the local communities. But there has been little change apart from a reduction in the numbers of security men. Movement in and out of the mine site is still severely restricted and our delegation was not able to enter the site because of fears for our security. We talked to people in a neighbouring area including some small-scale miners. They told us intimidation is still happening. We were told that the security company, Diostar, were carrying high-powered Armalite M16s. 'You can't see the guns. They're meant to carry revolvers or shotguns, which they do at the gate, but inside they have repeater weapons.'

We were also told that guards were still confiscating goods belonging to the local residents and earlier in the year had knocked down some local houses occupied by the local community. A week after we left we heard that one man had been shot at when he attempted to get his goods back. Standing in a beautiful house, a testament to his earlier prosperity, one small-scale miner told us:

'Before TVI came, even small children could earn a little bit of money but now no-one can. People could also catch monkeys and cut rattan-vine to make furniture but because of de-forestation the source of our livelihood has disappeared.'

Eddie Cayabyab who was under arrest at the time of the meeting and has received threats from the company told us:

'As small-scale miners we used to make 20,000 pesos a week. Now we make very little. The mining veins are still 90 per cent rich but we need capital to develop it. But the company want rid of us and are commissioning stories to show the damage done by small-scale mining. It's propaganda. They have a Mining Act which gives them protection for 25 years and we have a Small Scale Mining Act which gives us rights for two years. It's too short a time. We agree we need to operate to higher standards but we need capital and time.'

Rhetoric and reality

'TVI is committed to exploring and developing projects that provide positive social and economic benefits in the communities where it works. In the municipality of Siocon near the Canatuan project, working with the local communities is essential. Here we are consulting with the public and the government agencies to ensure that our development meets the needs of *all* affected communities: the small-scale miners, Canatuan's ancestral people, the Subanon and municipal residents.'

Since the high-profile trip to Canada by the local group, the company has attempted to have local 'consultations' in nearby Ipil, which surprisingly a Canadian government official attended. But talks broke down and the local group walked out complaining that the process was dominated by the company and that the community representative was continually prevented from making his point. The talks have not been resumed.

Is this consultation in line with what the company describes as its '*unwavering commitment to local social and environmental issues*'? It has been almost impossible for the Canatuan Subanen to bring the company to account for human rights abuses caused by its employees. Geography doesn't help as Canatuan is remote and isolated. Getting around is expensive. On a recent trip to England in July 2001 Onsino Mato said:

'It's expensive to charter a motorbike to take you a few miles up the road. You have to do it with a group of other people. How much harder is it to hire a lawyer and how much more impossible to get the company to the court. Even then the Philippines government is the secret lawyer of the mining company.'

As with Crew, TVI's consultation with local communities is deeply flawed. Individuals are hand-picked to agree with the company and do not represent the community's concerns. In no way can this deliver the consensual endorsement the law requires.

Conclusion

The Mining Act of 1995 has opened up almost the entire Philippines to mining, with detrimental effects on many of the country's rural poor, whose traditional livelihoods are now threatened. Filipinos are very much aware of the devastating effects mining operations can bring about, especially following examples such as the sustained mismanagement of the Placer Dome copper mine on the island of Marinduque, where resistance has been vociferous. Yet despite the fact that Crew and TVI do not have the prior informed consent of local people to mine, their operations have gone ahead – in the case of TVI using direct intimidation and violence. Although developments in Aglubang have been stopped temporarily this is only one of many Crew claims and there is little doubt they will be able to pursue their claim through other means. Despite international appeals, the Canadian government are not taking any action to protect the interests of local people.

International regulation is needed to hold companies and their investors to account for their actions overseas. It is clear that the implementation of the IPRA is fraught with difficulties. The Mining Act of 1995 and the influential mining lobby created loopholes to unburden the industry of constraints in its exploitation of natural resources. The Philippine 1992 Small Scale Mining Act goes some way towards giving rights to small-scale miners but these last only two years and contrast markedly with the 25 year powers given to large mining companies under the Mining Act.

Case study four: Peru – the perils of liberalisation

This case study by the Provincial Women's Federation of ICA – a Christian Aid partner – on working women in the Peruvian asparagus industry demonstrates some of the perils of liberalisation. A combination of a lack of state regulation of private companies, an industry that produces solely for the export market and the introduction of more flexible labour conditions are all undermining poor women's rights and livelihoods.

On the southern Peruvian coast lies the Ica Valley, which, despite its limited access to land and water, is one of Peru's most important agricultural districts. Under the hot Peruvian sun and the watchful eyes of foremen and supervisors, thousands of women work the land here for an asparagus crop destined for the markets of Europe and the United States. They exhaust themselves for a product that will not be consumed by their families. Despite working the fields all day (and sometimes all night), the women often can't take enough food home to feed their children.

Export-oriented policies under liberalisation

Peruvian woman have not always been involved in asparagus farming. For many decades, their fathers and grandfathers worked on cotton fields and on sugar plantations, while their mothers and grandmothers raised the children. Due to political unrest and a subsequent decline in income and living conditions, many women started to work alongside the men.

Liberalisation policies were adopted in Peru during the late 1980s, prescribed by the World Bank and IMF. The implementation of a neo-liberal agriculture model – characterised by the state withdrawing from the economy, ending subsidies, raising interest rates, lowering prices and liberalising the land market – coincided with a boom in asparagus farming. Between 1980 and 1995, the production of non-traditional crops increased from 8.7 per cent to 44.3 per cent. In less than a decade, asparagus production grew from 3,750 metric tons to 85,288 metric tons.

The government's policies attracted large investors keen on exploiting a cheap labour force and climatic advantages. Intensification of asparagus production in countries like Peru was driven by increasing demand in Europe and the US. Unable to produce more asparagus cost-effectively in their own countries, companies went in search of areas that could do so – and they found the Ica Valley. Low labour costs and suitable weather conditions made Peru an ideal location for investment.

Peruvian farmers were encouraged to farm for the export market and to abandon traditional crops. Farmers produced less and less of products that are traditionally farmed in Peru, with grapes and cotton production being the hardest hit. Women who turned towards agriculture for increased security for their families found an industry that had exports as its cornerstone. Many acres in Ica were bought up and used for export-oriented asparagus farming. In order to meet the needs of Peruvian people, food is increasingly imported. Peruvians are at the mercy of international price fluctuations and production trends, and food dependency has increased.

The concentration of land ownership on the Peruvian coast accelerated between 1994 and 2000. The establishment of medium-sized and large farms, exceeding 20 hectares, enabled the use of technology, which boosted yield. Fifty-six corporations controlled most of the area planted in asparagus, especially holdings of more than 50 hectares. Individual owners only accounted for 22 per cent of the total area of the province.

Asparagus farming is an expensive business, which partly explains why small growers have only a small role in production. Since asparagus is produced solely for the export market, investment delivers limited benefits to the domestic economy. As a luxury food, asparagus does not figure in Peruvian family diets, and most of the profits return to the home countries of the foreign investors. However, there are a number of locally owned farms that benefit from the export opportunities presented by liberalisation. Jobs for women have been created, but working conditions are far from satisfactory.

Prices for asparagus on world markets throughout the 1990s showed enormous variation. The instability in the asparagus market over the past two years can partly be attributed to oversupply and the increasing export of Chinese asparagus. Workers carry the costs of these fluctuations and instabilities by job losses or reductions in pay.

Poor working conditions

The policy reforms secured advantages for foreign and local companies alike. They have made it easier for management to dismiss workers and have led to a fall in real wages. Institutional reform introduced in the labour market has been imposed in a harsh manner and with little consultation.

The state does not require workers to sign contracts with their employers. In the Ica Valley, worker-employer relationships remain private and are, therefore, unregulated, giving companies near absolute power over their workforce. Despite these abuses, workers are very dependent on the jobs that the farms provide and would rather work under the adverse conditions than have no work at all. Without regulation by the state, employees can be exploited,

'I've been working for a year and a half now. It's seasonal, but right now I'm working. They say they'll lay us off in June and pay us for time served. Maybe, if I'm lucky, I'll get work again next season.'

Juana, a plant worker

leaving only companies empowered. The fear of being fired is used to create conditions of precariousness, low wages and greater exploitation for women working in the Ica Valley. The pattern has been described as 'flexploitation'.

In the mid-1990s, there was high unemployment in the rural area of the department of Ica. Asparagus cultivation opened the door to thousands of jobless workers. They were in no position to negotiate better terms, due to the lack of labour unions and the removal of protection under new labour legislation. Although wages have increased nominally since 1980, they have decreased by 70 per cent in terms of purchasing power. To keep costs down many workers are employed only during the harvesting season, which effectively

'They're always looking for a pretext for firing someone. That's happened to me because I'm clear about what I think. Out of necessity and fear, you stop talking. You're afraid and don't speak up. If you lose your job, what are you going to do? Where are you going to get money?'

Josefina, a field worker

means they have jobs for only 180 days in the year. Peru's 'comparative advantage' consists of low-cost labour with almost no legal protection. It is this that brings profits to foreign companies.

There is widespread discrimination against women working on the asparagus farms. 33.5 per cent of asparagus workers in Ica are women, the majority seasonal workers. Of the 1,777 permanent workers only two per cent are women. Most of these women are still very young: half are under the age of 30 and more than 80 per cent are under 40. Traditional family structures are giving way to single-parent families. Most of the women live in appalling conditions: 68 per cent of working

'Sometimes the companies spread poison. They don't care if we're protected or have gloves to hold the asparagus. Sometimes we're cutting and they spread poison, and they don't give us any protection, not gloves or boots or even a handkerchief. They don't care if it rains, they want us to stay late. They don't care if we're all wet or how we are, because if we leave early they threaten us or the next day they punish us by making us weed longer.'

Josefina, a field worker

women have inadequate housing, 45 per cent have no sanitation and 26 per cent have no running water. When the women turn 40 they gradually leave the labour market, because they cannot meet the levels of production required by companies. But even the younger workers often lose their income: the number of jobs may drop sharply from 100 to 20 from one week to the next, or sometimes from one day to the next.

Apart from working on different crops, Peruvian women today also work under different conditions from those of their grandparents. In order to increase productivity, farmers are increasingly using pesticides, which should be handled according to exact guidelines to protect the health of workers and consumers. On the asparagus farms, however, spray-

'When I started this work I weighed more. Now I weigh 45 kilograms. You get sick because of the travel, because you walk bent over. I've had anaemia and bronchitis and have also had kidney problems. You also get cold because you're in the water, your legs, knees and bones hurt.'

Mirtha, a field worker

ing is often done without adequate protective equipment and clothing.

Agro-industrial production has led to many job-related accidents and illnesses. The most common job-related accidents among women are cuts, both in the field and the factory, and falls or slipping. Job-related illnesses include pain in the spine and kidneys. However, few complaints are received since women are afraid of losing their jobs. Accidents and illnesses are a result of the long workdays and repetitive and demanding physical effort. In addition, there are no maternity benefits for the women. Given the seasonal nature of their employment, they try to work as long as possible before their babies are born – up to two weeks before delivery – to secure some income.

This is part of Peruvian agriculture's adaptation to a globalised economy. What matters is the women's productivity, rather than whether their lives are shortened. The government's priority is to serve the needs of capital, not to improve the quality of life of its citizens.

Case study five: the scorched earth – oil and war in Sudan [382]

The need for international regulation of companies operating overseas is nowhere more obvious than in the case of oil production in Sudan. Sudan began exporting oil in 1998 and since then human rights violations have been steadily increasing. One of the bloodiest and longest of Africa's wars is now being fuelled by oil. In the contested south of the country there is systematic depopulation of the oil concessions, as oil exploitation takes place. Sudanese government troops and militias are terrorising, raping, killing and displacing thousands of ordinary people to make way for oil production by European and other oil companies. The rights of foreign companies in exploiting the oil concessions are taking precedence over the right of the Sudanese civilians to live in peace.

> 'Christ was sold for 30 pieces of silver and our people are being sacrificed in exchange for barrels of oil.'
>
> Sudanese Catholic Bishops' Conference, September 2000

The presence of international oil companies is fuelling this war. Companies from Asia, North America and Europe, including the UK, have helped build Sudan's oil industry, offering finance, technological expertise and services, to create a strong and growing oil industry. Their very presence enables the government to secure revenues to enable it to intensify the war. Oil industry infrastructure – the same roads and airstrips which serve the companies – is used by the army to conduct the war. Opposition forces are attacking government-controlled towns and villages, causing further death and displacement.

> 'The Sudanese churches believe that the oil in southern Sudan is a national resource that should be used for all the peoples of Sudan. Instead, oil revenues have been used for the purchase of weapons used for killing and displacing people in the oil areas. As shepherds of the population in the Sudan and eyewitnesses, we call upon the international community to take immediate action... [and for] the withdrawal of the oil companies.'
>
> The Sudanese Councils of Churches, in a statement issued in late 2000

However, there is no way to hold the companies to account for international human rights or development standards or to make them accountable for the repercussions of their activities. There is nothing to stop these companies continuing to fuel the war, operating as they do in a regulatory void.

Christian Aid visited southern Sudan to gather first-hand information on the impact of the companies' involvement.

'Now the gunships are like rain'

'The worst thing was the gunships,' said Zeinab Nyacieng, a Nuer woman driven hundreds of miles from her home late last year, after two of her children were killed in a raid. 'I never saw them before last year but now they are like rain.'

'Before our region was peaceful,' Malony Kolang, a Nuer chief told Christian Aid. 'People were cultivating their cattle. When the pumping began, the war began. Antonovs and helicopter gunships began attacking the villages. All farms have been destroyed. Everything around the oil fields has also been destroyed. Oil has brought death.'

'During my visit I gathered further evidence that oil exploitation leads to an exacerbation of the conflict with serious consequences on the civilians. More specifically, I received information whereby the government is resorting to forced eviction of local population and destruction of villages to depopulate areas and allow for oil operations to proceed unimpeded. I was informed that all the villages around Nhialdiu, in Nimne, south of Bentiu, have been burnt to the ground and crop has been destroyed. Similarly, all the villages along the road up to Pulteri, in the surrounding of the oil fields at Rier, have been razed.'

Gerhart Baum, UN Special Rapporteur on Sudan, Human Rights Commission, 29 April 2001

Eyewitness accounts show that government forces are ruthlessly clearing the way for oil over an ever-larger area. A new road built in the concession of Sweden's Lundin Oil has been accompanied by massive human rights violations. Government troops and militias have burned and depopulated dozens of villages along and close to the oil road. In August and November 2000 Christian Aid found thousands of Nuer civilians displaced from villages along this road, hundreds of miles away in Dinka Bahr el-Ghazal. They all told the same tale. Antonovs bombed the villages to scatter the people. Then the government troops arrived by truck and helicopter, burning the villages and killing anyone who was unable to flee – in most cases the old and the very young.

A UN official familiar with the area said all the villages that once existed along the road to Pulteri have been razed to the ground:

'As one flies along the new road, the only sign of life are the lorries travelling at high speed back and forth to the oil field... small military garrisons are clearly visible every five kilometres. The bulk of the population that once lived in the villages along the road and within walking distance of LS airstrips are now nearly beyond reach. Communities in need cannot be assisted.'

Escalation of the war

Sudan, which two years ago was an oil importer, is now an exporter of oil and, with oil money, able to fund an expansion of the war. Exports of Sudan's estimated reserves of two billion barrels of oil are paying for the build-up of a Sudanese homegrown arms industry as well as paying for more arms imports. With oil, the civil war being fought between the government of Sudan and the main opposition force, the Sudan People's Liberation Army (SPLA) is escalating. 'Sudan will be capable of producing all the weapons it needs thanks to the growing oil industry,' General Mohamed Yassin claimed just 11 months after the oil began flowing out of the new pipeline into the supertankers at the Red Sea port. The government now earns roughly US$1 million a day from oil – equivalent to the US$1 million it spends daily fighting the war. The equation is simple, the consequences devastating.

The Western Upper Nile now has the highest proportion of people in need anywhere in Sudan. Its children are at the highest nutritional risk. Common Article 3 of the Geneva Conventions, which includes the protection of civilians during war, is being violated every day. Organisations such as Christian Aid and its 24 local partner organisations cannot fulfil their humanitarian mandate. Permission for aid flights is routinely denied and with it the end of a vital lifeline of emergency food and medicine.

Extracting oil in a country at war with itself is problematic. In Sudan, geography compounds the problem. Although the oil is being exploited by the government, most oil reserves lie in southern Sudan – in areas where the SPLA and other southern groups are fighting against the government in pursuance of demands for a more equitable share of economic and political power. The oil is transported north through a 1,600 km pipeline built with foreign hardware, including British pumping stations and engines. Khartoum has signalled its intentions by selling oil concessions across the entire south. These are the areas next in line for armed clearance.

Company complicity

Oil companies such as Canada's Talisman Energy, Sweden's Lundin Oil, Austria's OMV, Malaysia's Petronas and China's state-owned China National Petroleum Corporation (CNPC) are business partners of the government of Sudan and complicit in the human rights violations.

- The very presence of oil operators is fuelling the Sudan government's displacement campaign and war. Companies such as Lundin, Petronas and CNPC are complicit in the 'scorched earth' strategy by permitting government forces to

Which companies are involved?

A network of companies, including many British-based firms, has built the Sudanese oil industry piece by piece.

Talisman Energy (Canada): leads Sudan's largest operating consortium, the Greater Nile Petroleum Operating Company (GNPOC) with a 25 per cent share. GNPOC runs the major oil fields in Blocks 1, 2 and 4. It also owns the 1,600 km pipeline to the Red Sea and the supertanker facilities near Port Sudan.

Petronas (Malaysia's national oil company): owns a 30 per cent stake in GNPOC and 28.5 per cent in Block 5a.

CNPC (China National Petroleum Corporation and China's state oil company): owns a 40 per cent stake in GNPOC.

Sudapet (Sudan's national oil company): owns a 5 per cent stake in GNPOC.

Lundin Oil (Sweden): a family-run Swedish oil company based in Geneva. Lundin is the lead operator in Block 5a, with 40 per cent of shares.

OMV (Austria): owns 28 per cent of Block 5a and 25 per cent in Block 5b along with Lundin and Petronas. The Australian government has a 35 per cent share of OMV.

Totalfinaelf (France): it holds the huge concession Block 5 but is not yet operational. It has reportedly been asking for guarantees from the government of Sudan that it is safe to work there.

British Petroleum (UK): has a $578 million stake in PetroChina, a major subsidiary of CNPC, the largest operator in Sudan. BP claims that its investment is ring-fenced and none of the profits from its investment pass to the parent company but this cannot be proved.

Rolls Royce (UK): suppliers of diesel engines and technical personnel support to the pipeline, it has been operational in Sudan for over three years. The company is also rumoured to be considering building a major electricity power station in Sudan.

Weir Pumps (UK): suppliers of pumps and pumping stations (their first contract was worth £20 million). They also provide operational support for the pipeline and have trained personnel.

According to the UK Department of Trade and Industry (DTI) at least 46 UK companies were exporting to Sudan in 2000.

clear new areas for them to exploit. The offensive that will be necessary to take control of TotalFinaElf's concessions will take the scorched earth close to the borders of Uganda and Kenya.

- Oil company infrastructure, including airstrips and oil roads, is being used by government forces fighting in southern Sudan. Lundin Oil, for example, has allegedly paid for the construction of an oil road, which is controlled by the government, and government troops and militias have used them in their displacement campaign.

- The oil companies have never to Christian Aid's knowledge, spoken out against the denial of relief to people in need. The government's military operations have at times caused a number of airstrips to be put off limits by the UN's Operation Lifeline Sudan (OLS) security office. By the end of the planting season in mid-2000 for example, one of the most important traditional relief centres in Western Upper Nile received no OLS flights. The people had nothing left to plant and received no food aid to fill the gap. Our information is that in February 2001 19 locations were denied relief flights throughout southern Sudan. Throughout the past year OLS have been consistently prevented from reaching people in need. The community development and relief projects that some of the companies promote are little more than public relations exercises and are minuscule compared to the effects of the denial of massive UN relief and the scale of the suffering of the Sudanese people.

- Some companies have asked for and received protection from forces responsible for human rights violations. The companies require protection so that they may operate unhindered and so their staff are secure. However many of the security staff employed by the companies have been linked to human rights violations. Oil companies will not disclose the terms of their security agreements.

- The companies have expressed 'concerns' about 'allegations' of human rights violations and some have spoken out against them in general but none has ever acknowledged a single instance in their areas of operations or investigated them fully. In a letter to Christian Aid of 30 November 2000, Ian Lundin of Lundin Oil stated that 'we have not received any reports concerning human rights violations taking place in our block'. The sheer scale of the destruction and displacement that Christian Aid has documented makes the claim that the company is unaware of human rights violations occurring in its concession area quite incredible. The Canadian Harker commission and Amnesty International both refer to human rights violations in Lundin's concession, as well as other oil company areas, as does the report of the UN Special Rapporteur.

It is no longer possible for companies to claim ignorance of the effects of their operations. Investigation after investigation, by the UN's Special Rapporteur on Sudan, Amnesty International, Canada's Harker commission, church agencies and Christian Aid condemn foreign corporate complicity and tell the story of systematic, overwhelming human rights violations of innocent people. Yet, despite the evidence, the oil companies remain largely silent on this subject. Those directly engaged in production claim that they have no knowledge of oil-related human rights violations on their land and that, however deplorable, human rights violations are not linked to their activities or to their need for government-supplied security. Indeed, both Talisman and Lundin have gone to great lengths to publish material to defend themselves from these charges.

Instead, the companies, notably Talisman, argue that their presence will lead to positive change – 'islands of peace', as Talisman has expressed it. Talisman and Lundin have told Christian Aid of their concern for human rights in the area and their desire for peace. Yet neither will admit that the human rights are linked to oil nor will they or any of the other operational oil companies agree to meet Christian Aid to talk about the situation. Both Talisman and Lundin have brought in some humanitarian relief. But in the wider context, deliveries of tents for temporary shelter for displaced villagers, or support for water boreholes or a 60-bed hospital is only a sticking plaster while disaster spreads. It's also a clever way of averting attention from the atrocities that have already been committed.

The need for new national and global regulation

Sudan needs oil: its people, north and south, need oil wealth. But under current conditions oil revenues are not translating into wealth. Western governments and oil companies are talking the language of human rights and corporate social responsibility. But if it is to have any meaning it needs to be acted upon. If the ethical criteria declared publicly by these companies – for instance BP's signature to the UN Declaration on Human Rights, and Talisman's signature to the International Code of Ethics for Canadian Business – are to have any worth, they must be rigorously applied. Companies directly involved in Sudan must end their 'business as usual' approach and must take their very public commitments to corporate responsibility seriously. Investors, such as BP, must take a serious look at its portfolio. Likewise, Western governments, including the UK, must stop promoting business in Sudan until a just peace is negotiated. 'Business as usual' is no longer tolerable in a situation where thousands are being pushed off their land and being made victims of a war on resources, while profits flood back to rich countries.

There is currently no legislation to make companies, such as those based in North America, Europe and the UK, abide by human rights standards overseas. As signatories to international law on human rights, national governments including the UK must apply these standards, not only within their own boundaries to their own citizens, but to their own companies operating abroad. Governments must adopt new national legislation which translates the principles and standards they have ratified as states, especially the Universal Declaration on Human Rights, and apply them directly to companies registered within their countries to ensure that companies operating overseas abide by international human rights standards.

New international mechanisms are also needed to enforce global standards on human rights and sustainable development and to make companies accountable for the impact of their operations overseas, especially in least developed countries such as Sudan. The failure to monitor and regulate companies' activities overseas at an international level needs to be addressed by a global regulatory authority (GRA).

In Sudan, oil and war are inextricably linked. For this reason Christian Aid and its partners recommend that:

- all oil companies directly involved in oil in Sudan, such as Canada's Talisman Energy and Sweden's Lundin Oil, should immediately suspend operations pending a just and lasting peace agreement

- suppliers stop supplying equipment until a peace agreement is reached

- the EU invokes a temporary ban on all new investment in the Sudanese oil industry

- BP and other indirect investors should divest their shares in PetroChina, a subsidiary of CNPC

- the Government of Sudan and the armed opposition force, the Sudanese People's Liberation Movement/ Army (SPLM/A) should abide by the Geneva Conventions and respect the rights of civilians and negotiate a lasting peace agreement based on the IGAD Declaration of Principles.

Case study six: Ugandan coffee – surviving the volatility of global markets

'It's impossible to make a living,' says Emmanuel Mubiru, 'I used to harvest about 40 bags of coffee, but now I'm lucky if I manage to get ten. I used to be paid 300 shillings (US$0.17) per kilo and now I am paid less than 150 shillings (US$0.08).'

Mubiru's coffee plantation is over 40 years old and covers three acres. Mubiru himself is now 60 years old and is concerned that his children do not want to maintain the coffee plantation. 'I am getting old so I can't manage the whole plantation any more,' he says, and continues:

'I am trying to educate my children in coffee growing but I fear they may want to leave the country and go to Kampala. And the coffee wilt disease has halved my stock of bushes anyway. They will have to plant new varieties resistant to the disease but each plant costs 500 shillings and won't produce coffee for at least two years. The maximum I can now earn is 500,000 shillings (less than US $300) a year. I am becoming poorer and poorer, my house is half falling down and I am struggling to keep my children in school. Primary school is free but I have to make sure they have school clothes and food to eat at lunchtime.'

Uganda is highly dependent on coffee and Ugandan farmers have relied for generations on selling their coffee crop for cash. Because 98 per cent of coffee is grown on small-scale, family farms, it has provided funds for education. Many of those whose education was paid for by coffee have now successfully made the transition from rural subsistence to urban middle-class life. Trading coffee has been a powerful force for development in the past, but it may now be a spent force.

'There are three problems with coffee in Uganda at the moment,' says Joseph Nkandu, Director of the Uganda Coffee Farmers' Association, a trade union for coffee growers. 'The first is Tracheo Mycosis – coffee wilt disease. The second is the weather, which is changing and is less predictable than it once was. The third is declining prices which make it hardly worth farmers harvesting the cherries [ripe coffee beans].'

Nkandu is himself a beneficiary of coffee cash. He grew up on a coffee farm and was able to attend school because his father was able to afford the fees. He subsequently studied agriculture at Makerere University in Kampala. 'If it wasn't for coffee money I would not be here,' he says. 'I would be subsisting somewhere in the bush. The trouble is, farmers are giving up on their coffee and slipping back to subsistence.'

Coffee has been grown in Uganda for over 100 years. When the British took control of the region the governors insisted that each family farm grow coffee. They instructed farmers to harvest the cherries when they were ripe and lay them out on the ground to dry in the sun, loosening the skin. 'If farmers didn't follow these instructions they were beaten by their colonial masters,' says Nkandu. 'That's why we call this method of growing and drying coffee "kiboko" which is a Ugandan word meaning "whipped".'

Life for Uganda's coffee farmers changed beyond recognition in 1991 when the World Bank and IMF introduced liberalisation in the industry. The Ugandan Coffee Marketing Board (UCMB), the parastatal which bought coffee from the farmers and sold it on the international market, was scrapped and farmers were left to deal directly with traders and big food companies.

Few farmers miss the UCMB. 'Under the parastatal, farmers would be paid less than 20 per cent of the market price of coffee, if they were paid at all,' says Nkandu. 'Very often the people from the Marketing Board would pocket the money and leave farmers with nothing. Liberalisation meant farmers were better off almost overnight because they were suddenly being paid 50 or 60 per cent of the global price.' But with the global market the story is one of severe fluctuation in coffee prices. Since liberalisation, Ugandan coffee farmers have been exposed to huge variations in what they receive for their crop.

Most recently, the price of Robusta coffee of the type grown in Uganda has fallen on world markets from US$0.63 per lb in August 1999 to US$0.25 per lb in August 2001. According to industry analysts, this is due to over-production. The price cycle, they say, is currently at an all-time low and will recover. Martin Whatton from the International Coffee Organisation, the intergovernmental forum for coffee importing and exporting countries, agrees and argues that the market will take care of the large coffee stocks. 'Farmers will have to stop harvesting if it doesn't pay, and in two or three years' time stocks will diminish,' he says.

The concern for Uganda is what happens in the meantime, while the price paid for coffee is low. Already this year, government revenues from coffee are down by 36 per cent and since coffee revenues account for over two thirds of Uganda's exports, the country is suffering from severely reduced export earnings. This reduces its ability to purchase vital imports, such as oil, the price of which has recently risen. As a result, Uganda is suffering from extremely poor terms of trade.

President Museveni of Uganda has thrown down the gauntlet to foreign companies, inviting them to invest in Uganda's coffee industry. Certainly, adding value to raw coffee beans would help Uganda earn more money from coffee. Finance Minister Gerald Ssendaula agrees with the President. 'While the green bean price has been falling, the price of a jar of instant coffee in London, New York or even in Kampala has not dropped,' he says. 'All the roasters in the developed world are doing is blending. We should be able to roast and blend but it is impossible for us without us going into partnership.'

However, coffee market analysts are downbeat about the prospects of Uganda being able to develop its own coffee industry. There is no internal market for coffee in Uganda, they say, and who will want to buy beans roasted and shipped when they can buy beans freshly roasted in their own country? As a result, no big companies are likely to invest in Uganda.

None of this helps the coffee farmers. 'The farmers have lost morale,' says Sam Ssekitto, a coffee farmer and chair of the Coffee Farmers' Association in

Semuto sub-county in Luweero district. 'I had two acres of coffee but the whole lot was wiped out by the disease. I am starting again and replanting but a lot of farmers say that the price is so low you are wasting your time.

'I have cleared an acre but I need to plough,' continues Ssekitto. 'I am hoping to sell two pigs so that I can buy a plough, but after that I need support because it will be around two years before I am able to begin harvesting coffee.'

For Uganda, supporting farmers is not an option. WTO rules forbid either the continuation of current subsidies except in the short term, or the introduction of new forms of support or protection. So even if Uganda had the resources to shield farmers in times when the global coffee market is depressed, it would not be permitted to do so. What is more, the rules do not allow the introduction of a price stabilisation scheme, which could help iron out extreme fluctuations in price.

As a result, Ugandan coffee farmers are entirely at the mercy of the global market. There are no safety nets or safeguards. Allen Ruhangataremwa of the Uganda Debt Network believes the WTO should learn the lessons of small-scale farmers exposed to global markets. 'Eighty per cent of Ugandan people are farmers and the vast majority are small-scale,' she says. 'I wish the people from the WTO would go and look at the situation of the coffee farmers. How are they supposed to survive when the price is so low?'

Working for the UCFA, Joseph Nkandu is trying to bring farmers together into groups in order to buy machines to wet process their coffee. 'Wet processing adds value,' he says. 'Traders will pay up to twice the price for wet processed coffee beans – it's one of the ways farmers can add value to their produce.' But it's an uphill struggle for Nkandu. Apart from his salary, the UCFA has few funds and can only offer advice to farmers rather than the financial support many of them need.

It makes little sense for a century old industry, and one so important to hundreds of thousands of family farmers, to be killed-off by low prices as a result of the volatility of the global market. But under the current trade regime, Uganda is unable to invest in or otherwise support its coffee industry, and it can offer little incentive for foreign companies to set up coffee processing businesses in the country.

Christian Aid believes that governments of developing countries, which are the most vulnerable to market volatility, should have the freedom to sustain viable industries through the hard times in the expectation of expansion and development when market conditions change. Countries such as Uganda should be permitted to intervene to support small-scale farmers in order to boost traditional commodities or encourage diversification. Poor countries should also be able to benefit from price stabilisation schemes while they are still heavily reliant on key commodities.

The institutions of global trade

The GATT and the WTO

Until 1945, there was no global institution to regulate international trade. At the end of the Second World War, the Allied countries met with some other key international players at the Bretton Woods conference, to draw up a plan for managing the post-war international economy. They envisaged three global organisations to manage the world economy: the International Monetary Fund (IMF) would ensure economic liquidity, making sure countries' economies were not harmed by short-term shortages of funds; the International Bank for Reconstruction and Development (World Bank) would lend funds to countries devastated by war, to help them rebuild their economies; and the International Trade Organisation (ITO) would promote employment through the promotion of free trade accompanied by different instruments to protect labour rights, prevent undue domination by large corporations, assist weaker economies in gaining access to capital and technology and prevent prices for traded commodities becoming too low.

The success of the ITO depended on US participation, but US businesses successfully lobbied against ratification by the government, arguing it did not adequately protect their interests. With the failure of the ITO, the General Agreement on Tariffs and Trade (GATT) was created as an interim organisation in the hope that the ITO might still be established. Although it dealt with only one part of the ITO, namely the reduction of tariffs, the GATT became the main forum for international trade negotiations. Unlike the ITO, the GATT did not include provisions for economic development. From 1948 to 1994, the GATT provided the rules for much of world trade. Agreements were of two kinds.

- Tariff reduction: the first years of the GATT focused on tariff reduction, as countries agreed to reduce the tariffs that restricted imports.

- Rule making: as negotiations proceeded, they moved beyond tariffs and into other areas of government trade policy. Issues like subsidies, domestic legislation on intellectual property, investment and health and safety were all put on the agenda by countries which hoped to gain advantages for their companies if rules were made in those areas. Each new area was justified on the grounds that these were aspects of domestic policy which affected trading relations and which should therefore be included in trade negotiations.

Most GATT trade negotiations took place in 'trade rounds', the first two of which were in Annecy, France (1949) and Torquay, UK (1951). The structure and content of these rounds were dominated by the interests of the major powers, and only seven developing countries were members of the GATT during the first round of talks; only a further eight had joined by the end of the second round.

The first few trade rounds mainly involved negotiations on reducing tariffs imposed on imported goods. Countries demanded concessions from each other in return for reducing tariffs, hence the need for negotiations. The first round of negotiations resulted in 45,000 tariff concessions affecting $10 billion of trade (a fifth of the world total). By the end of the Torquay Round 58,000 items were subject to reduced import tariffs. For the newly-independent countries of Africa and Asia, the GATT was the only forum where they could hope to influence world trade in their favour. Another 32 developing countries joined the GATT during the 1960s, and by the time the fifth round (the Kennedy Round) of trade negotiations ended in 1967, 47 of the developing countries were members of the GATT.

The seventh round of negotiations – the Uruguay Round (1986-1994) – was the first in which a large number of developing countries took part: 60 countries were members of the GATT at the start of the Round, and another 22 joined during the negotiations. Under pressure from the TNCs based in rich countries, the Uruguay Round led to a considerable expansion of the scope of multilateral trade talks. Issues such as agriculture and textiles, as well as services, intellectual property rights and investment were put on the agenda. The Uruguay Round moved the GATT further beyond agreements on tariff reductions, and towards rule-making on international trade.

It also established the World Trade Organisation (WTO) which incorporated the GATT. Like the GATT, the principle of trade liberalisation is enshrined in the Final Act of the Uruguay Round, which establishes the World Trade Organisation as a body in which countries will negotiate 'reciprocal and mutually advantageous arrangements directed to the substantial reduction of tariffs and other barriers to trade and to the elimination of discriminatory treatment in international trade relations'.

The WTO, based in Geneva, has more powers than the GATT.

• It is recognised as the only forum for multilateral trade negotiations.

- It monitors countries' implementation of agreements (through the Trade Policy Review Body).

- It has greatly reinforced instruments – the dispute settlement mechanism – for member countries bringing complaints against each other if WTO rules are being violated, and can authorise one country to impose sanctions on another (through the Dispute Settlement Body).

The WTO now has more than 140 members. Unlike other global economic institutions such as the IMF and the World Bank, it has a relatively small secretariat. The secretariat works to administer agreements and establish negotiations, but real power in the organisation lies with the members. The strategic importance of trade policy means that WTO members keep tight control of the activities of the organisation. It is a hugely important institution – and rare among international institutions for having an enforcement mechanism. This means that, in practice, WTO agreements tend to override other international agreements. For example, just the threat of WTO action (brandished by an infant formula company) persuaded the Guatemalan government to backtrack on its compliance with the World Health Organisation ruling on breast milk substitutes in 1995.

UNCTAD

Although developing countries are always members of the GATT and the WTO, both are institutions founded and shaped by the agendas of the major powers. In response to a sense of dissatisfaction with the GATT, the United Nations Conference on Trade and Development (UNCTAD) was set up in 1964. Unlike the GATT and WTO, UNCTAD's role is not to promote trade liberalisation as necessarily the best way of increasing developing countries' gains from trade, but more to help develop an international trading system that is favourable to development and poverty reduction.

UNCTAD plays an important role in assisting developing countries to develop trade policy and participate in trade negotiations and in providing analysis on trade policy. Through its programmes of research and capacity building it greatly increases the ability of developing country governments to make their voices heard in other international institutions. UNCTAD conferences are also important forums where trade issues are discussed. However, rich countries have ensured that UNCTAD, which often takes a critical view on WTO agreements, does not undermine the 'liberalisation' ideology. In 1992, for example, they managed to ensure the limitation of UNCTAD's mandate so that it could not negotiate trade agreements but simply be a forum for discussion, consensus building, analysis and technical assistance.

The World Bank and the IMF

Although they are not forums for negotiations, and in theory have little to do with the trading system, in practice the World Bank and the IMF have had a huge impact on developing countries' trade policy. Trade liberalisation has been central to the conditionality attached to the World Bank's structural adjustment programmes and the IMF's stabilisation packages. During the 1980s, in order to qualify for loans from these institutions, almost all countries had to agree to a series of policy measures based on policy prescriptions firmly in favour of free markets. Many of the conditions attached to loans related to trade policy, and most required governments to reduce tariffs on imports and remove restrictions on exports.

Regional Trade Agreements

Regional Trade Agreements (RTAs) are arrangements negotiated to reduce trade barriers between specific groups of countries. There was a huge increase in the number of RTAs in the 1990s, and almost all countries belong to at least one. For many countries, RTAs are as important as WTO rules in limiting their options for trade policy. The WTO, however, as the multilateral forum, sets the conditions for RTAs.

For developing countries the aim of economic integration is normally not solely the reduction of tariffs, but the creation of larger combined markets for economies of scale, more efficient production and diversification of industry. For powerful countries, their bargaining power within a smaller group means that they can put a wide range of issues on the agenda for RTAs – such as making stronger provision for services or ensuring more rigorous technical and environmental standards.

Mercosur

Mercosur comprises Brazil, Argentina, Paraguay and Uruguay and has been relatively successful in implementing an RTA without serious delays and complications. It has not been dominated by one state, but the big economies of Brazil and Argentina have counterbalanced each other, and integrated faster than Paraguay and Uruguay. Mercosur developed in a two-stage process; a transition period until 1994 when tariffs were removed from 85 per cent of regional trade, and then in 1995 it became a customs union with an agreed Common External Tariff. Countries were allowed to exempt 300 products while converting to the RTA. Paraguay was given 399 exemptions in recognition of its weaker market position. Their agreement encompasses the elimination of import and export tariffs between members, which took place firstly between Brazil and Argentina and then progressed to the whole group. They have not just worked for integration in the area of trade but have also worked to form common agendas on education, justice, health, industry and culture.

NAFTA

The North American Free Trade Area (NAFTA) agreement – comprising the US, Canada and Mexico – was signed in 1992, coming into effect in January 1994. The US and Canada have gained from the opening up of the Mexican market, but it has been estimated that Mexico has gained comparatively less because on the products negotiated the tariffs for Mexican imports were comparatively low. Specifically, duties on automobiles and computers were immediately removed.[383] NAFTA also covers newer areas of competition policy, investment and intellectual property rights.

NAFTA seeks almost complete free trade and investment through the phasing out of all industrial and agricultural tariffs, over 10 to 15 years, and the elimination of most import quotas and agricultural export subsidies. NAFTA's provisions for investment liberalisation are the most far-reaching outside the EU and it also contains a comprehensive services agreement (allowing companies to sue governments for regulations and laws which have the effect of reducing companies' profits) with most services eventually being subject to de-regulation. Other provisions of the agreement are: extensive intellectual property rights; a government procurement code that greatly reduces domestic preference schemes; and a ban on export restrictions to the extent that the US can demand access to Canadian water and energy resources.[384]

NAFTA has been criticised for its top-down approach and lack of consultation with civil society in the negotiation process, benefiting large-scale capital at the expense of workers and vulnerable communities. Of particular concern has been the unequal impact that it has had on the development path of Mexico. Geographical areas close to the border and attached to private capital flows are developing rapidly at the expense of less connected communities, exacerbating inequality.

Even when they are not directly involved in a RTA, the interests of powerful rich country economies shape the formation of developing country RTAs. In southern Africa, the Southern African Development Community (SADC) has been strongly influenced by US and EU policies. Both the US and EU gave assistance when the RTA was being developed, and they influenced the negotiations through their trading relations with individual SADC members. Some of the most contentious issues discussed during the SADC negotiations were those associated with the agreement's relationship to other trading partners.

Bilateral trade deals

Although multilateral institutions get most of the attention, bilateral deals are often as important as multilateral rules in determining trade policy in developing countries. Like WTO agreements, regional trade agreements and World Bank conditionalities, bilateral deals are usually aimed at opening up markets.

The recent deal agreed between the EU and South Africa was signed at the end of 1999 after 22 rounds of talks over four years. Agriculture was one of the most controversial areas of the talks. At the beginning, the EU wanted to exclude large parts of agricultural trade from the agreement, but the South African negotiators succeeded in getting most sectors included, since this is one of the areas where South Africa is most likely to have a comparative advantage. In the end, South Africa managed to secure duty-free access to the EU for 62 per cent of its agricultural exports, but EU farmers will be able to export 81 per cent of their goods into South Africa duty free.

The full impact of the agreement will not be known until it is fully implemented in 2011. However, some of the effects can be predicted. Although some South African companies will gain from increased access to the EU market, the overall impact on the South African economy may well be negative. One estimate is that the countries of the Southern African Customs Union will suffer declines in revenue of up to £350 million a year.[385] A number of studies indicate that imports from the EU to South Africa will increase more than exports from South Africa to the EU – in other words, South Africa's trade balance will worsen. This may cause problems for the balance of payments, as

The EU and RTAs

The EU sits at the centre of a web of RTAs in a system that cuts across continents and development levels and has been categorised as a hub with many spokes. Some of the agreements are truly multilateral in nature and some increasingly bilateral with individual developing countries entering into negotiations with the whole EU. The EU agreement with South Africa came into being in 2000, an agreement with Mexico has been signed, and there are longer-term plans for agreements with Mercosur, Chile and a number of post Lomé partnership agreements. The EU's agreements typically call for harmonisation of standards to EC rather then international levels. Each agreement or spoke negotiated is subject to different rules. The EU is the only common denominator to all of its agreements, and as a result it is Europe that is likely to draw the main share of investment and be a more attractive location for production.

South Africa pays more for imports than it earns in exports, and there may be increased unemployment and financial instability which further undermines investment.[386] The impact on the southern African region may also be negative, as cheap goods from Europe flood into the markets of neighbouring countries through South Africa, and undercut local production.

The fact that South Africa, one of the more powerful of developing countries, felt that this agreement was the best it could get from the EU, illustrates the dire situation of developing countries in negotiating bilateral trade deals. Many commentators argue that developing countries are more likely to get positive results from multilateral negotiations, or from negotiating as trading blocs with industrialised countries. However, bilateral deals are an important instrument of trade policy for developed countries for the same reason – they are more likely to be able to pursue narrow self-interest through making a bilateral deal with one weak negotiating partner, than through deals with a range of countries at once.

The impact of liberalisation in five countries: the perspective of UNCTAD experts

An UNCTAD report from July 2000 contains analyses of the impact of liberalisation policies on agriculture in different countries, with a view to recommending what trade policies need to change to improve domestic food security in each country. The analyses consider the impact both of SAPs and the WTO agreements and all mention both positive and negative impacts in a series of country presentations by country experts. Five country presentations are highlighted here in full – although experiences have been different, they clearly show the need for the policy changes outlined in chapter 2.

Bolivia

'Bolivia uses only one quarter of its agricultural potential as a result of both external and internal factors. In 1996 a new regulatory framework was introduced with the aim of enhancing the use of agricultural potential and alleviating poverty while preserving the environment. This involved new laws on land, forests, water and the environment. As land constituted the only capital for indigenous peasants, their access to public land was central to the effort to reduce extreme rural poverty. The policy of Bolivia aimed at increasing agricultural productivity rather than bringing new land into production, which could have negative environmental implications. Bolivia's wheat production declined to negligible levels in the early 1990s as a result of competition from food aid shipments. A new policy introduced in 1992 among the major donors, the agricultural producers and the flour mills to maintain prices provoked a spectacular increase in land planted with wheat, from 3,500 hectares in 1994 to 112,000 hectares in 1997. The certified seed production policy had also been a success – seed production rose from 764 tons in 1981 to 43,155 tons in 1998 as a result of public and private sector co-operation, including research and transfer of technology. Soybean and oilseed production also increased dramatically, accounting for ten per cent of total exports. Bolivia eliminated its development banks at the beginning of the last decade, and no subsidized credit is available to producers. Micro-credit for small-farmers is now provided by NGOs. The main problem facing small farmers has been unfair competition from food aid and subsidized exports. Bolivia considers that the negotiations in the WTO should eliminate such unfair practices, since they create dependency and condemn the net food importers to remain in that category. Market access should be improved by attacking subsidies and high tariffs, as well as problems arising from sanitary and environmental regulations and standards. The concept of multifunctionality could lead to increased protection. If non-trade concerns are to be addressed in the ongoing negotiations, the focus should be on poverty reduction.'

Guinea

'Since 1986, Guinea, a least developed country, has adopted a new development policy based on the economic liberalisation and privatisation of productive and commercial activities. The rural sector and agricultural development have been at the core of these institutional and structural reforms. In 1991, the government elaborated the first Agricultural Development Policy (LPDA – Lettre de Politique de Développement Agricole) aiming at food security, export promotion and preservation of the production base. In 1997, the second LPDA was initiated within the framework of the medium- to long-term development strategy named "Guinea Vision 2010". In conjunction with those reform measures, Guinea became a member of the WTO in October 1995. The effect of market liberalisation since 1991 had, in some instances, led to a substantial increase in food imports. The lowering of the tariff on rice from 27 per cent to 22.5 per cent in 1992, for instance, was followed by a strong increase in rice imports from 1992 (182,160 tonnes) to 1995 (290,750 tonnes). Guinea also dismantled quantitative restrictions against a large number of imports, though certain measures are maintained for the protection of health, security and moral order. The domestic production of rice, potatoes and onions faces competition with subsidised exports of those products from other countries. The price gap between the locally produced rice and imported rice fell from 136 FG/kg in 1993 to 131 FG/kg in 1997. The ratio of imported rice to local consumption remains at 39 per cent. Given this high dependence on imports, the price fluctuations affecting imported rice (mainly from Asia) in the last six years have initiated an increase in the consumption of manioc and maize as substitutes for rice. With respect to agricultural exports, the reduction in tariff barriers and non-tariff barriers, as well as the continuation of preferential market access of which Guinea is a beneficiary, encouraged agricultural exports from Guinea. Looking at year-to-year growth of agricultural exports between 1998/1999 and 1999/2000, export quantities of pineapples, melons and water melons more than doubled. Exports of cotton and coffee also showed significant growth. The principal destinations of exports are the

European Union and Maghreb countries. There is a channel of commercial information for determining the needs for Guinea's products in major importing countries, supported by both the public and the private sectors. The current major objective in the agricultural sector is the horizontal and vertical diversification of export products. Guinea seeks to receive technical assistance from international organisations primarily in the following fields: increasing productivity of family farmers; organising the production and distribution of agricultural inputs; and introducing measures against plant disease affecting potatoes and citrus fruits.'

Guyana

'Guyana's agricultural sector is dominated by sugar (cane) and rice production, together comprising more than 50 per cent of total agricultural output. Exports of both sugar and rice depend on preferential marketing arrangements in Europe. Following the liberalisation of the economy in the early 1990s, there was a surge in imports, particularly of dairy products and of wheat and cereal preparations. The impact of adjustments in agricultural support budgets of developed countries will be felt increasingly by Guyana's agricultural sector. This is particularly so in the case of sugar, which is exported primarily to the EU (accounting for 90 per cent of total sugar exports) under preferential agreements. For rice, the impact of limited access to markets is already being felt in Guyana's traditional Caribbean markets, due in large measure to government-supported competition from the United States. Most of the rice entering the Jamaican market has been coming under the US non-donation food-aid programme (PL480), and is thus not subject to import tariffs. The impact of food aid on the competitiveness of developing country production should therefore be studied carefully. The poultry industry represents a case of an industry which has come under significant pressure from imports. Since the opening up of the economy, domestic producers have faced stiff competition from US poultry imports, consisting of frozen leg quarters. US poultry exporters enjoy considerable levels of export subsidies and export credits from their government. The domestic market for most other products (mainly tropical fruit and vegetables) has not been significantly affected either by trade liberalisation or by WTO reforms. The developments in 1998-1999 were more in line with the long-term declining trend in agricultural commodity prices. Moreover, it seems much clearer that the continued use of agricultural subsidies by developed countries is having an added depressing effect on world prices. In this respect, developing countries such as Guyana have an overriding interest in the existence of an international trading system that is as open and transparent as possible. In the WTO agriculture negotiations, therefore, strategies aimed at achieving swift and sharp cuts in government support measures will have to be worked out by developing countries with the ultimate aim of achieving world prices that are remunerative and sustainable. There is an understanding that the WTO process should deal specifically with commodities that are of export interest to developing countries, which would require an in-depth analysis of commodity-specific issues. UNCTAD, in conjunction with FAO and other international organisations, is encouraged to conduct a quantitative assessment of the levels of support and market access restrictions maintained by developed countries, and the economic effects that such measures are having on developing countries, at the commodity and country levels. On the issue of sanitary and phytosanitary measures (SPS), the position of some of the WTO members is that the SPS Agreement should not be open to negotiation. This should be of concern to the developing countries, since the SPS Agreement, as it is structured, leaves too much room for non-transparent procedures.'

Mali

'Mali is a sub-Saharan least developed country with 44 million hectares of cultivable land. Agriculture and animal breeding constitute the main activities in the rural areas of Mali. Food production is dominated by the production of cereals, mainly for subsistence purposes. Mali, like other sub-Saharan LDCs, has been engaged in structural adjustment programmes. In the 1980s, the goal of these programmes was to help the country to emerge from economic and social crises. Macroeconomic and sectoral programmes were used, including a programme for agriculture (PASA). All these programmes aimed at increasing productivity and the development of exports. The country has been continuing its structural adjustment efforts since 1992, the principal objectives being to: promote and diversify agricultural production; increase food security; and improve the use of natural resources. As a result, the agricultural sector has expanded, mainly in the subsectors of cereals and cotton. All in all, the agricultural sector has contributed positively to the recent economic performance of Mali, and it has accounted for 40-45 per cent of GDP since 1992. Animal breeding has also increased. In the case of cereals and cotton, the improvement can be explained by weather conditions and the expansion of the surface used for production. For rice, an additional factor has been higher yields. These changes took place thanks to the PASA. In short, SAPs have had a positive impact on the economy, while they have also had some perverse effects owing to the withdrawal of the State from certain support activities, such as subsidisation and supply of inputs, including credit, when the private sector was not ready to take them over. Agriculture in Mali is dependent on weather conditions. Despite the recent increase in agricultural production, Mali remains a net food-importing country. No domestic subsidies or internal support have been provided to the agricultural sector. The Uruguay Round has had no incidence on export opportunities, which continue to be based mainly on natural comparative advantage. Mali remains more vulnerable to changes in the prices of raw materials and to fluctuations in exchange rates than to the changes stemming from multilateral trade liberalisation. In conclusion, Mali will have to diversify its exports and gain access to new markets. However, to fight marginalisation in the global market, competitiveness needs to be combined with development aid.'

Tanzania

'Like many LDCs, the United Republic of Tanzania depends largely on agriculture. Since the mid-1980s, the Tanzanian economy has undergone gradual but fundamental transformation that has redefined the role of the government and the private sector in, inter alia, direct production, processing and marketing activities. However, the agricultural sector has failed to become an engine of growth, and has been disappointing in its role in poverty reduction and food security improvement. A number of constraints such as low investment, poor rural infrastructure, limited capital and access to financial services, and inadequate supporting services, including a weak and inappropriate legal framework, land tenure and taxation policy, have prevented the agricultural sector from performing well. The liberalisation process has activated the private sector in agricultural trade, and farmers were enabled to sell their products at the farm gate for cash, without the interference of any crop board. However, farmers often suffer from a lack of bargaining power, which they had enjoyed before as members of the now-defunct co-operative societies. The lack of market information and of sound storage facilities for stocking the harvest, as well as the de facto ban on cross-border trade of food crops, are among the most serious obstacles to the performance of farmers in this sector. With regard to the impact of the multilateral trading system on the United Republic of Tanzania, the Uruguay Round has had no or little beneficial effects in terms of market access, largely because the country is an insignificant producer from a global point of view. Reductions in export subsidies by developed countries have not been enough to increase Tanzania's exports of products where it has a comparative advantage. Other factors hindering increases in Tanzania's exports include the persistence of tariff peaks, tariff escalation and non-tariff barriers (eg SPS regulations) in major importers of Tanzania's products. The United Republic of Tanzania requires measures to overcome the constraints stemming from: the small domestic capital base for investment; the lack of trade, finance and working capital; the inadequacy of market information flows; the lack of commercially oriented extension services; poor technology and product quality; inadequate measurement, standards testing and quality systems; limited knowledge of regional and international markets, among other problems. In addition, the country needs technical assistance to develop sanitary policies and legislation. Regarding future negotiations, the main concerns of the United Republic of Tanzania relate to the possible rise in food prices and therefore an increase in the food import bill, the potential for erosion in concessions and preferences for agricultural products, and tariff escalation in respect of processed products. Issues of development must be addressed decisively.'

Draft Universal Human Rights guidelines for companies[i]

Preamble

Recalling that the Universal Declaration of Human Rights proclaims a common standard of achievement for all peoples and all nations, to the end that governments, other organs of society, and individuals shall strive by teaching and education to promote respect for human rights and freedoms and by progressive measures to secure their universal and effective recognition and observance,

Recognizing that even though governments have the primary responsibility to promote and protect human rights, companies, as organs of society, are also responsible for promoting and securing the human rights elaborated by the Universal Declaration of Human Rights,

Realizing that companies, their officers, and their workers are further obligated directly or indirectly to respect international human rights and other international legal standards in many UN treaties and other international instruments such as the Convention on the Prevention and Punishment of Genocide; the International Convention Against Torture and Other Forms of Cruel, Inhuman or Degrading Treatment or Punishment; the International Convention on the Elimination of All Forms of Racial Discrimination; the Convention on the Elimination of All Forms of Discrimination Against Women; the International Covenant on Economic, Social and Cultural Rights; International Covenant on Civil and Political Rights; the Convention on the Rights of the Child; the four Geneva Conventions for the Protection of Victims of Armed Conflict; the Nuremberg Charter; the Declaration on the Right and Responsibility of Individuals, Groups and Organs of Society to Promote and Protect Universally Recognized Human Rights and Fundamental Freedoms; the Rome Statute of the International Criminal Court; the Convention Against Transnational Organized Crime; the Convention on Civil Liability for Oil Pollution Damage; the Convention on Civil Liability for Damage Resulting from Activities Dangerous to the Environment; the Charter on Fundamental Rights of the European Union, the OECD's Convention on Combating Bribery of Foreign Public Officials in International Business Transactions, and other instruments,

Aware of the labour and other standards elaborated in the conventions and recommendations of the International Labour Organization and its Tripartite Declaration of Principles Concerning Multinational Enterprises and Social Policy as well as the Organisation for Economic Co-operation and Development Guidelines for Multinational Enterprises, and the UN Global Compact initiative which challenges business leaders to 'embrace and enact' nine basic principles with respect to human rights, labour, and the environment,

Conscious of the efforts of the ILO Committee on Multinational Enterprises, the OECD Committee on International Investment and Multinational Enterprises, and similar mechanisms, including the ILO Committee on Freedom of Association which has named companies implicated in governments' failure to comply with ILO Conventions 87 and 98, and seeking to supplement and assist their efforts to encourage companies to protect human rights,

Taking note of global trends which have increased the power and influence of companies – and particularly transnational corporations – on the economies of most countries and in international economic relations; and the growing number of companies which operate across national boundaries in a variety of arrangements resulting in economic activities beyond the reach of any one national system,

Noting that companies have a human rights impact on the lives of individuals through their employment practices, environmental policies, relationships with suppliers and consumers, interactions with governments, and other activities,

Taking into account the universality, indivisibility, interdependence, and interrelatedness of human rights, including the right to development that entitles every human person and all peoples to participate in; contribute to; and enjoy economic, social, cultural, and political development in which all human rights and fundamental freedoms can be fully realized,

Reaffirming that companies already have human rights responsibilities and that setting forth these human rights guidelines will supplement existing internationally recognized laws and standards and will aid in the clarification of those responsibilities,

Solemnly proclaims these Universal Human Rights Guidelines for Companies and urges that every effort be made so that they becomes generally known and respected:

A General obligations

1 While governments have the primary obligation to respect, ensure respect for, and promote internationally recognized human rights, companies also have the obligation to respect, ensure respect for, and promote international human rights within their respective spheres of activity and influence.

2 Nothing in these Guidelines shall diminish the human rights obligations of governments.

Commentary

a Companies shall inform themselves of the human rights impact of their principal activities and major proposed activities, so that they can avoid complicity in human rights abuses. Companies shall have the responsibility to ensure that their business activities do not contribute directly or indirectly to human rights abuses, and that they do not knowingly benefit from these abuses. Companies shall further refrain from activities that would undermine the rule of law as well as governmental and other efforts to promote and ensure respect for human rights, and shall use their influence in order to help promote and ensure respect for human rights. The Guidelines may not be used by governments as an excuse for failing to take action to protect human rights, for example, through the enforcement of existing laws.

B Right to equal treatment

3 Companies shall pursue policies which promote equality of opportunity and treatment, with a view towards eliminating discrimination based on race, colour, sex, religion, political opinion, nationality, social origin, social status, indigenous status, disability, age (over the age of majority), marital status, capacity to bear children, pregnancy, sexual orientation, genetic features, or other status of the individual unrelated to the individual's ability to perform his/her job, unless the selectivity is specifically designed to promote equality in employment or to protect health.

Commentary

a Companies shall treat each worker with equality, respect, and dignity. No worker shall be subject to direct or indirect physical, sexual, racial, psychological, verbal, or any other discriminatory form of harassment or abuse as defined above. No worker shall be subject to intimidation or degrading treatment; or be disciplined without fair procedures.

b All policies of companies, including, but not limited to those relating to recruitment, hiring, discharge, pay, promotion, and training shall be non-discriminatory as defined above. Companies shall establish a work environment in which it is clear that such discrimination will not be tolerated.

c In view of the prevalence of sex discrimination particular attention should be devoted to the consequences of company activities that may affect the rights of women.

d Companies shall treat other stakeholders, such as indigenous peoples and communities, with equality, respect, and dignity.

C Right to security of persons

4 **Companies shall not engage in nor benefit from war crimes, crimes against humanity, genocide, torture, forced disappearance, hostage-taking, abuses in internal armed conflict, and other international crimes against the human person.**

Commentary

a Companies, which supply military, security, or police products/services, shall take stringent steps to prevent those products and services from being used to commit human rights or humanitarian law violations.

b Companies shall not produce or sell weapons that have been declared illegal under international law. Companies shall not engage in trade that is known to lead to serious human rights abuses.

5 **Security arrangements for companies shall observe the law and professional standards of the country in which they operate in so far as those laws do not conflict with international human rights standards.**

Commentary

a Companies shall observe emerging best practices developed by the industry, civil society, and governments; and international human rights standards, particularly the UN Principles on the Use of Force and Firearms and the UN Code of Conduct for Law Enforcement Officers.

b Company security arrangements shall be used only for preventive or defensive services and they shall not be used for activities that are exclusively the responsibility of the state military or law enforcement services. Security personnel shall only use force when strictly necessary and only to an extent proportional to the threat.

c Security personnel shall not violate the rights of individuals while exercising the rights to freedom of association and peaceful assembly, to engage in collective bargaining, or to enjoy other related rights of workers as recognized by the Universal Declaration of Human Rights and the ILO Declaration on Fundamental Principles and Rights at Work.

d   Companies shall establish policies against hiring individuals or working with
    units of state security forces or contract security firms that are known to have
    been responsible for human rights abuses. To the extent of their resources and
    capabilities, companies shall ensure that guards in their employ are adequately
    trained, guided by, and particularly trained concerning relevant international
    limitations and caution with regard, for example, to the use of force and
    firearms as well for the handling of demonstrations. If a company contracts
    with a state security force or a private security firm, the relevant provisions of
    these Guidelines (4 and 5 as well as the related commentary) shall be incor-
    porated in the contract.
e   Companies using public security forces shall consult regularly with host govern-
    ments concerning the impact of their security arrangements on local
    communities, communicate their policies regarding ethical conduct and human
    rights, and express their desire that security be provided in a manner consis-
    tent with those policies by personnel with adequate and effective training.

D Rights of workers

6 Companies shall not use forced or slave labour.

Commentary
a   Companies shall not use slave, forced, indentured, or compulsory labour, as
    forbidden in ILO Conventions 29 and 105 (Forced and Bonded Labour).
    Workers shall be recruited, paid, and entitled to other working conditions so
    as to avoid debt bondage or other contemporary forms of slavery.
b   Workers shall have the option to leave employment and the employer must facil-
    itate such departure by providing all the necessary documentation and facilitation.

7 Companies shall not use child labour and shall contribute to its abolition.

Commentary
a   Child labour is defined as the employment of any person in regular work duties
    before the completion of compulsory schooling or the employment of any child
    below the age of 15 years, which employment is harmful to their health or
    development, will prevent the child from attending school or performing
    school-related responsibilities, or otherwise is not consistent with ILO Conven-
    tion 138 and Recommendation 146 (Minimum Age), ILO Convention 182
    and Recommendation 190 (Worst Forms of Child Labour), and the Conven-
    tion on the Rights of the Child.
b   Companies using child labour must create and implement a plan to eliminate
    child labour. Such a plan should assess what will happen to the children who

are no longer employed in the company and include measures such as withdrawing children from the workplace in tandem with the provision of suitable opportunities for schooling, vocational training, and other social protection for the children and their families, for example, by employing the parents or older siblings.

8 Companies shall provide a safe and healthy working environment.

Commentary
a Companies shall provide a safe and healthy working environment in accordance with the national requirements of the countries in which they are located and with international standards such as those found in ILO Conventions 81 (Labour Inspection Convention), 115 (Radiation Protection Convention), 119 (Guarding of Machinery Convention), 127 (Maximum Weight Convention), 129 (Agriculture Labour Inspection Convention), 135 (Workers' Representatives Convention), 136 (Benzene Convention), 148 (Working Environment (Air Pollution, Noise and Vibration) Convention), 155 (Occupational Safety and Health Convention), 161 (Occupational Health Services Convention), 162 (Asbestos Convention), 167 (Safety in Construction Convention), 170 (Chemicals Convention), 174 (Prevention of Major Industrial Accidents Convention), 176 (Safety and Health in Mines Convention), and other relevant recommendations. Such a safe and healthy work environment shall aid in the prevention of accidents and injuries arising out of, linked with, or occurring within the course of work.
b Companies shall make information about the health and safety standards relevant to their local activities available to their workers in the local language and in both written and oral form. The information shall also include arrangements for training in safe working practices and details on the effects of all substances used in manufacturing processes. In particular, companies shall make known any special hazards that tasks or conditions of work involve and the related measures available to protect the workers.
c Companies shall examine the causes of safety and health hazards in their industry and work to implement improvements and solutions to those conditions, including the provision of safe equipment at least consistent with industry standards. Companies shall investigate work-related accidents and keep records of all such incidents stating their cause and remedial measures taken to prevent similar accidents.
d Companies shall not require any worker to work more than 48 hours per week. Voluntary overtime for workers should not exceed 12 hours per week and should not be demanded on a regular basis. Compensation for such overtime should be at a rate higher than the normal rate. Each worker should be given

at least one day off in every seven-day period. These protections may be adjusted to meet the different needs of management personnel and professionals who have clearly indicated their personal desire to work more hours.

9 **Companies shall compensate workers with remuneration that ensures a lifestyle worthy of human existence for workers and their families in the context of their circumstances.**

Commentary

a Companies shall compensate workers for the work completed with just, favourable, and periodically regular remuneration ordinarily in legal tender at a level at least comparable to that received by similar workers (the prevailing industry wage) and adequate to ensure a lifestyle worthy of human existence for workers and their families in the context of their circumstances, as well as consistent with ILO Convention 100 (Equal Remuneration for Men and Women Workers for Work of Equal Value) and ILO Convention 111 (Discrimination in Respect of Employment and Occupation).

b Companies shall not deduct from a worker's wages already earned for disciplinary measures; nor shall any deduction from wages not provided in national law be permitted without the express permission of the worker concerned.

c Companies shall keep detailed written records on each worker's hours of work and wages paid. Workers shall be informed periodically as to the wages, salaries, and additional emoluments to which they are entitled. At the time workers are paid for their work, they shall receive an accounting in writing of hours worked and wages paid for the pay period.

10 **Companies shall ensure that all workers shall have the right to form and join organizations of their choosing, including trade unions, for the protection of their employment interests and for collective bargaining.**

Commentary

a Companies shall recognize the right of workers to establish and join organizations of their own choosing without previous authorization and without distinction whatsoever, subject only to restrictions consistent with ILO Convention 87 (Freedom of Association) and other international human rights law. Companies shall also recognize the rights of workers' organizations to draw up their constitutions and rules, to elect their representatives, to organize their administration and activities, and to formulate their programmes. Companies shall further refrain from any interference that restricts these rights or impedes their lawful exercise.

b Companies shall recognize workers' organizations for the purpose of collective bargaining consistent with ILO Convention 98 (Right to Collective Bargaining). Companies shall respect the right of workers to submit grievances, including grievances as to compliance with these Guidelines; to have those grievances examined by fair and impartial persons who have the authority to redress any abuses found, pursuant to the appropriate procedure; and to be protected from suffering prejudice for using those procedures.

c   Companies shall enable representatives of their workers to conduct negotiations on their terms and conditions of employment with representatives of management who are authorized to make decisions about the issues under negotiation. Companies shall further give workers and their representative access to information, facilities, and other resources, as consistent with ILO Convention 135 and Recommendation 129 (Workers' Representatives Convention) that are relevant and necessary for their representatives to conduct negotiation effectively without unnecessary harm to legitimate employer interests.

d   Companies shall abide by provisions in collective agreements that provide for the settlement of disputes arising over their interpretation and application and also by decisions of tribunals or other mechanisms empowered to make determinations on such matters.

e   Companies shall take particular care to protect the rights of workers as to such procedures in countries that do not fully implement international standards regarding the freedom of association, the right to organize, and the right to bargain collectively.

E Respect for national sovereignty and local communities

11 Companies shall recognize and respect the national laws; regulations; administrative practices; the rule of law; self-determination; values; development objectives; social, economic, and cultural policies; and authority of the countries in which the companies operate, in so far as they do not conflict with international human rights standards.

Commentary

a   Companies, within the limits of their resources and capabilities, shall endeavour to encourage social progress and development by engaging in constructive business activities and expanding economic opportunities – particularly in developing countries and most importantly in the least developed countries.

b   Companies shall respect the right to development in which all peoples are entitled to participate in, contribute to, and enjoy economic, social, cultural, and political development, in which all human rights and fundamental freedoms can be fully realized and in which sustainable development can be achieved so as to protect the rights of future generations.

c Companies shall respect the rights of local communities affected by their activities. Companies shall particularly respect the rights of indigenous peoples and similar communities to own, develop, control, protect, and use their lands, other natural resources, and cultural and intellectual property. Indigenous peoples and communities may not be deprived of their own means of subsistence. Companies shall respect indigenous control, use, and occupancy of their lands and resources. Companies should avoid endangering the health, environment, culture, and institutions of indigenous peoples and communities in the context of projects, including road building in or near indigenous peoples and communities. Companies shall use particular care in situations in which indigenous lands, resources, or rights thereto have not been adequately demarcated or defined.

d Companies shall protect and enforce intellectual property rights in a manner that contributes to the promotion of technological innovation and to the transfer and dissemination of technology, to the mutual advantage of producers and users of technological knowledge in a manner conducive to social and economic welfare, and to a balance of rights and obligations.

12 **Companies shall not offer, promise, give, accept, or demand a bribe or other improper advantage, nor shall they be solicited or expected to give a bribe or other improper advantage to any government or government official.**

Commentary

a Companies shall enhance the transparency of their activities in this regard; openly fight against bribery, extortion, and other forms of corruption; and cooperate with state authorities responsible for combating corruption.

13 **Companies shall respect the rights to health, adequate food, and adequate housing, and refrain from actions that obstruct the realization of those rights. Companies shall also respect other economic, social, and cultural rights, such as the rights to primary education, rest and leisure, and participation in the cultural life of the community and refrain from actions that obstruct the realization of those rights.**

Commentary

a Companies shall observe standards that promote the availability, accessibility, acceptability, and quality of the right to health as identified in Article 12 of the Covenant on Economic, Social and Cultural Rights, and the General Comment on the right to the highest attainable standard of health.[ii]

b Companies shall observe standards which promote the availability of food in a quantity and quality sufficient to satisfy the dietary needs of individuals, free from adverse substances, acceptable within a given culture, accessible in ways that are sustainable and do not interfere with the enjoyment of other human rights, and otherwise in accordance with Article 11 of the Covenant on Economic, Social and Cultural Rights, and the General Comment on the right to adequate food.[iii]

c Companies shall further observe standards which protect the right to adequate housing and are otherwise in accordance with Article 11 of the Covenant on Economic, Social and Cultural Rights, and the General Comment on the right to adequate housing.[iv] Companies shall not forcibly evict individuals, families, and/or communities against their will from their homes and/or land which they occupy, without the provision of, and access to, appropriate forms of legal or other protection pursuant to international human rights law.

d Companies shall observe standards that protect other economic, social and cultural rights and are otherwise in accordance with the Covenant on Economic, Social and Cultural Rights, and the relevant General Comments.

e In making siting decisions – particularly as to larger tracts of land – and decisions to depart from a community, companies shall assess the foreseeable consequences of their activities as to displacing people from their habitats and shelter, upsetting food security, diminishing health care, and decreasing the availability of primary education.

14 **Companies shall respect other civil and political rights, such as freedom of movement; freedom of thought, conscience, and religion; and freedom of opinion and expression and refrain from actions, which obstruct the realization of those rights.**

Commentary

a Companies shall observe standards that protect civil and political rights and are otherwise in accordance with the Covenant on Civil and Political Rights and the relevant General Comments.

F Obligations with regard to consumer protection

15 **Companies shall act in accordance with fair business, marketing, and advertising practices and should take all reasonable steps to ensure the safety and quality of the goods and services they provide.**

Commentary

a Companies shall adhere to relevant international standards so as to avoid variations in the quality of products that would have detrimental effects on consumers, especially in states lacking specific regulations on product quality.

b Companies shall disclose to the public all appropriate information on the contents and possible hazardous effects of the products they produce through proper labeling, informative and accurate advertising, and other appropriate methods. In particular, they shall warn if death or serious injury is probable from a defect, use, or misuse.

c Companies shall supply appropriate information to the relevant authorities regarding the characteristics of products or services that may cause injury to the health and safety of consumers, workers, or others as well as restrictions, warnings, and other regulatory measures imposed by several countries on the grounds of health and safety protection as to these products or services.

G Obligations with regard to environmental protection

16 Companies shall carry out their activities in accordance with national laws, regulations, administrative practices, and policies relating to the preservation of the environment of the countries in which they operate and with due regard to relevant international agreements, principles, objectives, and standards with regard to the environment as well as human rights; shall take due account of the need to protect the environment, public health, and safety; and shall generally conduct their activities in a manner contributing to the wider goal of sustainable development.

Commentary

a Companies shall respect the right to a clean and healthy environment in light of the relationship between environment and human rights; concerns for intergenerational equity; and internationally recognized environmental standards, for example, with regard to air pollution, water pollution, land use, biodiversity, and hazardous wastes.

b Companies shall be responsible for the environmental and human health impact of all of their activities, including any products or services they introduce into commerce, including packaging, transportation, and by-products of the manufacturing process.

c In decision-making processes, companies shall assess the impact of their activities on the environment and human health including impacts from siting decisions; natural resource extraction activities; the production and sale of products or services; and the generation, storage, transport, and disposal of hazardous and toxic substances.

d Companies shall undertake environmental and social assessments on a periodic basis (preferably annually or biannually). Assessments shall, interalia, address particularly the impact of proposed activities on women. Companies shall distribute such reports in a timely manner and in a manner that is accessible to the United Nations Environmental Programme, the International Labour Organization, other interested international bodies, the national government hosting each company, the national government where the company maintains its principal office, and other affected groups. The reports should be accessible to the general public.

e Companies shall respect the prevention principle, for example, by preventing and/or mitigating deleterious impacts identified in any assessment. Companies shall respect the precautionary principle, which indicates, for example, that when preliminary risk assessments indicate unacceptable effects on health or the environment, companies shall not use the lack of full scientific certainty as a reason to delay the introduction of cost-effective measures intended to prevent such effects. Companies should consider any reactions from stakeholders in endeavouring to prevent environmental and human rights consequences.

f Upon the expiration of the useful life of their products or services, companies shall be responsible for collecting or arranging for the collection of the remains of the product or services for recycling, re-use, and/or environmentally acceptable disposal.

g Companies shall take appropriate measures in their activities to reduce the risk of accidents and damage to the environment by adopting best management practices and technologies. In particular, companies shall use best management practices and appropriate technologies and enable their component entities to meet these environmental objectives through the sharing of technology, knowledge, and assistance, as well as through environmental management systems and sustainability reporting. In addition, they shall educate and train workers to ensure their compliance with these objectives.

H General provisions of implementation

17 Each company shall adopt, disseminate, and implement its own code of conduct or shall take other adequate measures to afford at least the protections set forth in these Guidelines.

Commentary

a Each company shall disseminate its code of conduct or similar measures, as well as implementation procedures, and make them available to all relevant stakeholders. The company code of conduct or similar measures shall be communicated in oral and written form in the language of workers, contractors, suppliers, customers, and other stakeholders of the company.

b Once a company's code of conduct or similar measures have been adopted and disseminated, companies shall – to the extent of their resources and capabilities – provide effective training for their managers as well as workers and their representatives in company practices relevant to the Guidelines.

c To the extent of its resources and capabilities, companies shall endeavour to assure that they only purchase products and services from contractors, subcontractors, suppliers, and licensees who follow these or substantially similar Guidelines. Companies using suppliers that do not meet the Guidelines should take all necessary steps to reform or decrease these violations and if a supplier will not change, the company should cease doing business with the supplier.

d Each company shall take adequate measures to afford at least the protections set forth in these Guidelines and shall endeavour to improve continually its further implementation of these Guidelines.

e Companies shall inform in a timely manner everyone who may be affected by conditions caused by the company that might endanger health, safety, or the environment.

f Companies shall provide adequate reparation to those persons who have been adversely affected by restoring, replacing, or otherwise compensating for any damage done or property taken.

18 Companies shall monitor and verify their compliance with these Guidelines in a manner that is independent, transparent, and includes input from relevant stakeholders.

Commentary

a Companies shall provide legitimate and confidential avenues through which workers can file complaints with regard to such issues. To the extent possible, companies shall make known to the complainant any actions taken as a result of the investigation. Companies shall not discipline or take other action against workers or others who submit complaints or assert that any company has failed to comply with these Guidelines.

b Companies receiving claims of violations of this code shall make a record of each claim and obtain an independent investigation of the claim or call upon other proper authorities. Companies shall actively monitor the status of investigations and press for their full resolution.

c Companies shall accept independent monitoring of their compliance with these Guidelines so long as the monitoring does not unduly interfere with work being performed. Companies shall also endeavour to assure such monitoring of their suppliers to the extent possible. In addition, companies shall comply with relevant governmental procedures, including, for example labour inspections.

d Companies shall endeavor to ensure the monitoring process is transparent, for example, by making available to relevant stakeholders the workplaces observed, remediation efforts undertaken, and other results of monitoring. Companies shall further ensure that any monitoring seeks to obtain and incorporate input from relevant stakeholders.

e Companies shall further enhance the transparency of their activities by disclosing timely, relevant, regular, and reliable information regarding their activities, structure, financial situation, and performance. Companies shall also make known the location of their offices, subsidiaries, and factories, so as to facilitate measures to assure that the companies' products and services are being produced under conditions that respect these Guidelines.

19 **Companies shall assess their major activities to determine their human rights impact in light of these Guidelines.**

Commentary

a Each company shall engage in an annual or other periodic self-assessment of its compliance with the Guidelines taking into account comments from stakeholders. The results of the self-assessment shall be made available to stakeholders to the same extent as the company's annual report.

b Assessments revealing inadequate compliance with the Guidelines shall also include plans of action or methods of redress a company will pursue in order to fulfill the Guidelines.

c Before a company pursues a major initiative or project, it shall, to the extent of its resources and capabilities, study the human rights impact of that project in light of these Guidelines. The impact statement shall include a description of the action, its need, anticipated benefits, an analysis of any human rights impact related to the action, an analysis of reasonable alternatives to the action, and identification of ways to reduce any negative human rights consequences. A company shall make available the results of that study to relevant stakeholders, and shall consider any reactions from stakeholders.

d Before entering into new business relationships, companies shall assess the compliance of these potential business partners with the standards set forth in these Guidelines.

20 **Nothing in the present Guidelines shall be interpreted as restricting or adversely affecting human rights recognized in international law, national or state law, or the activities of companies.**

I Definitions

21 **The term 'company' includes any business enterprise, regardless of the international or domestic nature of its activities; the corporate, partnership, or other legal form used to establish the business entity; and the nature of the**

ownership of the entity, including any privately-owned or government-owned entity.

22 The term 'stakeholder' includes stockholders, other owners, workers, and their representatives, as well as any other individual or group that is affected by the activities of the company.

Commentary

a   The term 'stakeholder' should be interpreted functionally in light of the objectives of these Guidelines and include indirect stakeholders when their interests are or will be substantially affected by the activities of the company. In addition to parties directly affected by the activities of companies, stakeholders can include parties which are indirectly affected by the activities of companies such as consumer groups, customers, governments, neighboring communities, NGOs, public and private lending institutions, suppliers, trade associations, and others.

b   The terms 'contractor,' 'subcontractor,' 'supplier,' and 'licensee' includes any natural or legal person who contracts with the company to accomplish the company's activities.

c   The phrases 'internationally recognized human rights' and 'international human rights' include economic, social, and cultural rights; and civil and political rights as guaranteed by the International Bill of Human Rights ᵛ and the other human rights treaties, as well as rights guaranteed by international humanitarian law, international refugee law, international labour law, and other relevant instruments promulgated by the United Nations.

NOTES

i   UN Commission on Human Rights, Sub-Commission on the Promotion and Protection of Human Rights, E/CN.4/Sub.2/2001/WG.2/WP.1/Add.1 (2001).

ii   Committee on Economic, Social and Cultural Rights, General Comment 14, The right to the highest attainable standard of health (Art. 12), UN Doc. E/C.12/2000/4 (2000).

iii   Committee on Economic, Social and Cultural Rights, General Comment 12, Right to adequate food (Art. 11), U.N. Doc. E/C.12/1999/5 (1999).

iv   Committee on Economic, Social and Cultural Rights, General Comment 4, The right to adequate housing (Art. 11 (1) of the Covenant) (Sixth session, 1991), Compilation of General Comments and General Recommendations Adopted by Human Rights Treaty Bodies, U.N. Doc. HRI\GEN\1\Rev.1 at 53 (1994).

v   The International Bill of Human Rights includes the Universal Declaration of Human Rights; the International Covenant on Economic, Social and Cultural Rights; the International Covenant on Civil and Political Rights; and the optional protocols to the Covenant on Civil and Political Rights.

Notes

1 AIM news cast, 1 January 2001
2 *South African Bulletin of Statistics*, Vol.34, No.2, December 2000, table 2.2.4
3 John Madeley, *Hungry for Trade*, Zed, London, 2000
4 'Feed Banned in Britain dumped on Third World', *Observer* (London), 29 October 2000
5 UNDP, *Human Development Report 1999*, p92
6 Mozambique News Agency, *AIM Reports*, No.204, April 2001
7 Institute of Development Studies, *Study on the economic impact of introducing reciprocity into the trade relations between the EU and CARICOM/ Dominican Republic*, Brighton, UK, Sept. 1998
8 G. Moon, *Free Trade: What's in it for women?*, Community Aid Abroad, Background Report No.6, 1995
9 UN Subcommission on the Promotion and Protection of Human Rights, *The realisation of economic, social and cultural rights: Globalisation and its impact on the full enjoyment of human rights*, preliminary report, 52nd session, 15 June 2000, p14
10 Moon, *Free Trade*
11 UN Subcommission on the Promotion and Protection of Human Rights, *Globalisation and human rights*, pp13-14
12 Moon, *Free Trade*
13 World Bank, *World Development Report 2000*, WTO, Sub-Committee on the Least developed Countries, 'Market access conditions for least developed countries', WT/LDC/SWG/IF/14/Rev.1, 20 April 2001, p2
14 Figures from World Bank, *World Development Report 2000*, based on totals for low-income countries. Total export earnings: $209,252 million (table 15, p302). Total ODA: $16,919 million (table 21, pp314-315, for ODA per capita; table 1, pp274-275 for population size).
15 WTO Annual Report, *International Trade Statistics*, Geneva, 2000
16 Uri Dadush, *in* WTO, Sub-Committee on the

Least Developed Countries, 'The policy relevance of mainstreaming trade into country development strategies', WT/LDC/SWG/IF/15/Rev.1, WTO, Geneva, January 2001, p112
17 World Bank, *World Development Report 2000*, table 15, pp302-303
18 UNCTAD, *Trade and Development Report 2001*, UN, New York/Geneva, 2001, p34
19 International Trade Centre, 'Product profile: Coffee', discussion document for the Third UN Conference on the Least Developed Countries, Brussels, 16 May 2001

CHAPTER 2

20 Roger Normand, 'Separate and unequal: Trade and human rights regime', background paper for the *Human Development Report 2000*, UNDP, New York, January 2000, p2
21 UNDP, *Human Development Report 1997*, OUP, New York/London, 1997, p82
22 *Hansard*, 24 January 2000, Col. 73W
23 FAO, 'Experience with the Implementation of the Uruguay Round Agreement on Agriculture: Synthesis of Fourteen Country Case Studies', Commodity Policy and Projections Service, Commodities and Trade Division, Rome, 2000
24 See WTO, Committee on Agriculture, proposal to the June 2000 special session by the group of 11 developing countries (Cuba, Dominican Republic, Honduras, Pakistan, Haiti, Nicaragua, Kenya, Uganda, Zimbabwe, Sri Lanka and El Salvador), 23 June 2000
25 UN General Assembly, Intergovernmental Preparatory Committee for the Third United Nations Conference on the Least Developed Countries, 'A compendium of the major constraints on development and desirable actions for the decade 2001-2010', A/CONF.191/IPC/18, 26 January 2001
26 UNCTAD, *Trade and Development Report 1999*, Geneva/New York, 1999, page v

27 UN Subcommission on the Promotion and Protection of Human Rights, *The realisation of economic, social and cultural rights: Globalisation and its impact on the full enjoyment of human rights*, preliminary report, 52nd session, 15 June 2000, p6

28 Office of the US Trade Representative, Charlene Barshefsky, 'The World Trade Organisation works for you', at: www.ustr.gov/html/wto4you.html

29 WTO, Committee on Agriculture, 'WTO negotiations on agriculture: Proposal by Kenya', 12 March 2001

30 Uri Dadush, Director, Economic Policy and Development Prospects Group, World Bank, *in* WTO, Sub-Committee on the Least Developed Countries, 'The policy relevance of mainstreaming trade into country development strategies', WT/LDC/SWG/IF/15/Rev.1, WTO, Geneva, January 2001, p112

31 56.1 per cent of the world's population – 2.8 billion people – lived on less than $2 a day in 1998, according to the World Bank, at: World Bank, *Global economic prospects and the developing countries*, 2001, at: www.worldbank.org/poverty/data/trends/scenario.htm

32 Statement to the Third UN Conference on the Least Developed Countries, May 2001

33 WTO, 'Mainstreaming trade', p3

34 Overseas aid to the least developed countries has dropped by 45 per cent in real terms since 1990. Although private flows have been increasing, per capita total capital inflows to the least developed countries have fallen by 39 per cent in real terms since 1990. Only 8 LDCs are on target to reach the UN goal of universal primary education by 2015, and only 7 expected to reduce infant mortality by two-thirds. *See* UNCTAD, press release, 'World's poorest countries losing ground, warns new UNCTAD report', 12 October 2000

35 B. Milancovic, 'True World Income distribution, 1988 and 1993: first calculation based on household surveys alone', World Bank, Washington DC, 1999

36 WTO, 'Mainstreaming trade', p63

37 www.wto.org/english/docs_e/legal_e/04-wto.pdf

38 J. Michael Finger and Philip Schuler, 'Implementation of Uruguay Round Commitments: the Development Challenge', paper presented at 606th Wilton Park Conference – Prospects for Trade Liberalisation in the New Millennium, July 2000

39 Quoted in Gerard Greenfield, 'The success of being dangerous: Resisting free trade and investment regimes', *Focus on trade*, No.57, Focus on the Global South, Bangkok, December 2000, p4

40 At least, this will be the case when China finally joins the WTO

41 Roger Normand, 'Separate and unequal', p21

42 WTO, 'Mainstreaming trade', p33

43 UNCTAD, 'Plan of action', TD/386, 18 February 2000

44 Uri Dudesh, WTO, 'Mainstreaming trade', p118

45 UNDP, *Human Development Report 1999*, New York/Geneva, 1999, p35

46 *Financial Times*, 30 May 2001

CHAPTER 3

47 Statement by the Organisation of African Unity, UNCTAD X, Bangkok, 12-19 February 2000

48 UNCTAD, 'Plan of action', TD/386, 18 February 2000

49 FAO, Commodity Policy and Projections Service, Commodities and Trade Division, 'Measures to enhance agricultural development, trade and food security in the context of the forthcoming WTO negotiations', presented to FAO symposium on agriculture, trade and food security, Geneva, September 1999

50 Interview with Christian Aid, in Geneva, October 2000

51 Bhagirath Lal Das, *The World Trade Organisation: A guide to the framework for international trade*, Zed/Third World Network, London/Malaysia, 1999, passim

52 Speech to the Third UN Conference on the Least Developed Countries, Brussels, 17 May 2001

53 See Aileen Kwa, 'The Agreement on Agriculture: Change requires a hero's journey', *Focus on trade*, No.57, Focus on the Global South, Bangkok, December 2000, p39; FAO, 'Experience with the implementation of the Uruguay Round Agreement on Agriculture: Synthesis of Fourteen Country Case Studies', Commodity Policy and Projections Service, Commodities and Trade Division, Rome, 2000

54 UNCTAD, Trade and Development Board, Commission on Trade in Goods and Services and Commodities, 5th session, 'Report on the expert meeting on the impact of the reform process in agriculture, July 2000', 26 February 2001, TD/B/COM.1.31, p16

55 FAO, 'Experience with the implementation of the Uruguay Round Agreement on Agriculture: Synthesis of Fourteen Country Case Studies', Commodity Policy and Projections Service, Commodities and Trade Division, Rome, 2000

56 UNCTAD, 'Reform process in agriculture', p18

57 Aileen Kwa, 'The Agreement on Agriculture: Meaningful Special and Differential Treatment', paper presented at seminar on WTO negotia-

tions on Agriculture: Setting the Right Agenda, Geneva, October 2000

58 Sophia Murphy, *Trade and Food Security – An Assessment of the Uruguay Round Agreement on Agriculture*, CIIR, London, 1999

59 Ceesay and Jagne, *Dumping and food security: A case study from Gambia*, ActionAid, London, 2000

60 FAO, 'Implementation of the Uruguay Round'

61 Cited in John Madeley (ed.), *Trade and the Hungry*, Aprodev, Brussels, 1999

62 UNCTAD, Trade and Development Board, 5th session, 'Report of the expert meeting on the impact of the reform process in agriculture, July 2000', 26 February 2001, TD/B/COM.1/31, p4

63 Ibid., p23

64 Cited in 'Cakes and caviar: The Dunkel draft and Third World agriculture', *The Ecologist*, Vol.23, No.6, November 1993, p220

65 See Kevin Watkins, 'Free trade and farm fallacies', *The Ecologist*, Vol.26, No.2, November/December 1996, p252

66 UNCTAD, Trade and Development Board, 'Report of the expert meeting on examining trade in the agricultural sector, April 1999', 5 August 1999, TD/B/COM.1/23, p5

67 WTO, Committee on Agriculture, Statement by Bolivia, 15 November 2000

68 UNCTAD, 'Subsidies, countervailing measures and developing countries', UNCTAD/DITC/COM/23, 4 July 2000, p12

69 Ibid., p23

70 Panos Konandreas, 'Overview of Implementation experiences and possible negotiating objectives', paper presented at seminar on WTO negotiations on Agriculture: Setting the Right Agenda, South Centre/IATP/Action Aid/Focus on the Global South, Geneva, October 2000

71 International Trade Centre, 'Product profile: Textiles and garments', discussion document for the Third UN Conference on the Least Developed Countries, Brussels, 16 May 2001, p16

72 UNCTAD, Trade in the agricultural sector', p10

73 Cited in Ruth Caplan, 'GATS Handbook', Alliance for Democracy at: www.afd-online.org/campaigns

74 'Towards GATS 2000', EU website at: gats-info.eu.int

75 Bhagirath Lal Das, *The World Trade Organisation*, pp325-30

76 WTO, Sub-Committee on the Least Developed Countries, 'Market access conditions for least developed countries', WT/LDC/SWG/IF/14/Rev.1, 20 April 2001, p7

77 Sarah Sexton, 'Trading health care away?: GATS, public services and privatisation', *Cornerhouse briefing 23*, July 2001, at: cornerhouse.icaap.org

78 'Trading into the future', WTO website: www.wto.org

79 Cited in World Development Movement, 'In whose service? The threat posed by the General Agreement on Trade in services to economic development in the South', London, December 2000, p4

80 Cited in Ellen Gould, 'The 2001 GATS negotiations: The political challenge ahead', The Alliance for Democracy, March 2001, at: www.thealliancefordemocracy.org/campaigns/2000/Globalization/2001_gats_negotiations.htm

81 Graham Dunkley, *The free trade adventure: The WTO, the Uruguay Round and globalism*, Zed, London, 2000, pp175-6

82 'What the General Agreement on Trade in Services can do', speech to the conference, 'Opening markets for banking worldwide', London, 8 January 1997

83 Cited in World Development Movement, 'Stop the GATastrophe', London, November 2000, p2

84 Cited in World Development Movement, 'In whose service?', pp5-6

85 Cited in *Corporate Europe Observatory*, No.9, June 2001, p13

86 Cited in *Corporate Europe Observatory*, No.6, April 2000

87 Speech by Lord Brittan of Spennithorne, 'Liberalising world trade: Why business must make its voice heard', February 2001, at: www.bi.org.uk. See also the website of *Corporate Europe Observatory* at: www.xs4all.nl/~ceo/ See also *Corporate Europe Observatory*, No.8, April 2001, p4

88 C.Raghavan, *Recolonisation: GATT, the Uruguay Round and the Third World*, Third World Network, Penang, 1990, p108

89 Communication from the United States to the WTO's Council for Trade in Services, S/CSS/W/4, 13 July 2000

90 Scott Sinclair, 'The GATS negotiations: State of play', *Briefing Paper Series: Trade and Investment*, Vol.2, No.2, Canadian Centre for Policy Alternatives, 19 February 2001, pp1-2

91 Ibid., p4. See especially the website of European Services Forum: www.esf.be

92 Ibid., p4

93 For excellent NGO analysis of the current state of GATS negotiations and potential threats of future agreements, see the Council of Canadians website, at: www.canadians.org

94 at: www.europa.eu.int/comm/trade/services/index_en.html

95 Communication from the United States, S/CSS/W/4

96 Cited in Sexton, 'Trading health care away?'

97 Ibid.

98 Scott Sinclair, 'How the WTO's new "services" negotiations threaten democracy', Canadian Centre for Policy Alternatives at: www.policyalternatives.ca, p5

99 See World Development Movement, 'In whose service?', pp13-16

100 Maude Barlow, 'A GATS primer', The Council of Canadians at: www.canadians.org/campaigns. The US chair of Xerox has also said, referring to education, that 'business will have to set the agenda… a complete restructure driven by competition and market discipline, unfamiliar grounds for educators'. Cited in Ruth Caplan, 'GATS Handbook', Alliance for Democracy at: www.afd-online.org/campaigns

101 Ellen Gould, 'Separating WTO fact and fiction', at: www.canadians.org/campaigns/ campaigns-tradepub-gats-fact_fiction-1.html

102 'Swedish advert ban breaches EU treaty', Financial Times, 9 March 2001

103 Aileen Kwa, 'Transparency and institutional issues a year after Seattle', Focus on trade, No.57, Focus on the Global South, Bangkok, December 2000, p17

104 High-level brainstorming meeting for African trade negotiators preparatory to the fourth WTO ministerial conference, Ethiopia, June 2001, at: www.uneca.org/eca_resources

105 Speech to the European Services Forum conference, 27 November 2000

106 'Should the WTO be abolished?', The Ecologist, Vol.30, No.9, December 2000, p20

107 Gerard Greenfield, 'The WTO agreement on Trade-related Investment Measures (TRIMs)', Briefing Paper Series: Trade and Investment, Vol.2, No.1, Canadian Centre for Policy Alternatives, 17 January 2001, pp1-2

108 See Bhagirath Lal Das, The World Trade Organisation, pp99-113, 139-50

109 WTO, Council for Trade in Goods, Philippines request pursuant to Article 5.3 of the Agreement on TRIMs, reply to written questions from the EU, G/C/W/170, 12 December 1999

110 B.Bora, P.Lloyd and M. Pangestu, Industrial Policy and the WTO, Policy Issues in International Trade and Commodities, Study Series No.6, UNCTAD, Geneva, 2000

111 High-level meeting for African negotiators, fourth WTO ministerial conference

112 Gerard Greenfield, 'WTO agreement on TRIMs', p7

113 Manuel Agosin and Ricardo Mayer, 'Foreign Investment in Developing Countries: Does it crowd in domestic investment?', UNCTAD discussion paper, No.146, February 2000

114 Eliminating world poverty:Making globalisation work for the poor, White Paper on International Development, Cm5006, HMSO, London, December 2000, para 154

115 DAC, Development Cooperation 1996 report, OECD, Paris, 1997, pp25, 50-51

116 Agosin and Mayer, 'Foreign Investment in Developing Countries'

117 UNIDO press release, Inter Press Service, 11 November 1996

118 UNCTAD, Trade and Development Report 2000, New York/Geneva, 2000, page vii

119 Gerard Greenfield, 'WTO agreement on TRIMs', p1

120 George Monbiot, Guardian, 15 April 1997

121 A subsidy is essentially a financial contribution by a government (or other public body) involving a direct transfer of funds (such as grants or loans) or a potential direct transfer of funds (such as loan guarantees). A subsidy is considered to exist if there is any form of income or price support, and a benefit is thereby conferred. UNCTAD, 'Subsidies, countervailing measures and developing countries', UNCTAD/DITC/ COM/23, 4 July 2000, p4

122 Bhagirath Lal Das, 'Strengthening developing countries in the WTO', Trade and development series No.8, Third World Network, www.twnside.org.sg, p6

123 Bhagirath Lal Das, The World Trade Organisation, pp241-9

124 Australian Bureau of Agricultural and Resource Economics, ABARE Current Issues, 'The US and EU agricultural support: who does it benefit', Canberra: ABARE/RIRDC

125 'Making the CAP fit', Financial Times, 17 April 2001

126 'Revealed: How Britain's richest man takes a £3m tax hand-out', Observer, 20 May 2001

127 WTO Secretariat, Committee on Agriculture, Special session, Domestic Support Background Paper, April 2000

128 FAO, 'Experience with the Implementation of the Uruguay Round Agreement on Agriculture: Synthesis of Fourteen Country Case Studies', Commodity Policy and Projections Service, Commodities and Trade Division, FAO, Rome, 2000

129 Nick Lardy, of the Brookings Institution, in 'Prospect of WTO entry looks distant for China', Financial Times, 14 March 2001

130 See Sibalwa Mwaanga, 'Forming the next government in Zambia: Which way will the

pendulum swing?', *Human Rights Review* (Afronet), Vol.4, 2000; Mercedes Sayagues, 'Southern Africa shifts food strategies', *Africa Recovery*, undated, at: www.un.org/ecosocdev/geninfo/afrec

131 UNCTAD, 'Subsidies, countervailing measures and developing countries', UNCTAD/DITC/COM/23, 4 July 2000, pp23-4

132 Ibid., p24

133 Dot Keet, *Alternatives to the WTO regime*, Alternative Information and Development Centre, Cape Town, November 2000, p27

134 UN General Assembly, Intergovernmental Preparatory Committee for the Third United Nations Conference on the Least Developed Countries, 'A compendium of the major constraints on development and desirable actions for the decade 2001-2010', A/CONF.191/IPC/18, 26 January 2001

135 Inge Nora Neufeld, 'Anti-dumping and countervailing procedures – use or abuse?', *Policy issues in international trade and commodities*, Study series No.9, UNCTAD, New York/Geneva, 2001

136 Cited in UNCTAD, 'Subsidies, countervailing measures', p22

137 Bhagirath Lal Das, *The World Trade Organisation*, pp153-62

138 Cited in UNCTAD, 'Subsidies, countervailing measures', p9

139 UN General Assembly, 'A compendium of the major constraints'

140 Cited in Aileen Kwa, 'The à la carte undertaking: A new form of special and differential treatment?', *Focus on trade*, No.57, Focus on the Global South, Bangkok, December 2000, p23

141 Bhagirath Lal Das, 'Some key issues relating to the WTO', at: www.twnside.org.sg

142 UNCTAD, 'Plan of action', TMD/386, 18 February 2000

143 UN General Assembly, 'A compendium of the major constraints'

144 Mehdi Shafaeddin, 'Free trade or fair trade: An enquiry into the causes of failure in recent trade negotiations', UNCTAD discussion paper, no.153, December 2000, pp20, 29

145 International Trade Centre, 'Product profile: Cotton and fibre', discussion document for the Third UN Conference on the Least Developed Countries, Brussels, 16 May 2001, p7

146 Cited in Aileen Kwa, 'The à la carte undertaking', p23

147 Taoufik Ben Abdallah, 'Africa between Structural Adjustment, globalisation and sustainable growth', at: www.africapolicy.org/rtable/tao0001.htm

148 Brian Groom, 'Getting Britain to the future first', *Financial Times*, 13 June 2000

149 UNCTAD, Trade and Development Board, 5th session, 'Report of the expert meeting on the impact of the reform process in agriculture, July 2000', 26 February 2001, TD/B/COM.1/31, p24

150 'White man's shame', *Economist*, 23 Sept.1999

151 See WTO, Committee on Agriculture, proposal to the June 2000 special session by the group of 11 developing countries (Cuba, Dominican Republic, Honduras, Pakistan, Haiti, Nicaragua, Kenya, Uganda, Zimbabwe, Sri Lanka and El Salvador), 23 June 2000. This refers to a study showing that, when compared to the non-tariff barriers of the 1990s, the EU's final tariff bindings for the year 2000 were almost two-thirds above the actual tariff equivalent for 1989-93. For the US they were more than three-quarters higher.

152 In *Eliminating world poverty: Making globalisation work for the poor*, White Paper on International Development, Cm 5006, HMSO, December 2000, para 245

153 WTO, Sub-Committee on the Least Developed Countries, 'The policy relevance of mainstreaming trade into country development strategies', WT/LDC/SWG/IF/15/Rev.1, WTO, Geneva, January 2001, p66

154 UN Department of Public Information, 'Opening doors for LDC exports', DPI/2190/C, April 2001

155 Effective from July 2001. Norway accords duty free access to all goods except flour, grains and feeding stuffs. Canada, as at May 2001, allows 90 per cent of LDC exports duty-free access. WTO, 'Mainstreaming trade', p31

156 *The Economist*, 25 September 1999, from World Bank study

157 UNCTAD, Trade and Development Board, 'Report of the expert meeting on examining trade in the agricultural sector, April 1999', 5 August 1999, TD/B/COM.1/23, p3

158 UN Department of Public Information, 'Opening doors for LDC exports', DPI/2190/C, April 2001

159 UNCTAD, *The changing supply and demand market structure on commodity prices and exports of major interest to developing countries*, Geneva, 1999

160 Sophia Murphy, *Trade and Food Security – An Assessment of the Uruguay Round Agreement on Agriculture*, CIIR, London, 1999

161 Figures from Customs and Excise, based on duty for chocolate of 8.3 per cent, with additional duties depending on sugar and milk content of up to 18.3 per cent

162 Chris Stevens and Jane Kennan, 'The impact of the EU's "Everything but arms" proposal: A report to Oxfam', IDS, Sussex, January 2001

163 Pascal Lamy, speech to the US Council for International Business, New York, 8 June 2000

164 Myriam van der Stichele, *Gender, trade and the WTO*, p51

165 Caroline Lucas, 'An unhealthy attitude to trade', *Financial Times*, 28 March 2001

166 For several of the promises broken by rich countries in the WTO, see Bhagirath Lal Das, 'Strengthening developing countries in the WTO', Trade and development series No.8, Third World Network, www.twnside.org.sg, pp7-8

167 Interview with Christian Aid, Geneva, Oct. 2000

168 UNCTAD, 'Impact of the reform process in agriculture on LDC's and Net Food Importing Developing Countries and ways to Address Their Concerns in Multilateral trade negotiations', Geneva, 2000

169 Action Aid, *The Marrakesh Ministerial Decision on Measures concerning the possible negative effects of the reform programme on least developed and net Food-importing developing countries*, London, 2000

170 Ibid.

171 FAO, Commodity Policy and Projections Service, Commodities and Trade Division, 'Measures to enhance agricultural development, trade and food security in the context of the forthcoming WTO negotiations', presented to FAO symposium on agriculture, trade and food security, Geneva, September 1999

172 Spencer Henson and Rupert Loader, 'Barriers to agricultural exports from developing countries: The role of Sanitary and Phytosanitary requirements', *World Development*, Vol.29, No.1, 2001, p99

173 See UNCTAD, 'Trade in the agricultural sector', p12

174 Sophia Murphy, *Trade and Food Security*

175 Interview with Christian Aid, Geneva, Oct.2000

176 T.Otsuki, J. Wilson and M. Sewadeh, *Saving Two in a Billion: A case study to quantify the trade effect of European food safety standards on African exports*, Development Research Group, World Bank, Washington, 2000

177 Statement made by Bolivia to WTO committee on SPS, 15-16 Sept. 1998, ref. G/SPS/GEN/93

178 Interview with Christian Aid, Geneva, Oct. 2000

179 All quotes and evidence from Inge Nora Neufeld, 'Anti-dumping – use or abuse?'

180 Ibid.

181 'WTO puts the brakes on anti-dumping bandwagon', *Financial Times*, 6 March 2001

182 International Trade Centre, 'LDCs' Trade: An analytical note', discussion document for the Third UN Conference on the Least Developed Countries, Brussels, 16 May 2001, p8

183 UNCTAD, '*Positive Trade Agenda and Future Trade Negotiations*', New York/Geneva, 2000

184 Ibid., p220

185 Ibid.

186 Ibid.

187 Ibid.

188 UNDP, *Human Development Report 1999*, New York/Geneva, 1999, p6

189 Interview with Christian Aid, Geneva, Oct. 2000

190 Patents relate to scientific and technological innovations in various industrial and service sectors. A government registers the patent and thereby confers certain exclusive rights on the patent-holder regarding the subject of the patent. The patent holder has the right to prevent any other person from making, using, selling, offering for sale or importing the patented product without the consent of the patent holder. Many rich countries have laws which protect the 'intellectual property' of companies – that is, inventions of new products or production processes, copyright on names, logos or trademarks. Companies argue that in order to invest in research and development of new products, they need to have the security that patents offer. Unless a company knows it will benefit from a new discovery, it will not invest in possibly costly new ventures. However, it also means that during the period of a patent, a company can charge very high prices for the product. See Bhagirath Lal Das, *The World Trade Organisation*, pp360-7

191 Bhagirath Lal Das, *The World Trade Organisation*, pp355-70

192 All examples from RAFI, 'Out of Control', *Occasional Paper*, Rural Advancement Foundation International, Winnipeg, Canada, 31 October 1998. See www.rafi.org. See also Actionaid, *AstraZeneca and its genetic research: feeding the world or fuelling hunger?*, London, 1999

193 Actionaid, *Crops and Robbers*, London, 25 November 1999

194 UNDP, *Human Development Report 1999*, New York/Geneva, p68

195 UN Subcommission on the Promotion and Protection of Human Rights, 'The realisation of economic, social and cultural rights: Globalisation and its impact on the full enjoyment of human rights', preliminary report, 52nd session, 15 June 2000, p7

196 UNDP, *Human Development Report 1999*, pp68-70. Emphasis added

197 RAFI, 'The Benefits of Biodiversity', *Occasional Paper*, Rural Advancement Foundation International, Winnipeg, 30 March 1994

198 UNDP, *Human Development Report 1999*, p71

199 See Graham Dunkley, *The free trade adventure*, p189

200 UNDP, *Human Development Report 1999*. In 2000, 75 per cent of all patent applications were lodged by companies from just five countries – the US, Germany, Japan, the UK and France. Only 3.5 per cent came from all developing countries, compared to six per cent from the UK. 'Demand for patents up almost 25 per cent', *Financial Times*, 14 February 2001

201 Actionaid, *Crops and Robbers*, p4

202 UN Subcommission on the Promotion and Protection of Human Rights, 52nd session, 17 August 2000

203 C. Correa, *Intellectual Property Rights, The WTO and Developing Countries*, Zed, London, 2000, p39

204 The UNDP notes how much of the global market is controlled by the top ten corporations. In commercial seed, 32 per cent of a £23 billion industry; in pharmaceuticals, 35 per cent of $297 billion; in pesticides, 85 per cent of $31 billion. It states: 'The lesson is clear: privatisation does not automatically lead to competition'. UNDP, *Human Development Report 1999*, p67

205 Cited in Aileen Kwa, 'The à la carte undertaking', p28

206 UNDP, *Human Development Report 1999*, p6

207 Uruguay Round Final Act, Agreement on Trade-Related Intellectual Property Rights, Article 7

208 UNDP, *Human Development Report 1999*, p69

209 Ibid.

210 K. Balasubramaniam, *Consumers and the WTO TRIPs Agreement*, Consumers International, Penang, Malaysia

211 Graham Dunkley, *The free trade adventure*, p187

212 Jean Lanjouw and Iain Cockburn, 'New pills for poor people?: Empirical evidence after GATT', *World Development*, Vol.29, No.2, 2001, p268

213 TRIPs, Article 22, Protection of Geographical Indications, at: www.wto.org/english/tratop_e/trips_e/t_agm3b_e.htm

214 Ibid.

215 'EU afraid of real competition', *South African Wine*, 19 June 2001, at: www.winenews.co.za

216 Mira Shiva, 'Globalisation, TNCs and the undermining of health rights and democracy in India', prepared for Christian Aid, March 2001

217 Delhi, November 1999

CHAPTER 4

218 J. Michael Finger and Philip Schuler, 'Implementation of Uruguay Round Commitments: the development challenge', World Bank, July 1999 (mimeo)

219 at www.whitehouse.gov

220 Cited in Graham Dunkley, *The free trade adventure: The WTO, the Uruguay Round and globalism*, Zed, London, 2000, p232. Emphasis added.

221 Ibid., p228

222 Ibid., p20

223 Cited in S.Dryden, *Trade warriors*, OUP, New York, 1995, pp355-6

224 *Financial Times*, 6 December 1999

225 Election campaign statement 2000, at: www.centralsoya.com

226 Election campaign statement 2000, at: www.ndfu.org

227 Speech to Los Angeles World Affairs Council, 31 May 2001, www.whitehouse.org

228 at: www.ndfu.org

229 Council of the European Union, General Secretariat, Preparations for the 3rd United Nations Conference on Least Developed Countries, 5257/01, Brussels, 12 January 2001, pp15, 17

230 UNDP, *Human Development Report 1999*, New York/Geneva, p31

231 Pascal Lamy, 'The challenge of integrating Africa into the world economy', speech in Johannesburg, 21 June 2000, at: europa.eu.int/comm/trade/speeches

232 Speech to US Chamber of Commerce, Washington 8 March 2001, at: www.europa.eu.int

233 Speech to the European Services Forum international conference, Brussels, 27 November 2000. Emphasis in original.

234 Speech to European Services Forum international conference Brussels, 27 November 2000

235 Ibid.

236 *Eliminating world poverty: Making globalisation work for the poor*, White Paper on International Development, Cm5006, HMSO, London, December 2000, para 235

237 Tony Blair, statement to the WTO at the 50th anniversary of the GATT, Geneva, 19 May 1998. Emphasis in original.

238 *Hansard*, 9 December 1999, Col.1031

239 Margaret Beckett, *Financial Times*, 10 July 1997

240 *Eliminating world poverty*, paras 35-45

241 '...Developed countries must end the large subsidies to their farmers, which currently distort world prices and deter private investment in agriculture in poor countries'. Ibid., para 222

242 Ibid., paras 230-1

243 Ibid., para 246

244 Ibid., para 229

245 Ibid., para 226

246 Ibid., foreword by Tony Blair, p6

247 'Trade openness is a necessary but not sufficient condition for poverty reduction'. *Eliminating world poverty*, para 218. The key here is 'necessary'. The 'not sufficient condition' refers to other policies that often also need to be in place to benefit the poor (see para 90). But there is no allowance for non-'liberalisation' trade policies.

248 Government policy is basically opposed to protection in all its forms. The White Paper on globalisation makes no mention of how protection policies could benefit developing countries. *Eliminating world poverty*, para 217

249 *Eliminating world poverty*, paras 219, 222. Most countries in Africa, for example, are encouraged to believe that 'the best export prospects over the next few decades are in natural resource-based products'.

250 '...This means giving high priority to the multilateral liberalisation of agriculture'. *Eliminating world poverty*, para 235

251 Ibid., para 256

252 Ibid., para 185

253 Ibid., para 186

254 Ibid., para 187

255 Ibid., para 156

256 Ibid., paras 142-3

257 Ibid., paras 143, 144

258 Ibid., para 145

259 Ibid., paras 146, 148

260 Ibid., box 6, p46

261 Ibid., para 237

262 Ibid., para 37

263 Ibid., paras 162-4. Emphasis added.

264 'Despite the insistence by those members [ie, advocating for addressing the new issues in a new round], there is no consensus to negotiate and set up rules in these areas in the WTO... Most African countries are not in a position to agree to launch negotiations in these areas.' High-level brainstorming meeting for African trade negotiators preparatory to the fourth WTO ministerial conference, Ethiopia, June 2001, at: www.uneca.org/eca_resources

265 For example: 'developed countries must give greater weight to the needs of developing countries whose agreement is needed if another Round is to be launched.' *Eliminating world poverty*, para 233. Emphasis added. This reasoning also seems to apply to UK support for special and differential treatment for developing countries:

'To help countries manage their commitments we will press for special and differential provisions to be real and binding, and for any new WTO rules to reflect countries' implementation capacity.' *Eliminating world poverty*, para 238

266 UNCTAD, *The Least Developed Countries 2000 Report*, New York/Geneva, 2000, Internet version, p120

267 Cited in John Madeley, 'There's a food fight in Seattle', *New Statesman*, 22 November 1999

268 Speech to TABD, Brussels, 23 May 2000

269 Keith Richardson, 'Big Business and the European Agenda', Sussex European Institute, University of Sussex, Brighton, September 2000

270 John Madeley, *Big Business, Poor Peoples: The Impact of Transnational Corporations on the World's Poor*, Zed, London, 1999, p38

271 *Corporate Europe Observatory*, Issue 4, July 1999

272 Ibid.

273 'Gates offers Ministers for Sale at World Trade Conference', *Independent on Sunday*, London, 22 August 1999

274 Cited in Ralph Nader, 'Introduction: Free trade and the decline of democracy', in *The case against free trade: GATT, NAFTA and the globalisation of corporate power*, Earth Island, San Francisco, 1993, p4

275 Julian Borger, 'Industry that stalks the US corridors of power', *Guardian*, 13 February 2001

276 See especially the newsletter *Corporate Europe Observatory*, and *Europe Inc: Regional and global restructuring and the rise of corporate power*, Pluto, London, 2000

277 Graham Dunkley, *The free trade adventure*, p228

278 For notes and sources see Christian Aid, 'Fair shares? Transnational companies, the WTO and the world's poorest communities', London, November 1999, p6

279 WTO, Sub-Committee on the Least Developed Countries, 'The policy relevance of mainstreaming trade into country development strategies', WT/LDC/SWG/IF/15/Rev.1, WTO, Geneva, January 2001, pp17, 19, 68, 70, 136

280 C.Milner and P.Wright, 'Modelling labour market adjustment to trade liberalisation in an industrialising economy', *Economic Journal*, Vol.108, No.447, March 1998

281 EU Trade Commissioner Pascal Lamy has said that 'we have proved again and again, and now in dramatically spiralling multiples, our ability to create fabulous wealth on this planet for the few. But we have not yet shown that we have the slightest idea how to get to a fairer, a wiser distribution of that wealth.' Speech to ARCO forum, Harvard University, 1 November 2000

282 For example, a *Financial Times* editorial states that 'if poor countries are to benefit [from liberalisation], they must recognise that their problem is too little globalisation, not too much. They need to attack the high trade barriers that have throttled development and open their economies to the world.' 30 January 2001

283 WTO, 'Mainstreaming trade', p18

284 UNCTAD, *Least Developed Countries*, Internet edition, p7

285 UNCTAD, *Trade and Development Report 2001*, New York/Geneva, 2001, pp14-15

286 UNCTAD, 'Foreign direct investment in Africa: Performance and potential, New York/ Geneva, 1999, p5

287 WTO, Committee on Agriculture, 'WTO negotiations on agriculture: Proposal by Kenya', 12 March 2001

288 Duncan Green, *Silent Revolution*, Cassell/LAB, London, 1995

289 Ha-Joon Chang, 'Industrial Policy of East Asia – the Miracle, the Crisis, and the Future', University of Cambridge (mimeo)

290 Ibid.

291 Ibid.

292 Duncan Green, *Silent Revolution*

293 WTO, 'Mainstreaming trade', p32

294 UNCTAD, *Least Developed Countries*, Internet edition, pp1, 110

295 World Bank, *Adjustment in Africa: Reforms, Results and the Road Ahead*, Oxford University Press for the World Bank, New York,1994

296 UNCTAD, *Least Developed Countries 2000*, p11

297 World Bank, *Sub-Saharan Africa: From Crisis to Sustainable growth*, Washington DC, 1989

298 J. Hanlon, *Mozambique: Who Calls the Shots*, James Currey, London, 1990

299 WTO, 'Mainstreaming trade', pp39-40

300 Ibid., p9

301 Ibid., p139

302 UN Subcommission on the Promotion and Protection of Human Rights 'The realisation of economic, social and cultural rights: Globalisation and its impact on the full enjoyment of human rights', preliminary report, 52nd session, 15 June 2000, pp15-16

303 Interview with Moses Tekere, Trade and Development Centre, Harare, Zimbabwe, March 2001

304 WTO, 'Mainstreaming trade', p17

305 Cited in World Development Movement, 'In whose service? The threat posed by the General Agreement on Trade in Services to economic development in the South', London, December 2000, p9

306 Nancy Birdsall and Robert Laurence, 'Deep integration and trade agreements: Good for developing countries?', in Inge Kaul et al, *Global Public Goods: International cooperation in the 21st century*, OUP, New York, 1999, cited in WTO, 'Mainstreaming trade', p75

307 Aileen Kwa, 'Transparency and institutional issues a year after Seattle', *Focus on trade*, No.57, Focus on the Global South, Bangkok, December 2000, p19

308 Aileen Kwa, 'The à la carte undertaking: A new form of special and differential treatment?', *Focus on trade*, No.57, December 2000, Focus on the Global South, Bangkok, December 2000, p27

309 Interview with Christian Aid, Geneva, October 2000

310 Bhagirath Lal Das, 'Strengthening developing countries in the WTO', Trade and development series No.8, Third World Network, www.twnside.org.sg, p5

311 Department of Trade and Industry, written answers to questions from UK Trade Network, September 1999

312 Interview with Christian Aid, Geneva, October 2000

313 Dot Keet, *Alternatives to the WTO regime*, Alternative Information and Development Centre, Cape Town, November 2000, p29

314 Cited in Walden Bello, 'WTO tries to subvert developing countries' resistance to new trade talks', *Focus on trade*, No.61, Focus on the Global South, Bangkok, April 2001

315 Statement released in Seattle, 2 December 1999

316 Statement by the Philippines to Fifth Special Session of the Committee on Agriculture, 5-7 February 2001, Geneva, WTO, G/AG/NG/W/90

317 Aileen Kwa, 'Transparency and institutional issues', pp17-18

318 Julian Borger, 'Industry that stalks the US corridors of power', *Guardian*, 13 February 2001

CHAPTER 5

319 UNCTAD, *World Investment Report 1999*, Geneva, 1999

320 *Measuring globalisation: the role of multinationals in OECD economies*, OECD, Paris, Nov. 1999

321 UN Commission on Human Rights, Sub-Commission on the Promotion and Protection of Human Rights, 52nd session, 25 May 2000, E/CN.4/Sub.2/2000/WG.2/Wp1, p2

322 Sarah Anderson and John Cavanagh, 'Top 200: The rise of corporate global power', Institute for Policy Studies, Washington, 2000, p1

323 Ibid.

324 UNCTAD, *World Investment Report 2000*, Geneva, 2000

325 Ibid., p1

326 28 January 2001, at: www.msbn.com

327 *Tax havens: Releasing the hidden billions for poverty eradication*, Oxfam, Oxford, 2000

328 J. Greer and K. Singh, 'A brief history of TNCs in India: An activists guide to research and campaigning on transnational corporations', Public Interest Research Group, New Delhi, 1997, at: corpwatch.org/corner/glob/history

329 Julian Borger, 'Industry that stalks the US corridors of power', *Guardian*, 13 February 2001

330 Sarah Anderson and John Cavanagh, 'The rise and fall of global corporate power', at: www.globalpolicy.org/socecon/tncs

331 'Findings on Nike put the spotlight on broader global issues', *Financial Times*, 22 February 2001

332 www.safer-world.org/e/countries/brazil.htm

333 'UK Judges Block Thor Chemicals Manoeuvre', *Guardian*, 1 October 2000

334 www.aph.gov.au/senate/committee/corp_sec_ctte

335 *Observer*, 18 June 2000; *Guardian*, 4 June 2001

336 UNDP, *Human Development Report 1999*, New York/Geneva, 1999, p100

337 UN Commission on Human Rights, Sub-Commission on the Promotion and Protection of Human Rights, 52nd session, 1 August 2000, E/CN.4/Sub.2/2000/1/Rev.1, p17. Emphasis added. See also Sub-Commission on Human Rights, 25 May 2000, p7

338 *Corporate Europe Observatory*, No.5, October 1999, pp4-5

339 Ibid., p5

340 Ibid., p4

341 UNCTAD, *World Investment Report*, Geneva, 1998

342 *Eliminating World Poverty: Making globalisation work for the poor*, White Paper on International Development, Cm5006, HMSO, December 2000, para 128, for example.

343 The exception concerns anti-bribery legislation, mentioned below. The government has also recently introduced legislation requiring pension funds to state the extent to which social, environmental or ethical considerations are taken into account in making investments.

344 *Eliminating world poverty*, para 204. Emphasis added.

345 *Eliminating world poverty*, para 201

346 One opinion poll conducted in 2001 among UK experts in the field of 'corporate social responsibility' (CSR) showed that 94 per cent of respondents believed that all large companies should have adopted social and environmental reporting by 2005, with a majority – 51 per cent – supporting mandatory social and environmental reporting. 62 per cent thought that all government departments should set a timetable for adopting and implementing a CSR policy within the next year. See ' "Good morning minister, here is your job description": The government mandate for corporate social responsibility', New Economics Foundation and Business in the Community, London, June 2001

347 S. Zia-Zarifi, 'Suing multinational corporations in the US for violating international law', *UCLA Journal of International Law and Foreign Affairs*, Spring/Summer 1999

348 UNDP, *Human Development Report 1999*, p5

349 UNCTAD press release, TAD/INF/2819, 23 October 1999

350 BP, 'What we stand for', at: www.bp.com/corp_reporting

351 Patti Rundell, 'Brussels spouts', *The food magazine*, January 2001, p52

352 Cited in *Corporate Europe Observatory*, No.7, October 2000, p16

353 See Transnational Resource and Action Centre, *Tangled up in blue: Corporate partnerships at the United Nations*, September 2000, at: www.corpwatch.org

354 Ibid., p12

355 Cited in *Corporate Europe Observatory*, No.5, October 1999, p2

356 Ibid.

357 Cited in Transnational Resource and Action Centre, *Tangled up in blue*, pp5-6

358 See Corporate Watch at: www.corpwatch.org

359 www.globalreporting.org

CHAPTER 6

360 UN Subcommission on the Promotion and Protection of Human Rights, 'The realisation of economic, social and cultural rights: Globalisation and its impact on the full enjoyment of human rights', preliminary report, 52nd session, 15 June 2000, p8

361 UNDP, *Poverty Report 2000*, New York/Geneva, 2000, p49

362 Ibid.

363 EDM No.260, 29 January 2001

364 The group of 11 developing countries, for example, has stated that 'all developing countries should be able to use a positive list approach to declare which agricultural products or sectors they would like disciplined under AoA provisions. That is, only the products which are

declared by a country are subject to AoA commitments'. See WTO, Committee on Agriculture, Proposal to the June 2000 special session by the group of 11 developing countries (Cuba, Dominican Republic, Honduras, Pakistan, Haiti, Nicaragua, Kenya, Uganda, Zimbabwe, Sri Lanka and El Salvador), 23 June 2000

365 Pascal Lamy, 'Trade is changing – so must Europe', *Financial Times*, 5 December 2000

366 Dot Keet, *Alternatives to the WTO regime*, Alternative Information and Development Centre, Cape Town, November 2000, p43

367 Ibid., p31

368 See also, for example, World Development Movement, 'Making investment work for people: An international framework for regulating corporations', London, February 1999, pp13-15

369 See UNCTAD, *Trade and Development Report 2001*, New York/Geneva, 2001, p15

370 WTO Committee on Agriculture, Proposal to the June 2000 special session by the group of 11 developing countries (Cuba, Dominican Republic, Honduras, Pakistan, Haiti, Nicaragua, Kenya, Uganda, Zimbabwe, Sri Lanka and El Salvador), 23 June 2000. It also stated the need to 'allow developing countries to re-evaluate and adjust their tariff levels. Where it has been established that cheap imports are destroying or threatening domestic producers, developing countries should be allowed to raise their tariff bindings on key products to promote food security.'

371 UNCTAD, 'Subsidies, countervailing measures and developing countries', UNCTAD/DITC/COM/23, 4 July 2000, p23. Trade negotiators from 27 African countries similarly called in June 2001 for 'substantial progressive reductions in export subsidies, leading to their eventual elimination' and reductions in domestic support in developed countries. See 'High-level brainstorming meeting for African trade negotiators preparatory to the fourth WTO ministerial conference', Ethiopia, June 2001, at: www.uneca.org/eca_resources

372 'High-level brainstorming meeting for African trade negotiators preparatory to the fourth WTO ministerial conference', Ethiopia, June 2001, at: www.uneca.org/eca_resources

373 UNCTAD, 'Subsidies and developing countries', p24

374 Ibid., p22

375 UNCTAD Trade and Development Board, 5th session, 'Report of the expert meeting on the impact of the reform process in agriculture, July 2000', 26 February 2001, TD/B/COM.1/31, p2

376 UNDP, *Human Development Report 1999*, New York/Geneva, 1999, p10

377 Letter, *Financial Times*, 20 February 2001

378 Whether patenting on, for example, plant varieties and seeds should be allowable at all deserves much closer international scrutiny. One of the key arguments put forward by defenders of patenting is that it is necessary to promote innovation and the development of new technologies. But a number of studies show that there is no clear link between intellectual property rights and innovation. See, for example, UNDP, *Human Development Report 1999*, p73

379 UNDP, *Human Development Report 1999*, p63

380 Joseph Hanlon, personal communication with Christian Aid

381 UNCTAD, 'Plan of action', TD/386, 18 February 2000

CASE STUDIES

382 See Christian Aid, 'The scorched earth: Oil and war in Sudan', London, 2000

383 Karemera and Ojah, 'An Industrial Analysis of Trade Creation and Diversion Effects of NAFTA', *Journal of Economic Integration*, No.3(3)

384 Graham Dunkley, *The free trade adventure: The WTO, the Uruguay Round and globalism*, Zed, London, 2000, pp89-92

385 *Financial Mail*, 23 April 1999

386 G. Wellmer, *SADC: Between regional integration and reciprocal free trade with the European Union*, World House Publications, Bielefeld

387 Anuario Brasileiro do Fumo 1999, Gazeta Grupo de Communicacoes

388 Ibid.

389 International Tobacco Growers Association

390 Anuario Brasileiro do Fumo

391 Ibid.

392 Ibid.

393 Afubra – The official union of tobacco workers

394 ASPTA

395 International code of conduct on the distribution and use of pesticides, UNFAO, November 1989

396 Adao Cosme Peres' son is being prescribed Gardenal and Idental, drugs normally used in the treatment of epilepsy.

397 Rodrigues da Silva, Falk, Pinheiro and Carvalho, 1996

398 Ibid.

399 Ellen Hickey and Yenyen Chan, 'Tobacco, farmers and pesticides: the other story', *Journal of the Pesticide Action Network of North America*, 1998

Glossary

AoA	Agreement on Agriculture
ATCA	Alien Tortes Claims Act
ASCM	Agreement on Subsidies and Countervailing Measures
ASIC	Australian Securities and Investment Commission
ATC	Agreement on Textiles and Clothing
BAT	British American Tobacco
BP	British Petroleum
CAP	Common Agricultural Policy
EBA	Everything But Arms
EMR	Exclusive Marketing Rights
EPZ	Export Processing Zones
ESF	European Services Forum
ESN	European Services Network
EU	European Union
FAO	Food and Agriculture Organisation
FDI	Foreign Direct Investment
FDL	Foreign Direct Liability
GATS	General Agreement on Trade in Services
GATT	General Agreement on Tariffs and Trade
GC	Global Compact
GDP	Gross Domestic Product
GNP	Gross National Product
GRA	Global Regulation Authority
GRI	Global Reporting Initiative
ICC	International Chamber of Commerce
IFSL	Group of International Financial Services, London
ILO	International Labour Organisation
IMF	International Monetary Fund
IPR	Intellectual Property Rights
ITC	International Trade Centre
ITO	International Trade Organisation
LDC	Least Developed Countries
LOTIS	Liberalisation of Trade in Services
MAI	Multilateral Agreement on Investment
MFN	Most Favoured Nation Treatment

MLI	Multilateral Institutions
MRC	Medical Research Council
NAFTA	North American Free Trade Agreement
NCP	National Contact Point
NFIDCs	Net Food Importing Developing Countries
NGO	Non-Governmental Organisation
OAU	Organisation of African Unity
OECD	Organisation for Economic Co-operation and Development
PhRMA	Pharmaceutical Research and Manufacturers Association
PRSP	Poverty Reduction Strategy Papers
QUAD group	US, Japan, EU and Canada
R&D	Research and Development
RTAs	Regional Trade Agreements
SADC	Southern African Development Community
SAP	Structural Adjustment Programme
SCM	(Agreement on) Subsidies and Countervailing Measures
SDT	Special and Differential Treatment
SPS	Sanitary and Phytosanitary Measures
SSP	Special Safeguard Provisions
TNC	Transnational Corporation
TRIMs	(The Agreement on) Trade Related Investment Measures
TRIPs	(The Agreement on) Trade-Related Aspects of Intellectual Property Rights
UN	United Nations
UNCTAD	United Nations Conference on Trade and Development
UNCTC	UN Centre on Transnational Corporations
UNDP	United Nations Development Programme
US ACTA	United States Alien Tortes Claims Act
USCIB	US Council on International Business
US CSI	US Coalition of Service Industries
USDA	United States Department of Agriculture
WHO	World Health Organisation
WTO	World Trade Organisation

Index

What to do now

Christian Aid is campaigning, with other organisations, to rewrite the rules that govern international trade.

With new rules, trade could work *for* poor people, not against them. It could create income, employment and investment for the world's poorest people. It could bring new products, new technology and new opportunities that would help countries tackle poverty.

Christian Aid is calling on governments and global institutions to put poverty eradication at the heart of new trade rules.

Your voice is vital: join the campaign and take action now.

Join the campaign

You will receive an *Action request* leaflet, containing suggestions for simple actions (like sending a postcard) that will help the campaign, and the latest news about the campaign, around five times a year. Phone **020 7523 2225** and ask to be registered as a campaigner.

Get others involved

If you can promote the campaign in your church or another group, you can become a campaign organiser – you'll receive *Action request* and all the latest action resources for groups. Phone **020 7523 2225** and ask to be registered as a campaign organiser.

Wear the badge

Show your support for the campaign by wearing the official symbol! The badge shows the scales that need to be tipped to make trade work for poor people. They are available in silver or red enamel, price £2 plus £2 p&p (for ten badges or more, p&p is free). The orderline number is 01252 669628.

Find out more

A range of free resources is available to promote the campaign. Phone **020 7523 2225** for more details.

Christian Aid is campaigning as part of the Trade Justice Movement. Other members include ActionAid, CAFOD, Friends of the Earth, Oxfam and the World Development Movement.

Please note that material from this book may be freely photocopied in order to promote Christian Aid's campaign on trade rules.